Bad Blood in Georgian Bristol
The Murder of Sir John Dineley

Redcliffe Press/The Regional History Centre,
University of the West of England, Bristol

Bad Blood in Georgian Bristol
The Murder of Sir John Dineley

Redcliffe Press/The Regional History Centre,
University of the West of England, Bristol

Steve Poole and Nicholas Rogers

First published in 2022 by Redcliffe Press Ltd.,
81g Pembroke Road, Bristol BS8 3EA
e: info@redcliffepress.co.uk
www.redcliffepress.co.uk

 Follow us on Twitter @RedcliffePress

Text © Steve Poole and Nicholas Rogers

ISBN 978-1-911408-97-0

British Library Cataloguing-in-Publication Data
A catalogue record for this book is available from
the British Library

All rights reserved. Except for the purpose of review, no part of
this book may be reproduced, stored in a retrieval system, or
transmitted, in any form or by any means, electronic, mechanical,
photocopying, recording or otherwise, without the prior
permission of the publishers.

Design and typesetting by Stephen Morris
www.stephen-morris.co.uk
Garamond 12/12

Printed and bound by Short Run Press, Exeter

Redcliffe Press Ltd is committed to being an environmentally
friendly publisher. This book is made from Forest Stewardship
Council® certified paper

Contents

Chapter One   The Chequered Fortunes of the House of Dineley-Goodere 7

Chapter Two   Prequel: Bristol at the time of Dineley's Murder 29

Chapter Three   Murder 47

Chapter Four   The Trial 67

Chapter Five   The Gibbet 85

Chapter Six   The Dineley Murder as Parricide 104

Chapter Seven   Fictions and Fratricides 118

Notes 149

Acknowledgements 164

Index 165

Sir John Dineley in old age, last surviving son of Captain Samuel Goodere.
Wellcome Collection

CHAPTER ONE

The Chequered Fortunes of the House of Dineley-Goodere

In 1841 Charles Knight, the printer and proprietor of the *Penny Magazine,* recalled his early days at Windsor, where his father was a bookseller. Among his recollections was the sight of one eccentric knight of Windsor, a pensioned aristocrat living out his days on the charity of the crown. Wearing a threadbare cloak called a roquelaure, the old man hobbled through the castle gate to run his errands in the town. On a pension of £60 a year, the man was parsimonious. His one extravagance, it seems, were his overtures of marriage to potential maids and matrons, printed on his own press. He claimed to be the owner of the Charlton estate in Worcestershire and worth a phenomenal £375,000, and he was prepared to press his claim to any lady of a hundred guineas in fortune. 'As the prospect of my marriage has most increased lately,' he declared, 'I am determined to take the best means to discover the lady most liberal in her esteem by giving her fourteen days more to make her quickest steps towards matrimony.'[1]

'Miss in your teens,' he wrote in 1802, 'let not this sacred offer escape your eye.' Become the 'mother of a noble heir', although at the age of 73 one wonders whether he was up for it.[2] Had a potential suitor encountered him at one of the festive parades of Windsor, she would have witnessed a man rooted in the mid-eighteenth century, attired in an embroidered coat, a silk-flowered waistcoat, velvet breeches and a newly powdered wig that was the worse for wear. He was Sir John Dineley, the fifth baronet of Charlton, an estate that had long passed into other hands. He could only dream of large acres and imposing mansions without a suitable match, and the prospects of obtaining one was the only thing that kept him alive.

Sir John Dineley was by birth a Goodere, the second of two twins to a naval captain who is one of the central characters in this drama. The name Dineley was one acquired by his uncle when he inherited the estates of his mother, a daughter to the Earl of Rockingham, one of the leading Whig families in the country. This uncle, Sir John Dineley-Goodere, is another central character, for he was murdered by the eccentric knight's father. How the Windsor knight lived with this fratricide is unclear although it is likely that it drove his twin brother insane and took his mother to an early grave.[3] Sir

John was only eleven years old when it happened and he became embroiled in the property disputes surrounding it until his forties. On one memorable occasion, in 1771, he had summoned the copyholders of Charlton and proclaimed that he was the true lord of the manor because his father had been cheated out of his inheritance there by his unscrupulous uncle.[4]

When he was born, in 1729, the Dineley-Goodere family was one to be reckoned with. His grandfather had recently retired as one of the two knights of the shire for Herefordshire. His father and two uncles had all been JPs and the latter were soon to be mayors of nearby towns.[5] The extended family was well situated in commerce, the navy, and in the landed society of the South-West. Yet when he died in 1809, aged eighty, Sir John Dineley was the last of the line of baronets and the family fortune had disappeared. In four generations this West-Country branch of the Goodere family prospered, declined and became extinct.[6]

The founder of this dynasty was John Goodere, who rose rapidly in the early East India Company from assistant in Basra, Macao and Persia, to factor and second-in-command in Surat, to deputy governor of Bombay.[7] He benefitted from the English company's success in defeating Portuguese ambitions in south-west India and successfully competed with the Dutch, who, from a firm base in the spice islands to the east, had wanted to expand their commercial sphere of operations in India. Relatively stable diplomatic relations with the Mughals enabled the English company to secure a profitable trade in Surat, which became a depot for the export of cottons, muslins, saltpetre, indigo and other dyestuffs needed for the English woollen and worsted industries. Under the leadership and mentorship of George Oxenden, John Goodere prospered from this opening of trade in Surat and Bombay, which became the chief settlement of the English on this coast some twenty years after Goodere's departure in 1669, when he was the deputy-governor of the post.[8] His business acumen and demographic good luck, for East India officers were highly susceptible to tropical diseases in India,[9] enabled him to purchase properties in at least three counties.

In Herefordshire John Goodere purchased an estate in Burghope over the objections of Thomas Prise, the knight of the shire, who believed the late owner had devised it to his father and subsequently to him. Prise tried to use his parliamentary status to buttress his claim, but his sisters, who were locked in an inheritance dispute with their brother, were taken by Goodere's attractive offer. The impecunious Prise was subsequently bought out.[10] John Goodere devised Burghope to Edward, his second, but first surviving son. At the time of his death, he also possessed mortgages, bonds and stock, not to mention

The Goodere–Dineley family tree

```
John Goodere (died 1697?) | Anne (dau of John Morgan)          Sir Edward Dineley (died 1706) | Frances (dau of Earl of Rockingham)
                    |                                                              |
   ┌────────────────┼─────────┐                          ┌─────────────────────────┼──────────── two sons died young
   |                |         |                          |
Edward Goodere Bt. MP ───── Eleanor Dineley
1657-1739                    1661-1714
   |
   ┌────────┬──────┬──────────┬────────────┬──────────┐
son      Edward  dau      John Dineley   George     Samuel         Henry         Eleanor m. Samuel Foote
d. age 11 1681-1706? d.1682 1685-1741    1687-1733?  1688-1741      1689-1733     1693-1774    1683-1754
                            m. Mary Lawford          m. Jane Nichols d.1721                    |
                                 |                       m. Eliz Watts 1723             ┌──────┴──────┐
                              Edward 1717-39                 |                    Edward Goodere Foote
                                                    Edward Goodere Dineley 1729-1761   John Dineley Foote
                                                    John Goodere Dineley 1729-1809    Samuel Foote 1720-1777
```

Notes:

The Dineley-Goodere family was created by the marriage of Edward Goodere and Eleanor Dineley in 1679. They produced eight children, two of whom died when still very young and a son, Edward, was dead by 1706.

Samuel Goodere (the murderer) became the second surviving son sometime in the mid-1730s on the death of George.

John Dineley (the murder victim) married Mary Lawford in 1717 and his sister Eleanor, born in 1693, married Samuel Foote in 1711. She was 18; he was 28.

Foote was sometimes thought to be MP for Tiverton, but not so. He was Mayor of Truro in 1719 on the Boscawen interest. His father or uncle had earlier been MP for Tiverton.

S.E. view of Burghope House, engraved by T. Cook after a drawing by I.W., published in *Gentleman's Magazine*, September 1791. Herefordshire History

plate gold, jewels, and necklaces to the value of £10,000.[11] He certainly had more than enough money to qualify as a director of the East India Company in 1670 and move from factor to financier. The fact that his sister Frances married into a powerful London family certainly helped.[12] The stage was set for another ascent. Daughter Pennington married Spencer Cowper, the second son of Sir William Cowper of Hereford Castle, who became a barrister and eventually a puisne judge of common pleas. Daughter Elizabeth married into a cadet branch of the Beaufort family, the premier nobles of the West Country.[13] Son Edward, who was born in India in 1657, joined hands with a young Worcestershire heiress. At the age of 22 when he tied the knot, Edward was fresh out of Oxford where he had matriculated in February 1676. There is no indication that he actually secured a degree; just enough social polish and cachet to attract the attentions of eighteen-year-old Eleanor Dineley and quietly court her before he secured her father's approval.[14] Her father, the baronet Sir Edward Dineley, thought it a poor match, probably because at that point the suitor was not the principal beneficiary of his father's fortune; but the mother, a daughter of the Earl of Rockingham, consented, and in 1679 they were married by license at Bodenham in Herefordshire.[15] Subsequently, on the death of his eldest brother, Edward became the beneficiary of two estates with a combined income of over £4000 a year. The

Worcestershire estate, in particular, was substantial, comprising over 3000 acres of arable land, and meadows and pasture of equivalent size, not to mention a further thousand acres of furze, heath and common pasture for cattle in Bricklehampton.[16]

As a new member of the greater gentry, Edward Goodere was now in a position to consider political ambitions, although his first entrée might well have been thrust upon him. His father-in-law had been considered by King James II as MP for the borough of Evesham, some two miles from his estate, and when a new charter was created for the borough in August 1688, Edward was touted as an alderman and justice of the peace. James II's wayward policies subsequently led to an annulment of this charter and may well have encouraged Edward Goodere to lay low in the reign of William for fear he might be branded as a Jacobite; that is, an adherent of James, the exiled king and his heirs. But in 1702 Goodere was to be found among Sir John Pakington's 'hounds' in the fiercely contested elections for Worcestershire.[17] As the electoral agent for this well-known Country Tory, he supervised the scrutiny and provided the malt for the entertainments that accompanied the contest. In 1705 he alerted Pakington's wife of a Whig plot to hold an election in his patron's absence. That year Edward Goodere became an alderman for Evesham and this set him up for his successful parliamentary candidature in 1708. The death of his father-in-law certainly helped, for it meant his wife, who was the principal legatee, could offer him an extra financial support. We may infer this because Sir Edward Dineley always feared his estate might be frittered away by his son-in-law's political ambitions. He shored up his estate with a strict settlement that ensured Edward Goodere could only benefit from the incomes of the Worcestershire property during his wife's lifetime.

Although Edward Goodere rose to prominence supporting Pakington he was classified as a Whig in 1708 and subsequently voted in favour of the naturalisation of the German Palatines; an immigration issue that consistently divided the two parties, the Tories being little-Englanders and the Whigs Protestant Europhiles. Goodere also supported the impeachment of the arch-Tory Henry Sacheverell for questioning the constitutionality of the 1688 settlement in a Gunpowder Plot sermon before the London Lord Mayor. The puzzle of his shifting political loyalties can be explained by the fact that Goodere secured a baronetcy from the Whig government in December 1707 and subsequently saw himself as a courtier. This did not stop him supporting his former patron, Sir John Pakington, in county elections and even hosting the other Tory candidate, Samuel Pytts, at Charlton in July 1710. Goodere had little difficulty adjusting to a moderate Tory position after the Tory landslide of 1710. He voted for the French Commerce bill in 1713 and in favour of the Quaker's affirmation bill. Here he trimmed his sails to suit the winds of local politics, the Quakers being an important electoral presence in Evesham. At the end of Anne's reign, he was identified with the Court Tory, Robert Harley, who was an important political figure in Herefordshire, where Edward Goodere's paternal and more modest estate lay. When Harley was disgraced after the Hanoverian succession for allegedly corresponding with the Stuart court, Goodere suffered accordingly. He was defeated at Evesham in 1715 but returned to the Commons in 1722 as a Country Tory candidate for Herefordshire, coming second in the poll.[18]

Sir Edward Goodere's parliamentary career over 19 years cost money and certainly put a strain on his finances. The situation was intensified by the fact that his wife Eleanor died in 1714, at which time the Charlton estate devolved on their first surviving son, John, who assumed the surname of his grandfather and became known as John Dineley-Goodere. This meant that Sir Edward was deprived of about £1000 per annum to sustain his opulent lifestyle as a baronet and consequently he became dependent on the goodwill and conscience of his son, John, who voluntarily gave him a life tenancy of the manor of Hanley Castle, an ample estate of farms, chase and park between the Severn and the Malvern Hills, about eighteen miles from Charlton.[19] Growing wheat, barley and oats, and with conspicuous resources of timber, the manor had been bought by Sir Edward Dineley in 1684 and brought in about £500 a year. This concession did not seriously affect John's financial fortunes, although a running dispute with his sister Eleanor, and his brother-in-law Samuel Foote, an attorney and commissioner of prizes in Truro, signalled the kinds of squabbles that would soon plague the Dineley-Goodere fortune. The Footes were troubled by a hastily drawn-up codicil to Sir Edward's will, dated November 1708, which left another £1000 to his 'daughter Elenover' and a similar sum to his 'grand[son] Samuel' once debts and charges had been paid for.[20] The Footes interpreted this to mean the granddaughter Eleanor, not the mother, who was well provided for during her lifetime. Granddaughter Eleanor, now Eleanor Foote, was already entitled to £2000 from her grandfather's personal estate, but the extra £1000 hinged on whether brother John had translated his grandfather's wishes correctly or not. The brother claimed the money was intended for Eleanor his mother, not his sister, and on that account would ultimately end up in his pocket. One way or another the Footes felt they had been shortchanged in the final settlement, especially since one of the other fraternal beneficiaries, George Goodere, had died by the time the personal estate of Eleanor's grandfather was distributed. The Footes were unhappy that the Dineley estate had gone exclusively to John, who they believed was never the favoured grandson. They wondered whether Sir Edward Dineley, who had a fit and was speechless at the end of his life, had been pressured into signing a codicil devising John the whole estate and much of the personal property.

They also feared that Sir Edward Dineley's personal estate, estimated to be worth £10-12,000, had been ruthlessly appropriated by Eleanor's parents to renew leases on the Cropthorne-Charlton estates owned by the Dean and Chapter of Worcester and to further Sir Edward Goodere's political ambitions.[21] In their suit they complained of the unseemly haste with which livestock were sold, including prize horses, and their own exclusion from the will, believing that Sir Edward and Eleanor Goodere had discriminated against them because their marriage had been concluded secretly behind their backs. The suit dragged on in Chancery, with John countering the Foote's charges by noting that sister Eleanor had borrowed a lot of money from her mother during her lifetime, and that the Footes' expectations of a 'very great Overplus' from Sir Edward Dineley's fortune were illusory. The matter was not settled until 1744, with ironic ramifications. Eleanor then had to deal with the trustees and beneficiaries of brother John's will; in effect, she was taking on her two sons, John and Samuel.[22] The jaunty exchange between Eleanor and Sam Foote over debts in 1743,[23] one that literary historians have loved to trot out, actually concealed altogether tougher negotiations.

John Dineley-Goodere was plagued with his sister's claim on his estate for thirty years. He encountered other kinds of difficulties as soon as he inherited his maternal grandfather's fortune. He was quickly appointed to the bench, but he just as quickly ruffled feathers. Reared as a merchant seaman in the East India trade, he only came into his landed inheritance because his eldest brother died at 11 and the next surviving brother, Edward, had been killed in a duel in Ireland in 1706. Under the conventions of primogeniture third sons normally had to make their way in the world, and practically speaking John came into his inheritance too quickly to adapt to landed society.[24] His nephew, the future dramatist Samuel Foote, remarked that a ship was 'not a proper academy for politeness', nor did it provide a 'necessary ingredient towards composing a social character', by which he meant it did not prepare men for the civilities and measured authority required of landed gentlemen who would officiate as justices of the peace. Another commentator thought that there was 'something in his [John's] cast of Thought, in his Turn of Mind, in his whole Frame and Constitution' that made it difficult to transform him into a 'social fine Gentleman.'[25] John thought nothing of hunting with the hounds on the Sabbath which seems to have bothered clerical JPs. He refused to contribute towards the maintenance of the highways, even though this was a task administered by the JPs, and he prohibited some of his tenants from devoting two to three days' labour to it, which they were technically obliged to do. John Dineley also appears to have treated his personal servants harshly. One, William Wilson, a sixteen-year-old lad, ran away in his blue livery with £6 in his pocket.[26] More serious was his vindictiveness towards a servant who had testified against him in the family suit with the Footes. He had her arrested as a vagrant and whipped in the county jail, to the disapproval of other members of the bench who released her.

Then in 1716 Justice Dineley arrested a woman suspected of being a witch and subjected her to the ordeal of swimming in a sluice with a rope around her waist. This was a test that had been introduced into England by King James I in his *Daemonologie*. It was based on the assumption that evil-doers and devil-worshipers were allergic to water because they were allergic to the holy sacraments, and consequently if a suspect was hog-tied and thrown into the water, the ordeal would test a person's innocence or maleficium [malevolence]. If the victims floated on the water, they were guilty; if they sank, they were deemed innocent, although they were then in imminent danger of drowning if they were not dragged out of the water in time. The practice had never won judicial approval, even in the days of rampant witch-hunting when it was widely practiced, and it signalled the growing divide between elite opinion and popular belief.[27] In 1712, when Jane Wenham was accused of witchcraft and offered to undergo the water test to prove her innocence, the examining justice in Hertfordshire said he would not approve it, since the ordeal was 'illegal and unjustifiable.' This did not stop Justice Dineley leading the pack in a local Worcestershire witch-hunt.

Swimming the witch continued to win favour in plebeian rural society for a considerable time longer. The register of Monks Eleigh parish in Suffolk, for example, contains the following entry: 'December 19, 1748. Alice, the wife of Thomas Green, labourer, was swam, malicious and evil people having raised an ill-report of her for being a witch.' Over twenty-five years later another Suffolk outsider, this time suspected of being a 'wizard', was subjected to the same ordeal in the river Deben 'in the presence of a great number of spectators'. He would have drowned, the *Ipswich Journal* reported, had it not been for the assistance of a humane looker-on.[28] Such unofficial ordeals persisted well after the official banning of witch-hunting in 1735, but even in its final years of dubious legality no-one expected a justice of the peace to endorse them.

John Dineley did. 'By God, she swims like a cork' he exclaimed, as the exhausted women was hauled out of the water. He then stripped down and swam about 'on his Back, exposing his nakedness to the Men and Women who were present.' Later, as he pulled on his breeches, he asked several women whether they would like to be 'knocked.' When asked why he had ordered the woman to be immersed in the water, he answered that it was because 'the hair of her cunt is too long and reaches under her feet.'[29] Whether Dineley was drunk or demented when he blurted out this absolutely bizarre remark is unclear, but his crude unorthodox behaviour brought about his dismissal from the bench. In fact, politics might well have influenced the decision, for the justice who exposed him to Lord Chancellor Cowper, the Reverend William Lloyd, was a Whig who had been removed by a Tory chancellor and reinstated in 1714 when the Whigs returned to power. John Dineley, like his father, was Tory-inclined, although he probably thought he might be immune to prosecution given his familial links to the Cowpers.

While John was offending gentlemen in Worcestershire he was also searching for a wife. He settled on one from the Bristol area, one Mary Lawford, the heiress to a fortune created by her grandfather, the grocer and alderman John Lawford, who had bought properties in Stapleton and Tockington, near Almondsbury. The two estates were worth about £1600 a year although they were burdened with a few encumbrances; two mortgages to the tune of £2900 and a lifetime annuity of £250 to Mary's mother Elizabeth out of the Stapleton estate.[30] Later, in 1731, Mary's whole estate, personal and real, was estimated at £24,000, some of it jewels and plate.[31] And so, in January 1716, the terms of the marriage were concluded. John Dineley received a marriage portion of £16,000, agreed to pay down the Gloucestershire mortgages and promised his young bride a jointure of £500 a year upon his death out of his Worcestershire estates.[32] This last obligation had been a condition of his inheriting his maternal grandfather's estate. It was explicitly written into Sir Edward Dineley's will.[33]

The marriage might have been a reasonable financial deal for the families, but it was a mismatch. Nearly twenty years separated the couple. John was a rough-mannered, irascible ex-seaman in his early-thirties; Mary was a ruddy-faced slip of a girl, aged fourteen, barely literate judging by her few letters that have survived, full of phonetic constructions with a Bristolian burr.[34] After his encounter with the Worcestershire bench, John, who showed early signs of being a manic-depressive, seems to have spurned respectable company and retreated into his own world and to the bottle. Mary, on the other hand, craved social company and sought it wherever she could find it. At first this did not matter since offspring came quickly: a son, Edward, who was born at Stapleton within eleven months of the marriage, and another at Charlton in 1722, who died at birth. After that, things started to go badly awry.

Mary's disposition to gad about started to bother John. He tried to curtail her socializing by keeping her short of servants, so that, as she later complained, 'I drest your victuals, clean'd your House, and wash'd your shirts, and had but one girl about thirteen years of age to help me.'[35] These 'servile' tasks, as she described them, did not stop her nocturnal revels. In February 1723 Mary returned to the house in Charlton around midnight and encountered an enraged husband, who kicked her out of the house and bolted all the doors. He turned on the nursemaid, Diana Mellichamp, and ordered her out of the house as well, together with the toddler Edward, swearing that if she did not take the child to its mother he would 'break its neck.'[36] The three of them managed to find shelter at the cottage of a neighbouring wheelwright, and the quarrel was patched up through the mediation of an elderly gentleman, Captain Jacob Meyrick. It was the first recorded confrontation of many.

In the summer of 1726 Mary visited her mother in Stapleton for two months, only to return to Charlton to find John had been philandering with the housekeeper, Elizabeth Atkins, described in a subsequent divorce petition as a person of a 'Mean extraction' and 'very indifferent Character & Reputation'. Mary ordered Atkins out of the house, but she haughtily refused to go unless her master John Dineley told her so. Mary was furious at her intransigence, and later complained that her husband kept 'whores in the home that had Ten Times more Power in it than I ever had.'[37] The situation escalated to a point where John grabbed his wife by the hair, called her a whore, and locked her in a garret. He then ordered his servant Joseph Baker to fetch a chain and two horse padlocks so he might pin Mary to the floor. The astounded servant refused, and so Dineley retrieved them himself, telling his wife he would 'keep her there and beat her to death if she would not carry herself civilly to Elizabeth Atkins.'[38] It seems he kept her there 36 hours, until neighbours intervened. Judging from a contemporary comment such brutal behaviour was not so extraordinary from enraged husbands. Sarah Chapone remarked that 'A good husband would not desire the power of Horsewhipping, confining, half-starving his wife; or squandering her Estate; a bad husband should not be allowed it.'[39] Mary certainly did not think so, and spread the word around about her shameful treatment.

After this serious and brutal confrontation, Dineley made an effort to accommodate his wife's desire for a larger social life. He befriended a local baronet named Sir Robert Jason who lived with his three sisters nearby at

Hinton-on-the-Green. The Jasons were frequent visitors to Charlton and sometimes stayed over. Sir Robert was closer to Mary's age than Dineley, in his early twenties in 1728, while John Dineley was well into middle age by the standards of the eighteenth century and worse the wear through heavy drinking. Sir Robert appeared a more compatible partner for Mary, and this precipitated fits of jealousy from the husband. On one occasion when Sir Robert visited and was sitting close to Mary by the fire, John entered the room 'in a great passion' and asked his wife 'if she would thrust her nose in Sir Robert's face'. He turned on the baronet asking him 'if he did not know the Penalty of Lying with other Man's wives'. Dineley became paranoid that his wife was having an affair with Sir Robert. He called her a slut, a whore, a trollop, a 'bitchington', a 'hell-fire bitch' and threatened her with a whipping. Sometimes he forced her to wear the redcap of whoredom in bed.[40] He was enraged when she came back in the early hours of the morning from drinking parties with the Jasons. He felt humiliated when he learned of Mary's alleged familiarities with Sir Robert in local alehouses and even in his own house. On one occasion Sir Robert was seen with one hand on her breast and the other up her skirts, at least according to Mary Sandiland.[41] On another, when Dineley was away, Sir Robert slept over in suspicious circumstances. He wasn't to be found in his normal sleeping place in the crimson chamber. There was a time when Mary asked Sir Robert to come over to Charlton 'at an unseasonable time of night.' And she was accused of undressing in front of him, something she strenuously denied.[42] Eventually John banned his wife from seeing Sir Robert, but it proved impossible to keep her away. During one drunken revel at Sir Robert's house in Hinton, a local neighbour, Mr John Acton of Bengeworth, declared 'Mr Dineley is a cuckold. He should go to Hinton and look after the drunken whore his wife.'[43] The allegation circulated through the neighbourhood like a bushfire.

The stage was set for a huge explosion in July 1730, on the day the horse races came to Chipping Camden. Mary had persuaded John to go, even though he was busy with the harvest, and she went ahead to collect her horse. She discovered that she had no housing for her side saddle and decided to go to Hinton to borrow some from the Jasons. Dineley took her departure to mean she intended to elope with Sir Robert. When he caught up with her, he asked her, rather oddly, where were her clothes and jewels? Sir John clearly feared his wife intended to bolt, and if so, he wanted to repossess her personal effects, especially the fine ingots of jewelry she inherited from her grandfather.[44] Mary was puzzled by the question and answered flippantly that they were scattered throughout the house. This retort threw Dineley into a paroxysm of rage. He horse-whipped his wife up a ladder into the garret and strapped a chain to her foot and to a chair. He then went to the races himself and ordered the servants to ignore her. The servants, to their credit, climbed the leads and managed to pass some small beer to her through the garret window; a neighbour provided some spirits of wine to bathe her welts and cuts. When Dineley returned from the races late at night, he allowed his wife a bed, but he tightened her ankle chains and imprisoned her there for four days. Neighbours remonstrated with him that it was 'very hard and barbarous that a gentlewoman should be so served' but he responded he 'desired her to reflect upon her present folly and resolve to amend in her future behaviour.'[45] Either that, or the madhouse, for husbands had the right to confine their wives in such places.

Mary Dineley defied her husband one more time. A few weeks later she spent a day and a night carousing with Sir Robert and his friends at the Angel Inn in Pershore. She left with Sir Robert at midnight and did not return to Charlton until four o'clock in the morning. John went berserk. He tracked Mary down to an inn in Bengeworth where she was recuperating from her revel and demanded to be let in. When the landlord refused him entry, he threatened to return with a posse and pull the house down.[46] In late July or early August 1730, she left for London claiming she feared for her life. Three months later, she launched a suit at the Consistory Court in Worcester for separation on grounds of cruelty, asserting she had been whipped and chained 'as never a Dog was used.' In her pleadings, which she had printed for public consumption, she denied the drinking and cavorting, 'tho if anything could excuse so Beastly an Action in a Woman 'twould be the Vile Inhumane Usage I have met with from you.' As for her time at Hinton, where she was accused of sexual trysts with Sir Robert, Mary protested much of her time was taken up trying to arrange a match between her brother-in-law Henry Goodere, and Sir Robert Jason's widowed sister.[47] In her pleadings she requested alimony and the recovery of her remaining personal possessions. She damned Dineley for his whoring, his financial laxity with regard to her fortune, his exceptional brutality and malice. Dineley, for his part, printed a notice that his wife had been 'entertained and secreted from her husband by some base designing Persons for wicked purposes.' When they were discovered, he declared, they would be prosecuted with all the severity the law allowed.[48]

Dineley's rage, it seems, knew no bounds. Just before Mary sued for a separation, she applied for a writ of supplication [a supplicavit] to restrain John from assaulting her. Her lawyer demanded impossibly high bonds of £6000 at the Court of Chancery, but even the award of two £2000 bonds enraged Dineley, who reputedly rode up to her wife's coach on her return from London and fired a brace of pistols into it, searing Mary's right arm. A month later, when she was travelling from Ashton Underhill to London, Mary stopped for refreshments at the Angel Inn in Pershore, one of her old haunts with Sir Robert Jason. John Dineley sprang into the room, she deposed, and 'in a Violent and passionate manner Insulted her.' He vowed that if he ever met her again he would strangle her, or again fire at her from his horse. He swore 'he knew ye consequences that he should be Hanged but it would be a sattisfaction to him if he lived but half an hour later.' As Mary left the inn, he grabbed her by the arm and swung her around. Holding her by the hair and cap, he invited the astonished crowd around him to join in humiliating her, crying 'Hallow, Hallow Boys, here is a Whore goeing to be Duck't.'[49] Fortunately, a gentlewoman intervened to guide her to the safety of a nearby shop.

After these assaults Mary demanded that the Court of Chancery execute the bonds. John responded with fifteen affidavits claiming that Mary had sensationalised if not fabricated these encounters. On hearing the evidence, the court refused to release Sir John from all the bonds, demanding that he restrain himself, and that order appeared to work.[50] Dineley seemed disposed to settle. Two months after the case was heard in Worcester, John agreed to drop all law suits and pay Mary £150 to clear her current debts. He agreed to hand over her personal clothes and jewellery and offered her an allowance of £200 a year for life, with a further £100 per annum on the death of his father. In return she agreed he would not be responsible for any debts she incurred after August 1730.[51] The agreement proved a dead letter because Dineley was really determined to find evidence of Mary's adultery with Sir Robert Jason and convict her on that account. Many of the rumours that circulated about their tête-à-têtes were tantalizingly inconclusive. They had allegedly slept together one night at the Golden Fleece at Bengeworth along with Sir Robert's sister Anne and Mary's maid, Ann Duncox. Mary claimed Sir Robert slept drunkenly in the chair. The maid claimed there was frolicking in the bed, whose motions shunted Anne Jason to the floor. She further testified that at 3am Sir Robert arose with his breeches down to his knees and went to fetch some cider.[52]

This evidence was probably enough to prove adultery on the part of Mary, but John Dineley wanted something firmer. Somewhat suspiciously he produced two witnesses who were prepared to testify that Mary and Sir Robert had sex in the plain light of day. Henry Grove claimed he saw them under a tree in the missionary position, with Mary on her back and her petticoats up. His wife, Esther Grove, confirmed another encounter *flagrante delicto* a few weeks later, two weeks before Mary left for London. Henry Grove later conceded that he had been suborned to provide this evidence. He had been bribed to give false testimony on the promise of a three-life lease of a farm let at £70 a year.[53] But at the time his evidence was compelling enough to allow Dineley to win a case against Sir Robert for a 'criminal conversation' with his wife, probably because John pursued the suit in Middlesex not Worcestershire, where John's volatile and violent behaviour was better known. In the patriarchal discourse of the law, Sir Robert had trespassed on the 'property' of John Dineley, that is, the body of Mary, for which he was ordered to pay £1000 in damages by the Court of Common Pleas.[54]

The decision in Common Pleas paid for some of Sir John's legal expenses, but more importantly it promised to give him some leverage in the protracted marital dispute. Nonetheless, the litigation before the church courts satisfied neither party. Despite the beatings and imprisonment in a garret, despite the pistol shots and public humiliations, the Worcester Consistory Court astoundingly thought Mary was not in a life-threatening situation, which was a necessary condition of alimony. At the same time, the proctor did not think John Dineley's claim that his actions were recriminations upon a known adultery sufficient to void the original suit.[55] This inconclusive verdict only escalated the dispute. Mary appealed to the Court of Arches, and when turned down, to the High Court of Delegates, which sat on the case for five years. She and Sir Robert Jason sued John Dineley at the Court of King's Bench for suborning witnesses in the crim. con. case, but Dineley was inexplicably acquitted for lack of evidence, despite the fact that Henry Groves had confessed before Justice De Veil of Bow Street that he had been bribed to give false testimony.[56]

John Dineley then retaliated by bringing Mary's maidservant to the stand to swear that his wife and Sir Robert had conspired to incriminate him for the subornation; that from the beginning it was a vexatious and malicious prosecution. Sir Robert was acquitted, but Mary was not. She received a small fine and was sentenced to a year in King's Bench Prison. Mary responded by racking up debts for fees and food at the Golden Lyon Sponging House within the rules of the prison; this was a preliminary detention centre for debtors destined for King's Bench, which also served as an alehouse for residents. The charges in such places were exorbitant, and John Dineley was expected to pay them in the absence of a viable separation agreement. Dineley fought off the move by successfully claiming that Mary was not entitled to the rules of King's Bench and he was therefore not responsible for the bill. He had made the claim earlier, when Mary was racking up debts in London, on the grounds that she had 'eloped'. This deliberate departure, he argued, absolved him from paying her bills.[57]

Then Sir John moved in for the kill, a bill for a full divorce before the House of Lords. This would have freed John of any responsibility for Mary's debts; it would have cancelled her jointure and cut off her right to dower on the Dineley estate. If passed, it would have granted Sir John the right to remarry and produce other legitimate heirs.[58] Dineley's case rested on the conviction of Sir Robert Jason at the Court of Common Pleas and his wife's adjudged adultery. Mary's counsel countered by producing the confession that Henry Grove had perjured himself, insisting that it was on this critical testimony that Dineley had won his case at Common Pleas. Their lordships were reluctant retroactively to reverse that verdict, although the evidence of Grove's perjury must have made an impression.[59] Sir John Dineley produced witnesses replicating the evidence brought before the Court of Arches of Lady's Dineley's 'familiarity' with Sir Robert. Lord Hardwicke's notes on the matter read a bit like a scandal sheet. Citing witness and event, the brief entries ran thus: Sarah Bates, 'the bed tumbled'; Eleanor Andrews, 'Sir Robert…under the bed' and then 'his leg over hers'; Richard Bevan, the two 'seen in the bedroom with the door locked.'[60] Lady Mary countered this salacious detail with the garret scenarios and allegations of rampant cruelty. She produced her own parade of witnesses. It was tit for tat, and in the end the Lords rejected the bill of divorce on 16 May 1739 before it reached the third reading. Sir John had won on dubious grounds at the Court of Common Pleas, but no ecclesiastical court had endorsed his version of events; a full divorce had to fulfil both conditions, evidence of adultery and a judicial separation before a church court. Judging from Lord Hardwicke's notes on the trial, this last issue was crucial. Their lordships were very reluctant to grant a petition of divorce without a clear sentence from a church court. Only two exceptions were known: those of the Duke of Norfolk and the Earl of Macclesfield; both noblemen of stature, not some rough-edged Worcestershire baronet. So Sir John did not get the verdict he desired, and he fumed about having to pay the expenses of Mary's witnesses before the Lords, which were calculated at £204. In the end, he stubbornly refused to do so.[61] He could not avoid his other obligations to her, however. Technically speaking he was still bound by the separation settlement of 1731, and his Worcestershire estate remained encumbered by her jointure of £500 a year after his death.

Nine years of litigation in some of the highest courts of the land diminished Dineley's fortune, notwithstanding his successful suit against Sir Robert Jason. We know that he hired Sir John Strange to represent him in Chancery and King's Bench and as a recently elected bencher of Middle Temple and solicitor general for Sir Robert Walpole's administration, lawyers of his calibre

Engraved portrait of Captain Samuel Goodere, made at the time of his trial for murder, 1741. From *The Trials of Samuel Goodere, Matthew Mahony and Charles White*, broadside, Bristol Libraries, B10146

were expensive.[62] Dineley claimed that his legal bills came to £14,000, over £2 million in today's terms, and he had been hampered by the fact that his father, Sir Edward Goodere, lived beyond eighty and deprived him of any revenues he might accrue from the Herefordshire estate at Burghope, not to mention the income from Hanley Castle which he had conveyed to his father.

Sir Edward Goodere died in March 1739. He was paraded to the public as a member of one of the 'ancientest families' in Herefordshire and as a 'true brave Englishman who never took an intended affront or ever gave one.'[63] On one occasion in 1702 he is said to have sorted out Beau Robert Fielding for a slight at the theatre in Drury Lane, causing a flutter among the ladies when he drew blood.[64] Whatever Sir Edward's public reputation, his son John Dineley-Goodere was shocked to learn of his will. Despite his generosity to his father, he was only given a life interest in the Herefordshire estate, which went to his younger brother Samuel. Although it was not unusual for younger sons to get an interest in a secondary estate, John seems to have been flummoxed by the arrangement.

This was because Sam's relations with his father had not always been amicable. In his youth he had fallen out with his father, threatened him for money, and whined that he had not used his political influence to secure him a captaincy in the royal navy.[65] Samuel had served as a first lieutenant in the War of Spanish Succession on HMS *Preston* and in 1719 he was responsible for the bombardment of San Sebastian and the neighbouring ports of Ferrol and St Antonio. His printed journal suggests he carried out his duties with courage and aplomb, burning three men-of-war, capturing a few shallops[66] and one small privateer, and landing troops near St Antonio at personal risk. But because he botched a landing of French troops on the island of St Clare, he was court-martialled by Captain Robert Johnson for misconduct. The Court decided that Goodere was 'very much wanting in the performance of his duty' in failing to land the troops and he was consequently dismissed from his ship, then HMS *Deptford*, in December 1719.[67] This was tantamount to leaving the service altogether and for many years Samuel Goodere was simply a lieutenant on half-pay awaiting a berth.

In the long run-up to the 1734 election Goodere was encouraged to use his interest in Evesham on behalf of a Tory candidate, William Taylor, and to secure the co-operation of his father and brother in the election; all on the promise of a captaincy. But Samuel decided he could better achieve his ambitions by supporting Taylor's opponents, the neighbouring Whig landlords Sir John Rushout and John Rudge. This placed him in opposition to his father and propelled him into the limelight as the Whig mayoral candidate for Evesham in 1733 against none other than his brother. The result was a tie, and in the riotous aftermath of this inconclusive election, Samuel had brother John physically ejected from the mayoral pew of the city's principal church, where the swearing-in was due to take place. This eviction set them on an acrimonious path for the rest of their lives.[68]

Samuel Goodere gained little from this political manoeuvre; merely a brief captaincy of HMS *Antelope*, a fourth-rate ship with fifty guns.[69] His father was unhappy with his antics, but over time he relented. Sir Edward could not have been upset with the result of the 1734 Evesham election, which returned two anti-Excise candidates, one a Tory. And Samuel's second marriage to a Monmouthshire widow proved more stable than his brother's.[70] He produced two sons and three daughters and spent more time at Burghope with his father in his old age. He seems to have insinuated himself into Herefordshire society and became a fitting representative of his family, serving on the bench and as a trustee of the Hereford turnpike.[71] According to one account, Sir Edward regularly confided in Samuel during his final years and probably felt his second son was entitled to the Herefordshire estate, leaving his eldest only a life interest in it. Sir Edward was disturbed by the reckless way John Dineley-Goodere was destroying his landed estate in a relentless, vindictive divorce against his wife.[72] According to Mary, Sir Edward desired his son 'to use me better'; his treatment of her 'almost broke his heart.' John, by contrast, was so angry at his father's will that he gave him a funeral well below his station, reputedly akin to a servant's or plebeian burial. Samuel was so outraged by this slight to his father that he turned up at Burghope in Herefordshire with six bouncers and demanded that John leave immediately, on the unsubstantiated grounds that his father had long ago given him the lease to the house. Samuel's wife begged him not to cause trouble and diffused the situation, while John reputedly shooed off his brother's bruisers with an unloaded blunderbuss.[73]

The stage was set for a bitter rivalry that would ultimately end in murder. Samuel had already irritated his brother by aiding Mary Dineley in her legal battles.[74] Now Sir John Dineley, as he was now titled, was determined to make the most of his life tenure at Burghope and deprive his brother of the possibility of inheriting the Worcestershire estate. In order to exclude his brother from that estate he had to break the entail, because his only surviving son, Edward, had tuberculosis and was not expected to live long, and according to his grandfather's will, the estate would devolve to Samuel and his heirs after Sir John and his male progeny. Edward had been neglected by his quarrelsome parents; he was never given any filial attention by his father, who in a paranoid frame of mind, suspected he was not his offspring. The poor boy was apprenticed to a sadler, hardly an appropriate training for a future baronet and proprietor of a large estate. He quickly fell into a life of dissipation and was at death's door when his father's attorney, William White, found him in Blackman Street, Southwark, poor, wretched, evading debtors.

Edward Dineley was at that point in the care of his mother, who could do so because Blackman Street was within the rules of King's Bench where she was imprisoned. She importuned him to sign over his estate to her, in 'possession, reversion or remainder', in what was clearly an attempt to frustrate Sir John Dineley's intention to exclude her from his will. Edward's will of 6 January 1739 gave Lady Mary full powers to dispose of her son's property 'notwithstanding her couverture.' In it, Edward declared that 'her husband, my father, shall not have the power to dispose of the same or any part thereof but it shall be to her separate use and be disposed of by her.'[75] He referred to her as his 'Dear Mother' which suggests either that he had begun to repair the differences between them or that his mother had squeezed the endearment out of him.

Sir John Dineley was keen however to frustrate the designs of his separated wife, and to deliver a blow to brother Samuel, who had been helping Lady Mary resist Sir John's efforts to secure a divorce. Although he knew his son was dying of tuberculosis, he had him moved across the Thames to his attorney's house in Fetter Lane. There he offered him £20 to pay his immediate debts and a £200 annuity in return for a recovery, a legal instrument that allowed Sir John to dispose of his estate as he pleased. His attorney William White had suggested a more generous offer, but Sir John was unwilling to give his son a penny more than he had to, doubting his own paternity. In his petition before the House of Lords Sir John had actually disowned Edward, although his legitimacy mattered here. In fact, John is alleged to have said that he was only happy with the annuity because he knew his son would not live to enjoy it, a mean-spirited comment if ever there was one.[76]

The recovery was carried out in very dubious circumstances. According to affidavits later exhibited before the Court of Exchequer, Edward was too debilitated to know what he was really doing. He had been persuaded to sign the recovery by his old nurse, Elizabeth Stiles, who was offered a 'great reward' to bring him round. Edward was so ill he had to be propped up by Stiles and a local glover named Mary Pursley in order to sign. His hand was so shaky he signed ineffectually, and on the wrong side of the seal. Accordingly, Sir John Dineley and attorney White ordered virtually everybody out of the room, and then ordered White's clerk, John Tapscott, to place a quill in Edward's hand and run it over the document. The witnesses were then called in to testify to the signature, although they were unhappy about it; especially William Stephenson, a glover who also happened to be the undertaker. Once he had signed, Edward was carried out of the attorney's lodgings in Fetter Lane as if he were a corpse, four men acting as virtual pallbearers. He died a few days later, on 20 January 1739. Allegedly Sir John drove the hearse himself, consigning his son's body to a pauper's grave to save on burial fees.

In his new will of 11 January 1739, Sir John excluded his brother Samuel from the entail, and devised his estates to his nephews John and Samuel Foote, the sons of his sister; that is, if he did not marry again and produce new heirs, for the decision of the House of Lords was then still pending.[77] John Foote, a naval lieutenant who was fighting in the Caribbean under Sir Chaloner Ogle, would inherit the Worcestershire estate; Samuel, the younger brother and future comedian, then raising eyebrows in Oxford where he was a scholar at Worcester College, was offered those he acquired by marriage in Gloucestershire. The arrangement was bound to be contentious. Samuel Goodere believed the recovery was a forgery and refused to accept its legitimacy. He alleged that his brother knew full well that moving Edward across the Thames might hasten his death and render him more vulnerable to his father's solicitations. His nephew Edward was 'in a most helpless and debilitated situation both in body and mind…and utterly incapable of judging or acting for himself.'[78] As far as Samuel was concerned, the recovery was fraudulent. This was evident from the very dodgy signature around the seal, and the crucial fact that the witnesses to the recovery were not in the room when it was signed. Sam had been cheated out of an inheritance. He challenged the legitimacy of the recovery in the Court of Common Pleas.[79]

For her part, Lady Mary believed she had a prior claim on the estate in the light of Edward's will, although it was not actually proved at the Prerogative Court of Canterbury until early April 1739. She continued to insist she was entitled to the jointure of £500 on the Worcestershire estates, as set out in Sir Edward Dineley's will and confirmed in her articles of marriage in 1716. She also argued that her husband had failed to pay off a mortgage on the Tockington estate owed to her grandfather, Thomas Cole, and by his will these debts were now owing to her.[80] After the murder of 1741 she was locked in a Chancery suit with the Foote family over their obligations to her. And quite predictably, the quarrel between the brothers lasted beyond the grave, with Samuel Goodere's son Edward, disputing his cousin John Foote Dineley's right to the Worcestershire properties by suggesting that Sir John's recovery was fraudulent and his new will invalid.[81]

The legal wrangles did not even end there. Creditors demanded to be paid before the families squabbled over the remaining assets. In Bristol, the families of Henry Parsons and Lawford Cole requested the repayment of outstanding mortgages on the Gloucestershire estates, as indeed, did lawyer Jarrit Smith, who had loaned Sir John more money to pay down those very mortgages. In Worcestershire new creditors emerged from the woodwork for debts due on the manor of Peopleton, and messuages in Norgrove, Offenham, Aldington, and Badsey.[82] It became very clear that Sir John had greatly neglected his properties, quite unlike his maternal grandfather, who was described as 'a very warry and frugal gent' who 'would seldom Permitt his Tenants to bee Longe in Arrears.'[83] Sir John had failed to fulfil his obligations under his marriage agreement; he overlooked commitments made by his grandfather, Sir Edward Dineley; he let Worcestershire leases lapse. He destroyed two good estates in his vindictive pursuit of a divorce, with the result that the Dineley-Goodere inheritance became a mere shadow of what it had been.

The fact that John Foote Dineley was a fun-loving, libertine naval lieutenant didn't help. He had just returned from a hard-fought, debilitating campaign against the Spanish at Cartagena, where he was in the thick of the battle with Captain Charles Knowles on HMS *Weymouth*. He had been in the advance party that took possession of Castillo Grande, before disease ripped into the troops ordered to mount an assault on Cartagena.[84] Lieutenant Foote seems to have left the *Weymouth* before he was able to profit from the spoils of war,[85] but he salvaged some money by clandestinely marrying an heiress with a small fortune, one Margaret White. When it came to family affairs, however, he confessed he was an 'absolute stranger'. He quickly found himself locked in a dispute with his mother who asserted he owed her £3456 and took possession of Charlton and Hadley Castle to reinforce her claim.[86] John protested that his uncle had arranged a mortgage of £2000 to satisfy her, but he proved to be an easy-going lieutenant on half pay who ran with the hounds, ran into debt and lacked the assiduity to attend to his Worcestershire legacy. Before he died in 1758, he disobliged his mother by selling Charlton to Lady Mary's new husband, the opposition printer William Rayner.[87]

Between John and his equally profligate brother Sam Foote, it came as no surprise that the Dineley estates were sold and dispersed. John Foote Dineley sold his properties in Sheriff's Lench to satisfy his mother's claim.[88] He released lands at Hanley Hall to accommodate Lady Mary's jointure. By 1770 the Dineley baronetcy was no longer linked with the estates in the three west-country counties. In the case of the Herefordshire estate, the eccentric Sir John, Samuel Goodere's son and future Windsor pensioner, sold it to an East Indian nabob who was considering reviving his electoral fortunes in that county.[89] As a result, Burghope entered and exited this family's turbulent history by way of the riches of the East.

Rather ironically, amid all the struggles over the Goodere-Dineley estates, Lady Mary Dineley emerged as the most successful claimant. She held on to her jointure and retained control of the Stapleton estate, thanks to the cunning of William Rayner, who forced the impecunious Samuel Foote to hand it over in return for paying his debts and a reversion on the estate. The aspiring actor and playwright was in no position to argue, since he was obliged to pay over £1200 to various creditors to secure his release from the Fleet in 1743. By the time he was in a position to reclaim his heavily encumbered Gloucestershire properties, Rayner had sold them off to accommodate creditors, especially Jarrit Smith, Sir John Dineley's principal creditor, who raised enough money to revive the dormant baronetcy of the Smyths of Long Ashton. Rayner also obliged Lady Mary by buying John Foote Dineley's diminishing share of the lands around Charlton and Cropthorne. A man who had a reputation as a social adventurer, Rayner then smartly sold them off.[90] He resembled a vulture picking and profiting from a crumbling fortune.

But in January 1739 that was in the future. At this point in time Sir John chose to overlook the disagreements that his sister Eleanor and husband had caused over the Dineley bequest and privileged their sons as remainders of his estate; no doubt to silence the older Footes while his petition before the Lords was still pending. A new marriage and new heir would outfox all his relatives and his wife. In framing his will of January 1741, he predictably overlooked the entitlements his estranged wife had on Stapleton and the jointure she might claim under their marriage settlement. Perhaps he felt, if he could not divorce her outright, he could beat down her demands after she had experienced the penury of a debtors' prison and the inflated price of legal fees. To the Lords she had complained that she had received a mere five guineas from her husband since her confinement in King's Bench and 'must have starved if some persons out of mere charity supplied her with common necessities.'[91] Mary was so desperate that she even fabricated another son, whom she claimed was born just before her departure from Charlton; just to confound Sir John's testamentary strategy once more. The ploy didn't work. There were no witnesses to the birth and her lawyer eventually admitted it was a fraudulent claim, which rather put her at the mercy of Sir John.[92] When he was murdered, Mary affected sorrow and horror. She told her cousin that the news of 'poor Sr Jon…have all most ben my Deth for I am frit outt of my wits.' Yet she spent the bulk of the letter thinking of the mourning dress she would wear 'in the very pink of ye mode', no doubt to attract prospective suitors.[93]

That was also in the future. In May 1739 Sir John Dineley had failed to crush his wife in a divorce suit that had cost thousands of pounds, although he probably derived some satisfaction from impoverishing her in the process. What Sir John did not reckon with was the all-consuming anger of his brother, who was determined to overturn the recovery, and failing that, pursue darker designs.[94]

CHAPTER TWO

Prequel: Bristol at the time of Dineley's Murder

In August 1740, Robert Fytche, Captain of the *Ruby*, dropped anchor at Kingroad near the mouth of the River Avon with Admiralty orders to impress some fresh sailors to fight the Spanish. Bristol's Society of Merchant Venturers took a dim view of activities like this. War was obstructive to international trade, their ships targeted for legitimate plunder and their crews forcibly waylaid and pressed onto Naval vessels as they made their way home. Fytche would have to parley terms with the merchant-dominated Bristol Corporation and agree to cruise the *Ruby* and an accompanying tender, *The Charming Sally*, between Kingroad and Ilfracombe, rather than remain rooted to the mouth of the river. By September, the job was proving difficult. Although eleven men had been picked up by the tender near Lundy, Fytche registered little success closer to Bristol. 'It is impossible to get any here', he reported, 'the Pilots' Boats meeting the ships below the Holmes and putting their men ashore before any Boats can board them'.[1] Despite these difficulties, he seized an additional thirty men the following week and was looking forward to setting sail with them before an outbreak of smallpox amongst the Spanish prisoners infected the rest of his crew. But in October, tragedy struck. Captain Fytche mounted the rails in the Gallery astern of the ship and sat himself down, then pulled out his pistol and shot himself through the head; although it was assumed by crew members, who came running at the sound of the shot but found no trace of his body, that he had fallen into the water and sunk.[2] Shortly afterwards, Samuel Goodere was sent to Bristol by the Admiralty as Fytche's replacement, and the scene was set for a second unnatural death aboard the *Ruby*.

While his official orders were to complete the work of impressment and then sail to engage the enemy, Goodere must also have recognised the opportunity his posting had given him to settle scores with his brother. Yet the plan he consequently hatched remains obscure. In the immediate aftermath of Dineley's death, Goodere maintained he sought only to confine his brother as a madman so that his inheritance could be legally restored without any further damage being done. Goodere knew that some of Dineley's legal affairs were being handled by the Bristol lawyer and future Tory MP Jarrit

Smith, whose house looked out over the city's fashionable College Green. Involving Smith as Dineley's trusted advisor in a familial meeting of reconciliation was one option, and if Dineley could be persuaded, in Smith's company, to restore the entail, any need for further action or legal expense might be avoided. On the other hand, Goodere was now the master of a man of war, anchored in the Bristol Channel and, by January, ready to sail. If Dineley could be somehow got aboard, he could be subjected to further persuasion, confined as a lunatic or even, if all else failed, be made to disappear beneath the deep waters of the Atlantic. However, the *Ruby* lay at anchor seven miles from the city harbour, and conveying a resistant Dineley through narrow streets and thoroughfares to a boat on the river or a coach on the road, without attracting unwelcome public attention, was unlikely to be easy. But before we address that problem, we turn our attention to the role played by the city of Bristol in the Goodere affair, in terms of its topography, its judicial and commercial status and the attitude of the governing elite to the maintenance of both order and reputation.

With a population of around 35,000 in 1741, Bristol was one of the busiest urban environments in the country. To the author of *The Present State of Great Britain*, it was 'next to London, the most trading and flourishing place in England, happily seated both for the Welsh and West India trade'.[3] Having successfully challenged the Royal African Company's former domination of the British slave trade, mid-century Bristol was fitting out an average of 36 ventures each year and was responsible for roughly forty per cent of British traffic to the Guinea Coast. American trade was in equally fine fettle, the tonnage of shipping arriving from transatlantic destinations rising from 9,830 in 1700 to 12,796 by 1742.[4] The Corporation spent lavishly on harbour improvements, snapping up old properties encroaching on the city's cramped quay space and levelling them to make it 'all flush from the conduit on the Back clear round to the Key'.[5] Visitors were often impressed. Defoe thought it 'the greatest, richest and the best port of Trade in Great Britain, London only excepted',[6] and Pope marvelled at the size of the harbour with 'as far as you can see, hundreds of ships, their masts as thick as they can stand by one another'. In fact Bristol was fast outgrowing its own infrastructure, a problem visibly demonstrated by the great four-arched stone Bridge that gave access to the city across the Avon, 'so incumbered with houses' complained one guidebook, 'that foot passengers are in great danger in going along'. In common with most of the city streets, it was 'much crowded with a strange mixture of Seamen, women, children, loaded horses, asses, sledges with goods dragging along'. Critics berated the Common Council for splashing out on

PREQUEL: BRISTOL AT THE TIME OF DINELEY'S MURDER

Andrew Bernard Lens, *West Prospect View of the City of Bristol* (1727). Bristol Culture: Bristol Museums and Archives, M988. Shipping entering and leaving the city on the Avon can be seen beside the ropewalk to the right

the harbour while the city's living space was so overcrowded. 'When we consider Bristol as a place of trade and riches', continued the guidebook, 'we are greatly surprised to find the houses so meanly built and the streets narrow, dirty and ill-paved'.[7]

Some thought the city's mercantile culture excessively materialistic, but both Corporation and clergy were happy to extol Bristol merchants as civic heroes. Trade was the *cause* of cities, ran one published sermon, 'and cities are as well the nurseries of learning and schools of politeness as the centre of trade and the seat of magnificence'.[8] And as the merchants enriched themselves, argued the eighteenth-century chronicler, William Barrett, 'they refunded great part of the wealth they acquired here to the city again' through charitable works. In the 1730s nearly a third of all apprentices indentured in Bristol were sponsored by charitable societies.[9]

Wayfinding demanded accurate mapping and it was not by chance that John Rocque, the most important and innovative map maker in the country during the first half of the eighteenth century, chose Bristol as the subject of his first foray into urban cartography in 1742. Until then, Rocque was known only as a surveyor of estate, garden and country houses, and he would soon be much better known for the great multi-sheet map of London that followed. But the

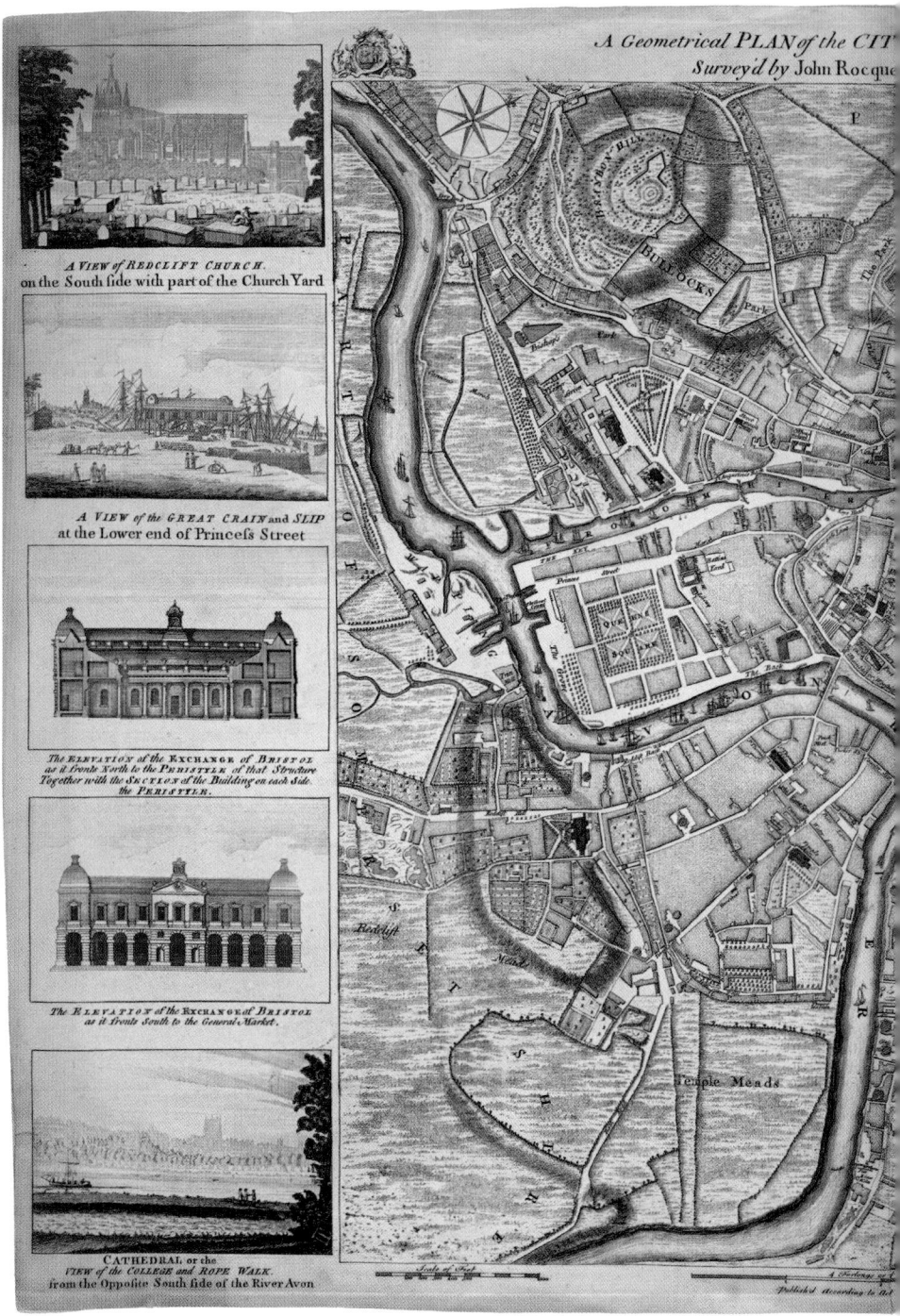

John Rocque, *Plan of the City and Suburbs of Bristol* (1742). Bristol Archives, 07770/1

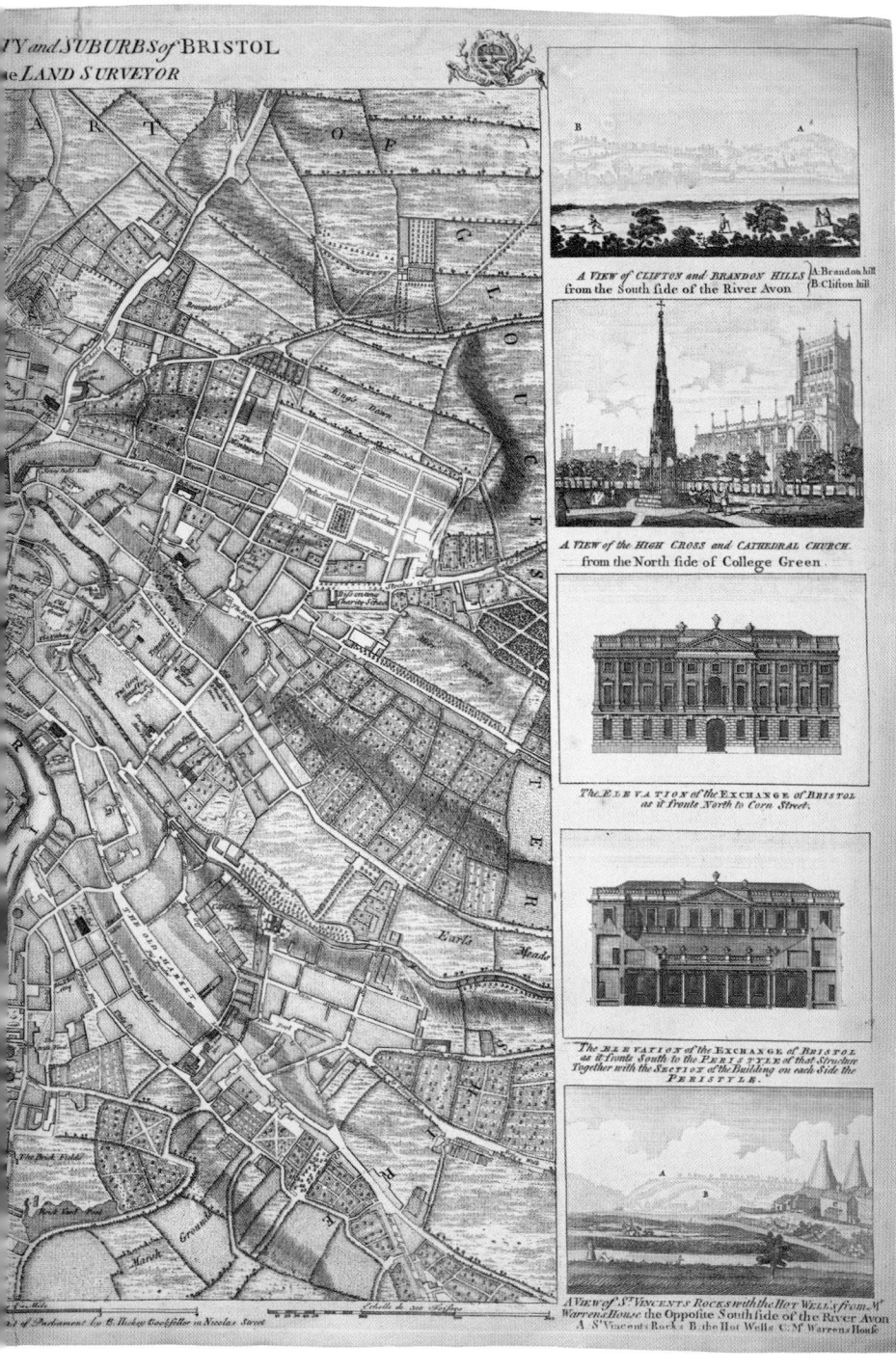

John Rocque, *Plan of the City and Suburbs of Bristol* (1742). Bristol Archives, 07770/1. Border vignette of the harbourside crane and slip

John Rocque, *Plan of the City and Suburbs of Bristol* (1742). Bristol Archives, 07770/1. Border vignette looking towards Hotwells with industrial glass houses in the right foreground

Bristol map, printed in four large interlocking sections, was his first. No other city in Britain could boast a map of such detail or complexity.

Roque's map superseded the earlier street maps of James Millerd, originally surveyed in 1670 and revised in several editions to 1732. It offered a grand vision of Bristol, more spacious than it actually was, with felicitous prospects of the Cathedral and St Mary Redcliffe in the margins along with several views of the new Exchange. Only the portrait of the Great Crane and Slip at the end of Prince Street, where Dineley's murderer Matthew Mahony landed on the morning of 19 January 1741, and the cone shaped refineries in front of St Vincent's Rock, convey a sense of the industrial landscape.

We get a glimpse of the narrow streets encircling the old medieval centre around Corn Street and Broad Street as it was at the time of the Dineley murder, although Marsh Street, where rough-edged sailors caroused, and the Pithay, the site of pawnbrokers and lodging houses, are impossibly spacious. Rather predictably, for a map designed to appeal to local merchants and gentry, Rocque zoned in on the grand and formal geometry of the town houses arranged neatly around Queen Square. To this fashionably Georgian prospect, Rocque added a flotilla of ships on the Avon and the Frome whose bustling quays separated the privacy of the Square from the genteel cross walks of College Green and its recently relocated centre piece, the city's stone cross. Here was the scene of Dineley's abduction, the ropewalks of Canons Marsh through which he was hustled, and the river's edge at Mardyke where he was pulled onto a waiting rowing boat for his last journey down river. And here too, Rocque added a small drawing of the gallows on the open country at the summit of St Michael's Hill, so recently occupied by Dineley's abductors. In 1742, when Rocque's map was published, the hillsides to the north and east of College Green were still largely undeveloped though a start had been made on the upmarket suburbs of Kingsdown and plans were afoot to create the new wide avenue of Park Street.[10]

Proud of the city's economic prosperity though its merchants may have been, they were also acutely aware of threats to it, including the very war that brought Goodere and the *Ruby* to the city in the first place. Although Bristol's overall share of international trade remained well ahead of both Liverpool and Glasgow, war with Spain and subsequently France, adversely affected both European and American markets, leaving the production of West Indian sugar the only significant area of economic growth in the 1740s.[11] The Navy's impress service was a notoriously regular visitor, never welcome, and sometimes the cause of murderous affrays, so by customary agreement, gangs were no longer sent openly onto the quays. Goodere's instructions were to leave the *Ruby* at anchor in Kingroad where homeward bound ships customarily waited for a favourable tide. There they could be boarded without fuss, their officers powerless to prevent the carrying off of their fittest men. This strategy was first trialled in 1734 when the Admiralty sent no less than five ships into the channel, some to Kingroad and others to cruise between Bridgwater and Milford, 'so not one ship can escape'.[12] But as fears grew of Spanish incursions in the British colonies of Carolina, Georgia, Gibraltar and Jamaica in the summer of 1738, impressment intensified. The hotter the press, the more likely it was to spark conflicts of interest between local government and the central state. Two years before Fytche's arrival in the *Ruby*, another man of war, the *Lively*, had sailed into Kingroad and set about harassing all homeward bound shipping. The *Lively's* crew impressed as many fit men as it could find, and then sent boats up the River Avon to the pilot village of Pill, where, it was reported, men could be seen jumping from trows and cutters into the water to evade capture. With no 'protections' [exemptions] offered by the Navy, even to the smallest coastal vessels, the Corporation were fearful that traders from neighbouring Severnside harbours would be too intimidated to risk a trip up the Avon, depleting supplies to Bristol's markets a few short weeks before the opening of the summer fair. It was a scenario that would be replicated in later wars.

Mayor Nathaniel Day despatched a messenger to treat with the *Lively's* captain, requesting safe passage for coastal vessels, but he was rebuffed with a 'regardless answer, uncommon from a Gentleman to a chief Magistrate of the second City of this Kingdom'.[13] The City took the matter up with the Admiralty, who initially agreed to protections from the press, but then sent another man of war, the *Spy*, the following summer. Once again, merchants and Corporation were powerless to prevent international shipping, coastal traders and even small fishing boats from indiscriminate boarding and interference with their crews. Captains trying to outrun the blockade were given short shrift; at least one mackerel boat receiving cannon fire across her bows to bring her round. With the coastal trade now officially embargoed by government order, the Corporation appealed once again for the protection of domestic shipping, 'because we are sure it is not His Majesty's Design to starve 100,000 of his People, as must be the consequence of stopping the Market Boats on both sides of the Severn'.[14] As in previous years, the Admiralty was keen to avoid confrontations on Bristol's quays so it did not send press gangs into the city, but instead ordered magistrates to furnish 'volunteers' for the navy. Hoping perhaps to ease the pressure on market traders down river, the Corporation sent constables out to comb the streets and take up as many able-bodied seamen and landsmen as they could lay their hands on, a sweep that also netted a number of 'idle and disorderly' vagrants. In all, some 200 men were crammed into Bridewell over three nights in July, to await inspection by the *Spy's* officers. However, only 70 were subsequently deemed fit for naval service and the rest were released.[15]

Since the spring of 1739, all the talk in the streets and coffee houses had been the plundering of Bristol ships by Spanish privateers in the West Indies and the Bay of Biscay, the loss of thousands of pounds worth of cargo and the illegal detention of Bristol captains and sailors. These attacks and seizures were not altogether unreasonable, for British merchants had been openly defying a monopoly imposed by Spain upon trade with its own American colonies. It was the case of an aggressive maritime power baulking at the overly pretentious claims of an old imperial power, defended by *guardacostas* whose seizures were questionably legal. Bristol was one of several towns to petition Walpole's government for protection from Spanish *guardacostas* but ministers prevaricated over a declaration of war until the end of October. In the intervening summer months, merchants took comfort from the arrival of letters of marque, sanctioning retaliation against Spain. They had, after all, already established something of a reputation for privateering earlier in the century.[16] The fitting out and manning of privateers, trumpeted the newspapers, would 'fire the breast of almost every single Cit with Martial Ardor and an Ambition of *plucking* off as many Spanish Ears as would serve to nail on every Gate throughout Great Britain', a reference to the alleged cropping of British captain Robert Jenkins' ear by *guardacostas* in 1731.

Within three weeks, four ships, the *Hanover*, the *Eagle*, the *Westmoreland* and the *Barclay*, were made ready to sail from Bristol and the Society of Merchants continued pouring money into privateering well into the autumn. By November some £5000 had been invested 'towards that glorious purpose' in the shipyards as various vessels, including a couple of old whaling ships were converted for battle, with further sums mooted.[17] Among the principal owners and investors of this privateering enterprise, at least down to 1744, were eleven members of the Merchant Venturers and two founding members of the newly minted Tory Steadfast Society, namely the linen draper William Berrow and the American merchant John Brickdale. Twelve owners of privateers are known to have been slave trade investors, including some of the largest: men like John Cross, an African merchant trading to St Kitts; Richard Farr, the sheriff in 1746; William Gordon, Isaac Hobhouse and James Laroche senior, the mayor in 1750.[18] Slaving, at least, was a bipartisan, non-denominational affair that spilled over into privateering.

The delicacy of negotiations between the Corporation and the Admiralty over impressment is indicative of Bristol's determination to protect its historic sovereignty. It was to have some bearing indeed, upon the Corporation's insistence on trying Goodere in the city's own courts rather than bow to the prisoner's initial attempts to get his trial shifted to the court of Admiralty; a measure requiring a judicial ruling and some legal argument to settle once and for all the precise extent of the city's jurisdiction into the open waters of the Channel. The importance to mayor Henry Combe of reasserting the right of the civilian courts to try the captain of a vessel sent by the Navy to impress

Bristol seamen should not perhaps be underestimated.

Neither were disputes of this kind between the Common Council and central government restricted to the activities of the Navy, for the land army too provided regular tests for Bristol's autonomy. In July 1738, mayor Nathaniel Day was visited by an officer from Brigadier Harrison's regiment and asked at short notice to supply them with billets. Day refused, arguing that the judge, John Fortescue Aland, had just arrived at Bristol to open the summer assize and that it would be highly irregular to have armed soldiers in the city until the session was over. But Day was ignored and a few days later a detachment of soldiers duly marched in, an affront 'highly resented, as well on Account of the little Regard paid to the request of the chief Magistrate of so great a City as the incommoding of the inhabitants at such a Publick time'. Furious and belittled, mayor Day took his case to Aland who summoned the officer, issued him with 'an especial reprimand' and ordered the soldiers back out of the city until the assize business was complete.[19] Soldiers billeted involuntarily amongst communities with which they had no shared interests were notoriously difficult to police. A fondness for drink, women, and a ready recourse to arms, assured soldiers a bad reputation and Bristol magistrates were not short on experience in trying to tame them. Two drunken recruits had been taken up a few months earlier, after laying into passers-by with their swords, cutting a finger off one man, hacking another across the head and slashing the clothes of a third.[20]

Whilst it can certainly be argued that relations between billeted troops and their civilian hosts were a common cause of friction in many English towns, Bristol seems to have developed a reputation for it. Back in 1729, a soldier convicted for shooting a civilian who threw a snowball at him was 'abused and provoked beyond sufferance by the unruly mob of that place who are notoriously and universally disaffected to the government and constantly insulting the King's servants when they can overpower 'em with numbers. Besides their aversion to soldiers in general, they took him, it seems, for an Irishman…'[21] But it was no better to be a Scottish soldier, as David Reid found to his cost after being convicted of sodomy in 1738. Apparently terrified that a lynch mob would break into the gaol and string him up on the spot, Reid petitioned the crown for clemency. 'The common people of the city of Bristol have so great hatred and malice against all your majesty's soldiers…they will, if possible, find means, tho ever so unjust, to persecute and oppress them', he wrote. 'I am perpetually terrified at the report of some people who, with malicious joy, tell me that their worshipful mayor has sent several expresses at the heels of each other to procure my speedy execution, so that I protest to your grace I die hourly'. Reid was still in Newgate awaiting a decision when Dineley's killers were thrown into the cells in 1741, and still there indeed a year after their execution, in 1742.[22] Trouble between citizens and soldiers rumbled on as war edged closer. 'We are not to be governed by a standing army and hope we never shall be', insisted one of the magistrates after forcibly freeing a townsman from military custody when fighting broke out in a Bristol inn.[23] By the summer of 1739, military recruiting parties were drumming for business on the streets just as naval impressment was warming up in the Channel. Two soldiers were taken up for cutting with sabres at a man who insulted them in the street, several more were interrogated over a series of armed robberies on Bedminster Common, and another on suspicion of murdering a man with a sword on Durdham Down.[24]

Defendants in Bristol murder cases were liable to be tried in the city's own courts, by the city's Aldermanic magistrates and a Recorder, whose introduction ensured some measure of external surveillance but who was nevertheless an appointee of the Common Council. As an ancient borough and county, the Corporation was empowered by a series of charters to maintain its own courts of quarter session and assize, and jealously guarded its jurisdiction into the Channel as far as a line drawn between the islands of Steep Holm and Flat Holm. Under its fifteenth-century charter, the city was entitled to try all cases, from misdemeanours to capital felonies 'within the city and liberties on land or water', and without reference to the Admiralty courts. This, as we'll see, would have a bearing on the fate of Dineley's killers. The Common Council was self-selecting and its members could only work their way up to becoming Aldermen and magistrates by first being selected as one of the two city Sheriffs, and then being chosen as mayor for a year. Bristol did not have the more open freeman constitution of London, where common councilmen were elected annually and aldermanic seats were contested like parliamentary elections. Only perhaps in ceremonial ritual could the two cities be compared. The Bristol Aldermanic bench, 'gentlemen of greatest worth and capital in the city', were particularly well turned out. 'They have the highest marks of honour granted to magistracy', visitors were assured, 'scarlet ermined gowns, gold fringed gloves, four swords…mace and cap of maintenance'.[25]

Bristol was no stranger to murder at the time Dineley's killers took their trial, nor to the idea that soldiers and seafarers were frequently implicated. In the period 1720-1741, we have traced 34 reports of murder in Bristol and its immediate Gloucestershire and Somerset peripheries. Most people derived their knowledge and understanding of crime from brief accounts in the newspaper press, where murder was invariably represented as brutal, impulsive and without rational motive. Readers of the *Gloucester Journal*, for example, would find 'barbarous' one of the most frequently used adjectives in the paper's murder reports, and killings seemingly carried out almost at random.[26] In 1723, they would have learned, a young colliery boy had his throat cut by a gentlemen who passed him on the road for giving 'impudent answers' when questioned. In 1728, an innkeeper's wife knocked down a pregnant woman who came to see her husband and killed her by stamping on her stomach. In 1734, three soldiers visited a shop near the Pithay gate and killed the owner by beating him about the head, and in 1737 the dismembered body of an unidentified woman was discovered in a sack on Durdham Down.[27] Qualitatively, it is often difficult to learn anything further. The Calendars and Gaol Delivery Fiats for Bristol's court of Oyer and Terminer have not survived before 1741 and there are no Coroners' Inquest papers or Town Clerk's correspondence to fall back on either.[28] But quantitatively we can dig a little deeper. About a third of our 34 cases concerned the deaths of children under the age of six, leaving an average of one adult murder case every year. Ten of those accused were either soldiers or sailors (nearly half), and, coincidentally, in five cases, a ships' captain had been either victim or defendant.

Unsurprisingly, murder cases involving ships' captains aroused a great deal of public interest and commentary. While local cases of this kind were clearly unexceptional in themselves, it was nevertheless unusual for them to end, as Goodere's did, in a public execution on St Michael's Hill because naval crimes were not often tried in civilian courts. For the brutal murder at sea of a cabin boy, Richard Pye, the Bristol captain, John Jeane was convicted by the High Court of Admiralty in London and hanged at Execution Dock in 1726. The trial was sensationalised, probably by Defoe, and Jeane's privileged Bristol background publicly exposed, in a widely circulated pamphlet entitled *Unparallel'd Cruelty*. Three years later, James Newth, another Bristol captain, was acquitted of murdering his cabin boy but later convicted for murdering his wife in a Bristol ale house. Newth was condemned to die on St Michael's Hill, but cheated the gallows by committing suicide in his Newgate cell.[29] Another Bristol Captain, Rice Harris, was apprehended in the city for the murder of a crewman in 1733, and like Jeane tried and convicted before the Court of Admiralty. Harris was subsequently pardoned, but almost immediately another Bristol captain was taken up for the suspected murder of three of his crew and closely questioned by the city magistrates. Unable to identify any witnesses, and with negligible evidence, they reluctantly ordered his release.[30] In 1737, a Bristol captain was once again in the news, not as a perpetrator this time, but as a victim. Edward Bryan was murdered with an axe in his own cabin during a mutiny on the Bristol slaving ship, the *Tewksbury*, and his body thrown overboard. Five men were hanged and gibbetted for this gruesome crime by an Admiralty court convened at Cape Coast Castle on the Gold Coast; a very long way from Bristol, but a tale that found its way back to the city through a pamphlet printed by Sarah and Felix Farley, the publishers of the *Bristol Journal*, and distributed by two booksellers in St Thomas and Wine Street.[31] Goodere may not have been the first ship's captain to pay with his life for a murder at sea, but he would be the first in living memory to be hanged for it at Bristol.

The popular print industry kept readers viscerally entertained with an array of murder stories in the years before the Goodere fratricide and one of the most salacious had taken place just a few miles from Bristol in the North Somerset village of Hemington only a year earlier. Here two outwardly respectable women, Elizabeth and Mary Branch were tried for neck-locking and whipping a young orphaned servant girl to death for being too slow on an errand to the dairy. The mother and daughter then privately buried the girl to avoid detection, but under pressure from the neighbourhood the coroner exhumed the body and brought in a verdict of 'wilful murder by persons unknown'. The two women tried to claim that the girl, Ann Butterworth, was ill and subject to epileptic fits. Whatever correction they inflicted on her was 'change medley', but the court was more persuaded by the testimony of the dairy maid, Ann Somers. She testified that Elizabeth and Mary Branch beat the girl with a shoe and broom stick until she was unconscious, and then tried to cover up the homicide by insisting that Ann Somers share a bed with her, or more accurately, with her corpse. When other cruelties to workhouse servants came to light, the evidence of murder seemed overwhelming. The two women had to be brought from Taunton to Ilchester under a strong guard, for fear the people should 'tear them to Pieces.' They were hanged together at Ilchester, quite early in the morning to avoid the anger of the crowd. At least three cheap pamphlet accounts of the case hit the streets as soon as it was over, their admonitory tone given away by their titles; *The Cruel Mistress*, complete with crude but vivid woodcuts of the Branches maltreating Butterworth, and *Inhumanity and Barbarity not to be Equal'd*.[32]

A rather different perspective on the capacity of the courts and magistrates to tackle disorder can be gained from a glance at their perrenial struggles with the colliers of Kingswood, a community just beyond their jurisdiction to the East. The Kingswood pits supplied the coal that fed the furnaces not only of the city sugar refineries but of the glass, copper and brass works and a range of other industries. The miners were well aware of their industrial strength, used it frequently and effectively in disputes with the mine owners and were not at all intimidated by the city magistrates. Demands that they be brought to heel for their effrontery in destroying new turnpike gates and refusing to pay tolls on the eastern approach roads in 1727 and 1731 grew steadily during the 1730s. Collier communities resisted any attempts to regulate and control them, however, and constables complained they were unable to serve warrants or collect rents 'without endangering their lives'. When coining was added to the colliers' growing list of indiscretions, magistrates requested 'to have a Regiment of Soldiers quartered…to reduce those stubborn People to a proper Obedience to the Law', and one man was eventually hanged for it, but the district remained unsubdued.[33] In October 1738, crowds of colliers protesting a pay reduction marched into Bristol 'some going thro' the Body of the City, hallowing'. They then headed for the pits at Brislington that had not come out on strike, sabotaged them and humiliated any colliers who still refused to strike by giving them rough music; 'a sound Drubbing, Riding the Cow-Tang etc.' For the next three days, roads between Kingswood and Bristol were blockaded and money extorted from passers by.[34] Mayor William Jefferies wrote to the Duke of Newcastle, asking him to order the Gloucestershire county bench into action so that some arrests might be made outside the city gates, and 'have examples made of some'.[35]

Early in November, Gloucestershire constables 'apprehended by Strategem' one of the colliers' leaders and secured him in the Bridewell. Simultaneously, magistrates sat for two days at the nearly Lamb Inn taking evidence of financial losses from riot victims. But they were forced to do so under armed miltary guard because the colliers threatened to attack the building and storm the Bridewell to release the prisoner. Several of them had acqured guns and 'fir'd diverse Times to bring their Arms in Tune, as they said, against [those] they went to War'. The mayor retaliated by sending soldiers into Kingswood to make further arrests and 'with orders absolutely to fire on the colliers if they made any opposition'. One more ringleader was taken up as a result and both captives were despatched to Gloucester Gaol to await trial on capital charges at the next assize. Uncowed, the colliers responded with further sabotage, blowing up one of the locks on the Avon navigation between Bristol and Bath and leaving an anonymous note behind them: 'what they had now done was nothing; the Damage was to come; that at present they assembled in a small Body but when they came again they would be 1000 strong'.[36] Attempts to make further arrests were hampered by 'swarms of subterranean bees', or 'colliers wives and old women of the wood' who beat shovels and pans to raise the alarm.[37] No-one was hanged as a result of these confrontations and the Gloucester assize cases were quietly dropped. Twenty colliers were eventually put before the Bristol assize in August 1739, charged with rioting and 'cutting and spoiling' the goods of a coal carrier. The grand jury returned a true bill against only one of them however, and he was simply bound over to appear at the next sessions.[38]

By this time it will have been clear to the colliers that however much the mayor and magistrates might talk of making examples of them, anxiety about the possible consequences was an active deterrent. When bread prices soared in 1740 and magistrates requested military assistance once again to keep protesting colliers in order, the soldiers' commanding officer was downbeat. 'Captain Porteous's unhappy fate was too fresh in my memory not to make me act with the utmost caution and security', he explained, well remembering how that captain antagonised an execution crowd in Edinburgh and was lynched as a consequence. He advised the mayor that he could do no more than continue the men under arms until he had explicit instructions from government. The mayor sent an express to Whitehall requesting just that, but the carefully worded reply he received made it clear he would have to take responsibility himself for any orders to use armed force. Fortunately all remained calm.[39]

Understandably, the threat posed so recently by the colliers would not be forgotten in the aftermath of the Goodere murder trial in 1741 when rumours began to circulate that Goodere, Mahony and White were planning an escape from their cells in Bristol's Newgate gaol. Captain Goodere, it was said, 'believed he should be rescued out of prison, to which end it was proposed that a body of colliers, for a certain sum, was to come in, seize the turnkey etc and to take him out by force of arms'. It seems unlikely that any such plot existed in reality, but a stand of firearms was reportedly taken to Newgate 'to give them a warm reception' and the doors to both Goodere's cell and the Turnkey's quarters reinforced with iron cladding.[40]

In the midst of these manifold disorders, challenges and uncertainties, the Corporation clung steadfastly to the civic rituals and public processions that had helped to shape an illusion of social stability for centuries. In the autumn of 1738, while the mayor and magistrates were relentlessly pursuing ringleaders from the October colliery riots and struggling to restore order to the mining districts, the Prince and Princess of Wales let it be known that they would be travelling to Hotwells to take the waters. Their route West would almost certainly take the Royal couple through Kingswood, so it was not a risk-free proposition. But these were years in which the commercialisation of the mineral waters at the spa, mainly for the treatment of consumption and diabetes, had begun to take off in earnest. An increasing quantity was being bottled and traded around the globe, encouraged by pseudo-scientific treatises advertising the water's efficacy for a much wider range of discomforts. The Prince's visit was therefore much anticipated as a sign that Bristol was ready to compete with neighbouring Bath as a place of fashionable and healthy resort.[41]

Whatever the potential hazards, the visit would not be downplayed or put off. In a well-planned and extravagant display of social unity, the Corporation rolled out the red carpet as though their troubles in Kingswood were all forgotten. Colonel Bridges opened up his parklands between Keynsham and Brislington to ensure a private passage for the Royal party's coaches well away from the rutted Bath road, unimproved since the turnpike riots, and well away from the unsettled colliery villages that co-ordinated them. Newspaper reports of guns being fired by some 'country people' along the route were unquestioningly attributed to outbursts of patriotic enthusiasm, and entry through Temple Gate kept the procession a safe distance from the Lamb Inn by Lawford's Gate, where statements were still being collected from rebellious colliers. Inside the city, some impressive civic organisation was revealed. Alongside the usual dignitaries, the sheriffs, aldermen, clergy, the recorder and leading merchants, representatives of 21 loyal trades, costumed in white and carrying objects representing their craft, composed the Royal escort to Queen Square. There were glass makers and saddlers, wool combers and weavers, 'in the midst of whom was a new loom erected on a pageant with a boy in it weaving a piece of shag along the streets'. No party disputes sullied these proceedings as they had done in similar circumstances in 1735.[42] Salutes were fired from Brandon Hill and from 121 cannon arranged around the quay. The Prince was invited to admire the city's shipping, 'which would have afforded a much pleasanter prospect had not Jack Spaniard plundered us of some of our best ships'. The royal party was then ushered into Alderman Henry Combe's town house in the Square to receive loyal addresses and to be given the freedom of the city. In return, the Prince led a toast to the city's continuing prosperity, which was drunk with sweet sherry. When that was over, the royal couple retired to Merchant's Hall for a lavish entertainment and ball with 500 of the gentry. Finally, at midnight, there was a reassuringly expensive display of fireworks around the Square's central statue of William III. The whole affair had cost the Corporation very nearly £1000.[43]

Through rituals such as these and some public spending, the Bristol elite signalled defiance in the face of anticipated economic decline and a reduced political influence. As we have seen, heavy investment in improvements to the harbour were one expression of it. Another was the commissioning of a grand new Exchange building in Corn Street, just across the road from the council house. This long overdue initiative would replace the ramshackle and ancient corn exchange on the Quay, a building that did nothing to enhance the city's trading reputation. By January 1741, Henry Combe's ingratiating hospitality to the Prince and Princess had paid off and he had become mayor, a position that carried with it a generous allowance of £1000 'to support the dignity of his office'.[44] In that month, he wrote to John Wood, perhaps the most fashionable architect of the period, and invited him to submit designs. On visiting the site, Wood was impressed at the way in which the Corporation had 'within the space of two years and at very great expense, purchased several estates in the heart of the city, pulled down the old houses, and cleared the ground of the superfluous materials'. Quickly getting the measure of Combe's ambition, Wood proposed 'an *Egyptian* Hall as the properest Center for an august Building; and the most convenient Place for Men of Business to assemble in'. The flattered Corporation instructed the architect to begin work at once, for it must be 'designed for the Preservation of the principal Citizens whose Health and Persons were every Day endangered while they assembled in the open street to carry on the Trade and Commerce of the City'.[45]

Combe's rise to local prominence as a member of the unaccountable oligarchy who ran the city and lorded over its law courts was remarkable, though not unique. He was a local boy made good, working himself up from linen draper's apprentice in 1702, to be warden and treasurer of the Society of Merchant Venturers, Common Councillor and Sheriff by 1727 and now 'one of the most considerable merchants of that city'. He married the daughter of a Virginia merchant and slave owner in 1725, financed slave trade voyages and purchased a plantation of his own, on Nevis. The income derived from the labour of enslaved Africans enabled him to purchase a fine new town house in Queen Square, a Palladian mansion in Somerset called Earnshill House, and invest in a block of substantial new houses on Prince Street. By the time he tried and failed to win a parliamentary seat for the city at the 1739 by-election, Combe was wealthy enough, or so it was said, to 'buy half a nation'. When he died in 1752, he was being listed in the local press as one of 37 Bristol merchants 'who within 50 years had but small beginnings but died rich'.[46]

As mayor, Combe found himself juggling two rather different responsibilities in the early spring of 1741. On 10 March he was standing at the Exchange building site, in full civic regalia on freshly prepared ground, tossing 'several handfuls' of coins into a small pit. To the applause of the Society of Merchant Venturers and a crowd of well-heeled burgesses, several gentlemen followed suit before the Foundation stone was laid on top and then another five guineas laid out for the workmen 'to make themselves merry with'. After the Aldermen had taken it in turns to knock the stone further into place with a mallet, other members of the crowd jumped down onto it from the surrounding scaffolding to finish the job amidst much cheering and the peal of Church bells. Combe, the Corporation and the merchants then processed back over to the Council House to formally toast the city's future prosperity while barrels of ale were set up on the Exchange ground and drink distributed to the people. The local significance of this extravagant new addition to the city streetscape can perhaps best be illustrated by the attention devoted to it in John Rocque's cartography in 1742. As we have seen, Rocque included ten vignette views of the city in the margins on either side of his great map. No fewer than four of them depict the Exchange.[47]

In many ways this had been a typically well-choreographed display of civic unity and cross-class celebration. But Combe was not in a position to celebrate for long for there were serious and pressing matters of a different kind to be addressed in the coming week. On 17 March, just seven days' time, he would preside with the Recorder, Michael Foster over the most talked-about and keenly anticipated law case of the year, the trial of Captain Samuel Goodere and two sailors, Charles White and Matthew Mahony, for the abduction and murder of Goodere's own brother, John. He had personally conducted the examinations of the prisoners and several witnesses at the Council House in January, and was fully conscious of the city's right to try the case without interference from the Admiralty court. Ironically, Combe would lead the traditional procession to St Marks' Chapel for divine service on the opening day of the assize, a mere stone's throw from the *White Hart* on College Green, where Dineley's abduction and murder was first conceived and planned.

CHAPTER THREE

Murder

At what point did Samuel Goodere decide to kill his brother? It is an interesting but speculative question; speculative because until his final confession Goodere never admitted to the crime and consistently denied that he had a 'secret design' against Sir John. His main refrain was that he intended to protect Dineley from himself. His brother was a madman who had frittered away his estate to a point that he was likely to be incarcerated as a debtor. He needed solace and rest, a quiet confinement, and that was what Samuel intended for his eldest brother, as any dutiful sibling might.[1] This was why Samuel was quite open about his intention to bring him on board the *Ruby* man of war. The crew was aware of it; it was no secret. In any case why should he kill his brother when he stood to lose £40,000 if he was held responsible for his death?[2] It made no sense.

The prosecution, of course, insisted that Goodere had planned the murder all along. They revealed that Goodere had hired privateers to capture Sir John, entertaining them at the White Hart Inn across from Jarrit Smith's residence on College Green where Sir John had repaired for business. Matthew Mahony, a former seaman with Captain James Mervin on the *Charles*, acted as a go-between. Mahony was a recently pressed man on the *Ruby*, but he was anxious to remain in Bristol because Captain Mervin owed him money. Curiously he doesn't appear on the muster roll of the ship, or in the list of supernumeraries, although he was possibly registered under an assumed name. He was really Goodere's hired man, having taken lodgings at the Scotch Arms in Marsh Street. He gathered together five ruffians from the *Vernon* privateer, who were persuaded to delay their voyage to Jamaica in return for a £50 reward and a protection from the press.[3] They were to kidnap Sir John as he left Smith's apartments and hustle him onto the barge of the *Ruby* at Hotwells. Mahony's reward for this intrigue was a discharge from the *Ruby* and a 'handsome reward besides.'[4] Some suggested as much as £200, with £150 to his accomplice.

Goodere laid the groundwork for his brother's capture on 12 January 1741. According to the landlord of the *White Hart*, Morris Hobbs, Goodere hired the upper room of the pub, in effect the small alcove over the entrance, from

47

John Rocque, *Plan of the City and Suburbs of Bristol* (1742). Bristol Archives, 07770/1, border vignette of College Green. Sir John Dineley's solicitor, Jarrit Smith's house was here

where he had a good view of the Green. The captain thought it offered 'a very fine Prospect of the Town.' He ordered a dish of coffee for the following morning, a somewhat unusual request, because the *White Hart* was not in the habit of serving coffee, which could be easily obtained at a nearby coffee-house. Mrs Hobbs took the trouble to get him one – it was a small pub without a servant – thinking that the captain intended to meet someone coming out of college prayers.

It quickly became obvious that a different encounter was intended. Goodere mustered his privateers downstairs where they were given ale and bread and cheese. Mahony, whom Hobbs assumed was some kind of footman, went back and forth. When Sir John appeared on the Green with his servant, both armed and mounted, Goodere decided to forego kidnapping him. He simply alerted his men to 'look well' but 'don't touch him.' He followed Sir John a small way himself, perhaps to ascertain the route he conventionally took to his lodgings, and then returned to pay the bill; just over four shillings.[5]

Mahony arranged a second booking of the room for the following Sunday, 18 January 1741, when Sir John was expected to go to dinner at Jarrit Smith's, his lawyer's residence. He irritated Hobbs and his wife by demanding tick for his porter and asked them to alert him at his lodgings if a gentleman in a black cap passed by. At three o'clock the privateers piled in. They asked to go upstairs but Hobbs refused to allow them because divine service had begun at St Augustine's church nearby. So they drank in the parlour, along with some of the *Ruby* crew; raucously, it would seem, for Hobbs complained of the noise and the constant slamming of the door as men scanned the green for Sir John and the captain. 'Don't break my House down about my Ears,' he screamed at Mahony, 'don't think you are in Marsh Street.'[6] When the brothers finally appeared, the men rushed out. Mahony paid the reckoning of half a crown. There were later rumours that the men had been ordered to drink tea to keep them sober, but if so, it is doubtful they complied. Ale and hot flip, a combination of rum, sugar, eggs and beer, warmed with a poker, were more to their taste.[7]

Through the mediation of Thomas Chamberlayne, Captain Goodere had met with Smith at the College Green coffeehouse, and asked the lawyer to arrange a meeting with his brother in an effort to patch up their differences. A fateful meeting between the brothers at Smith's own house on College Green was accordingly arranged, once Dineley had consented to come over from a convalescent visit to Bath. He sent Smith an incoherent note announcing his arrival that seemed only to confirm his mental discomfort. 'My head was well', he explained, 'yet I could perceive but little noyse but before I came to Bristol it was worse and last night it was very bad, but I thank God it is something easier.'[8] Was Goodere's reconciliatory intention genuine? Probably not. Samuel had too many outstanding issues with his brother to think that a single meeting on neutral territory would resolve anything. Although Samuel had married well, and enjoyed a Monmouthshire estate equivalent to that of Burghope,[9] his brother had broken the entail on the Charlton estate and deprived him of his entitlement under their maternal grandfather's will. He had not acted as an elder brother should. He failed to observe the reciprocities that bound elder brothers to their siblings and the desires of his father.[10] Sir John had also seriously run down the value of Burghope manor, where he had a life's tenancy before handing over the property to his younger brother. In May 1740 Samuel had taken Sir John to court for cutting down the timber on the estate, which had an impressive terrace garden but little in the way of broad acres. If this state of affairs continued, Samuel feared he would be left with a ramshackle inheritance, not enough to accommodate his sons and daughters in a manner appropriate to his landed status.[11] Possibly, just possibly, Goodere offered his brother a chance to make amends. According to Jarrit Smith, Goodere embraced his brother, refrained from drinking wine because his brother was abstemious, and ostensibly made every effort to turn the corner. But what he learnt from the hour-long encounter was that Sir John was trying to arrange a loan of £5000 from the attorney on the security of the Charlton estate. It was too much. Goodere believed Sir John could

The abduction of Sir John Dineley on College Green, from *The Trials of Samuel Goodere, Matthew Mahony and Charles White*, broadside (1741), Bristol Libraries, B10146. Samuel Goodere is on the left, looking the other way

not do this without his consent, despite his brother's efforts to break the entail.[12] He was confident he could successfully sue for the restitution of his grandfather's legacy, although Jarrit Smith doubted that he could. Months earlier, Sam had launched a suit in the Court of Common Pleas arguing that his brother's recovery of the entail was fraudulent, although he was frustrated by Sir John's refusal to answer it. More generally, the situation confirmed that Sir John was a spendthrift, a reckless wastrel of his own and other people's property. As Samuel was leaving, Jarrit Smith expressed the hope that the meeting would broker some agreement. He was pleased to have been the intermediary. Samuel muttered 'By God, this won't do.'[13]

Whatever Goodere's intentions before the meeting, he was hell-bent on destroying his brother thereafter. He had already ordered midshipman Thomas Williams to bring the barge to the Brick Kilns near Hotwells in preparation for Sir John's abduction down river to the *Ruby*. He had also requested eight of his crew to assist in getting his brother on board, although it would seem that they were not entirely clued into the plan.[14] Sir John was picked up by the privateers and Goodere's crew in the vicinity of the College Green coffeehouse, not far from St Augustine's churchyard.[15]

In the circumstances it would have been better had the *Ruby* moored in the river Frome. The tide was at 'three quarters flood',[16] enough to moor it near the Gibb, but Goodere very probably did not want the publicity. Obscured by the trees that then lined College Green, Sir John was hurried along the ropewalk of St Augustine's Back towards the Lime Kilns.[17] Dineley cried 'Murder, murder' and was threatened with a severe ducking if he didn't shut up. He was a portly man, fifty-seven years of age, and suffering from a long bout of alcoholism that he had only recently shaken off. At the trial the prosecuting counsel described him as of 'advanced in years and very ailing.'[18] Even so, Dineley made enough noise to attract attention as darkness descended on a January night.

Some members of the public gave the party a wide berth. As we have already noted, the *Ruby* was responsible for taking volunteers and pressed men down to Portsmouth to serve the navy in the War of Jenkins' Ear, an imperial venture against the Spanish. Citizens might well have thought the gang was conducting one of its impressment forays in the city, of which there had been quite a few in the months before January 1741. The muster book of the *Ruby* reveals there had been a recruitment drive in October 1740, and another on New Year's Day. A further foray was scheduled for the 25 January, 1741.[19] Recruitment by impressment had encountered resistance, not only on the quays, but by ship masters, who stripped down their crews before they approached Kingroad, allowing key topmen to disembark on the Somerset coast. In December one Mary Beard even had the audacity to hire a boat and rescue six pressed men from the *Ruby* when she was moored in Kingroad.[20] In an increasingly tense situation, in which regulating officers were beginning to lose patience with Bristolians, no one wanted to get entangled with the press gang.

Yet Dineley's dress and his demeanour, he wore a scarlet cloak and a black cap with earmuffs, declared he was hardly your typical seafarer. It was implausible that he was a deserter who had run off with the king's bounty and been taken back to the ship to stand trial. This was one of the stories that circulated about him.[21] In the light of his dress and his age, his cries attracted curiosity.

Another contemporary impression of Dineley's abduction. Here he is being frog-marched along the river bank by Goodere's hired sailors. From *The Genuine Trial of Samuel Goodere Esq, Matthew Mahony and Charles White* (1741). Bristol Archives, 14754/8

In the mid-eighteenth century, before regular policing, it was still the responsibility of the public to intervene in matters of public disturbance, to raise a hue and cry if a crime had been committed.[22] Carpenter Samuel Trivett came out of a pub on the ropewalk to ask what was the matter? He was told the man in custody had killed someone and was to be taken to the man-of-war down river for a court martial. He was abruptly ordered to 'standoff, or else we will knock your Brains out.'[23] Anchor-smith Stephen Perry also wondered what the fracas was about. Matt Mahony offered the same story. It was an unlikely scenario, for the civil power would have delivered the culprit in more pompous circumstances, not have sailors threaten inquisitive bystanders to mind their own business. Not that this mattered on this occasion. Espying Goodere marshalling his men, Perry was troubled by the possibility that a press gang would take him up despite the fact he was a substantial smith who employed other workers. This was a very real possibility since impressment extended to people whose 'Occupations and Callings are to work in vessels and boats upon rivers.'[24] An anchor smith was thus fair game, even Perry who had a 'counting house'. As he told solicitous spectators 'Do you know what you are about? I should not be in your Coats for a Thousand Pounds, it is Squire Goodere.'[25]

Every time the gang took a break in hauling, dragging and carrying the screaming Sir John along the ropewalk, people stepped out to inquire about this unsavoury hustle. At Lime Kilns, Dineley was recognized. A Mrs Elizabeth Darby had repaired a chair for him the previous summer.[26] She testified that sometime after 5 pm she and her daughter Hannah heard a 'Great Noise in the road' so 'they went to the door to see what was the matter.' They saw two sailors forcibly carrying Sir John under the arms, 'with a Great many other Sailors in Company.'[27] At the *King's Head*, just before Hotwells, Sir John blurted out 'for God's sake, go and acquaint Mr Jarrit Smith, for I am undone, they will murder me.'[28] Dineley was muzzled thereafter, his cries stifled in his scarlet cloak, but the word got out, and William Dupree, a soldier from Blakeney's regiment quartered at the *Crow* at the foot of Brandon Hill, was persuaded to report the incident to Jarrit Smith.[29] The lawyer learnt about the plausible capture of his client around 6 pm and went to Sir John's lodgings in Peter Street to inquire whether he had returned. Mary Barrow, the wife of the landlord, reported he had not. In his testimony Jarrit Smith said he did not have time to obtain the appropriate writ to have Dineley released; in the technical terms of the law, 'to replevy the man', to request his freedom on the security that he would return Sir John to answer any charges.[30] But inexplicably, and lethargically, Smith did not report the possibility of abduction to

Mapping Dineley's abduction. The section from Rocque's map of the city demonstrates the bravado of the kidnappers. Seizing Dineley as he left College Green (1) at a spot close to the wall of St Augustine the Less (2), Goodere's men hustled him along the busy quayside before turning to follow the tree-lined Ropewalk (3) towards Hotwells. The city gallows on St Michael's Hill where three of the party would pass their final moments three months later, is circled

An alternative view is offered by Samuel and Nathaniel Buck's *North West Prospect of the City of Bristol*, published in 1732 and showing the same scene but looking south from Brandon Hill: 1. College Green 2. Church of St Augustine the Less 3. the Ropewalk

Dineley is rowed out to the *Ruby* at Kingroad. From *The Trials of Samuel Goodere, Matthew Mahony and Charles White*, broadside (1741), Bristol Libraries, B10146

the mayor until the following morning.[31] By then it was too late.

Goodere's explanation for his brother's detention was that he needed to restrain him for his own sake. He was mentally unstable and reckless, to himself and his wider family. 'Have you not given the Rogues of Lawyers Money enough already?' he chided his brother on the barge. 'Do you wish to rot in jail as a debtor? I will take care of you that you will not spend your Estate.' Dineley retorted: 'I know better, you intend to kill me. Do it now, not on the ship'. Goodere replied he would 'do no such thing', but 'he would have him make his peace with God';[32] a very ambiguous phrase in a religious age, where madness constituted an affliction of the soul or diabolical possession. The retort could mean either psychological respite or death. The prosecution would emphasize the latter, so much so that the phrase was printed in upper case in the principal trial transcript and in italics in another.[33]

How long this bickering continued is unclear. Some seamen on the barge testified that it went on for some time, and Captain Goodere later confessed he had been moved by his brother's pleadings. 'My heart relented a little', he recalled, 'but I thought I had gone too far to retract or curb my fixed resolution.'[34] By 7 pm, when the barge approached the *Ruby* in Kingroad, Dineley was frozen into silence. Tom Williams described him as 'benumbed with cold.'[35] Goodere had removed his cloak on a rainy night, and hard westerlies curbed his verbal protests. Sir John was speechless by the time he was hauled on board the man of war and bundled into the purser's cabin in the cockpit.

No one seems to have questioned the captain's decision to bring his brother on board and confine him in the purser's cabin. If members of the crew did, they kept it under wraps. The captain was, after all, the sovereign of his ship whose word was not to be questioned. Moreover, attitudes towards madness were not standardized in the eighteenth century. There were plenty of people who made private arrangements to care for deranged relatives. In a ship of over 300 seamen, not every sailor knew who Sir John Dineley was. His brother, Samuel Goodere, had only recently taken command of the ship; over a third of the crew were relative newcomers, having entered the *Ruby* in the last six months.[36] But because Sir John had married a Stapleton heiress and had a seat at Tockington, just north of Almondsbury, less than ten miles from the centre of Bristol, gossip about his marital difficulties and irregularities must have circulated; enough to suggest he was an eccentric gentleman, if not a little crazy. The local Bristol gentry barely tolerated him. According to Goodere, conversations about Sir John's hostility towards him circulated the quays. 'As I used to walk on the Tolzey at Bristol', the captain remembered, 'I have heard things spoken of him, as if he intended to do me all the prejudice that lay in his power.'[37]

When Daniel Weller, the ship's carpenter, was dispatched to reinforce the cabin door of the purser, no one necessarily thought anything untoward was about to happen to Sir John. Captain Goodere could be simply protecting his brother from harming himself. He secured the cabin, provided an attendant, Matthew Mahony, and also a sentry. He had the surgeon's mate read Dineley's pulse, referring to him as a 'crazy old man.' Rest and solitude might calm his senses, especially with a little purging or shaving his head.[38] And the captain, aware of his brother's arthritic condition and his complaints aboard the barge, offered him some rum 'to bathe his thigh.'[39] Captain Goodere had apparently sought some sort of refuge for his brother in Bristol. He had approached a Mrs Gethins or Gettings to rent a garret for his brother in Prince Street, where he himself occasionally lodged when he came to town. He had assigned Matt Mahony the task of caretaker, at £5 a month.[40] But for some reason, this had not worked out; quite probably deliberately. It allowed Goodere to claim that he had to take Sir John on board because he could not find a proper sanctuary for him in Bristol.

Goodere's conspiracy to murder his brother nonetheless posed real problems. A ship is a cramped space. The purser's cabin was in the cockpit at the stern of the ship, near the after hatchway. The cockpit was deep in the bowels of the ship, below the lower deck and gunroom, a space sometimes allotted to senior midshipman or to the surgeon and his mate. In the *Ruby* it housed the purser's cabin, the surgeon's, the steward's and the slop room; at this time the sleeping quarters of the cooper and his wife. The latter was separated from the purser's cabin by a half-inch deal partition.[41] Everything that went on in the purser's cabin could be heard by someone, and because there was a chink in the partition, the cooper and his wife could spy on what went on there. It was not an ideal space for killing someone and getting away with it. Sir John Dineley recognized this. According to cooper Edward Jones, he said 'it was impossible it could be done [the murder] without somebody hearing or seeing it.'[42]

When Captain Goodere came on board the *Ruby* on the evening of 18 January he was committed to continuing the charade of harbouring his brother for reasons of insanity if not reaching some agreement over their disputed inheritance. He could not be seen to be openly malevolent, although some seamen in the barge must have wondered why privateers from the *Vernon* had been recruited to kidnap Sir John and doubtless relayed this to other crew members.[43] In Matthew Mahony, Goodere had one potential assassin, although Mahony alleged that the captain had told him he had confined his brother to 'bring him to reason'; that is, to force him to change his will, and by extension the new entail which left his estates to the Foote nephews.[44] Mahony was not happy that his assignment suddenly darkened to murder, but he was a vulnerable young sailor, 21 years of age, a pressed man and a fugitive from justice. He was born in Ennis, County Clare, and first found work as a farm labourer. According to the Reverend John Penrose, he was 'of too roving a disposition to be tied to such a grovelling occupation',[45] and opted for the sea where he revelled his life away in Mediterranean ports such as Leghorn [Livorno]. Mahony was accused of a rape in Calais, but he eluded the law by slipping out of the port for England. Fleeing from justice, he was undergoing a cure for venereal disease with Robert Gibson, a Redcliff apothecary, at the time of the murder.[46] In the circumstances he was under Goodere's thumb.

Mahony needed an accomplice to fulfil the deed and so he looked around for a suitable candidate on the ship. He thought he had found one in Elisha Cole, an able seaman who had been impressed on the *Ruby* and was soon to be assigned to the *Royal Sovereign*.[47] Cole was discovered sleeping off a hangover on top of a sea chest. He was too drunk for the task and disconcertingly misidentified Sir John Dineley as the former captain of the *Charles* who owed him back pay. So Mahony switched his attention to Charles White, a native of Drogheda in Ireland who had originally sailed as a cabin boy on Liverpool ships and had subsequently worked in the whaling, Baltic and Caribbean trades. He had entered the *Ruby* at the rank of able seamen in August 1739, and during his 17 months on board seems to have been liked by his shipmates. Edward Jones the cooper said he had been with him on the *Kinsale* man of war in the West Indies and 'never knew any harm by him.' William MacGuiness, the quarter gunner, said he was 'as good and civil a Man as need be.' His problem was drink and revelry, which led the Reverend John Penrose to write him off as a 'stout lusty fellow, thoughtless and prone to all manner of debauchery.'[48] White's heavy drinking and womanizing threatened to put him constantly in debt, which suggests, even when we divest his character of the clergyman's moralistic judgments, that he was vulnerable to bribery when in dire straits. Mahony certainly thought so. He hauled him out of his hammock and Goodere plied him with drink, asking him if he had killed any Spaniards during his time at sea. White replied he had not, but he must have understood the innuendo. If he did not, Captain Goodere laid it on the line. He was to 'make away with his brother'. Four or five glasses of rum brought White round. 'Mahony and myself worked him up to a proper pitch', the captain later recalled, 'so that he was ready enough to assist.' In White's own words, Goodere and Mahony 'robbed me of my understanding' and set him up as a tipsy accomplice to the murder.[49]

The murder was planned after midnight, when those in the cockpit were likely to be asleep and when the watch was inattentive. Prior to midnight Goodere went through the motions of attending to his brother's welfare. He insisted that the surgeon's mate, James Dudgeon, take Sir John's pulse that evening rather than the following morning, especially since Sir John complained of a severe headache and a cold contracted at Bath, where he had taken the waters.[50] Dudgeon told the captain his pulse was regular, but in light of his age believed Sir John had should be better accommodated in the cabin. Goodere replied that he had offered his brother different bedding but he had declined to take it. Later, in the presence of quarter gunner Duncan Buchanan, Goodere made other gestures for Sir John's welfare. He gave his brother a fresh pair of stockings, noting that his current pair was wet.[51] Dudgeon retired to his cabin around 8 pm but he was up until 9:30 pm. Being only nine feet away, he heard Sir John complain that he would have to do 'his affairs' in the cabin if no pot was brought in. 'Let me have a bucket to piss in', he cried.[52] Dudgeon remonstrated with the sentry to attend to Sir John's request, and this brought Goodere and Mahony to the cabin. Mahony gave Dineley a bucket to 'ease himself' and then tried to settle him down.[53] He offered him some rum, which Dineley refused since he had been abstinent for over two years. Goodere was heard to remark that he hoped this would be the gentleman's worst night. 'I told the people who heard him that he was mad and would cry out in the middle of the night when his mad fits came to him, but they must not mind him.'[54]

Captain Goodere changed the sentries at midnight, Duncan Buchanan replacing William MacGuiness, who was assigned to watch the gunroom.[55] Around 2 am Goodere came down to the cockpit and stood sentry himself; an unusual turn of events, which disconcerted both Buchanan and MacGuiness, who had a clear view of the cockpit and had just suffered verbal abuse from Mahony as he rushed through the gunroom to the ladder of the cockpit below.[56] It was at this point that White joined Mahony in the cabin and began the ordeal of strangling Dineley. The cabin was dark. The two men had trouble doing the job. They fumbled the task using Sir John's own cravat and their own hands, or as the Inquest would have it, a linen handkerchief. White then fetched a piece of rope, purportedly one that held the captain's writing desk or escritoire to the floor of his own cabin; although this may well have been journalistic embroidery to rivet Goodere to the murder.[57] Mahony pressed his knee against Dineley's stomach to get more leverage. Sir John pleaded for his life. He was not kneeling on the floor as represented in the frontispiece of the *Genuine Trial*, with the two assassins tugging on the rope from opposite ends. That version sometimes attributed to the nephew of the brothers, the future actor Samuel Foote, looks incredibly staged. So, too, does the one broadside on the murder, where the two assassins grapple with Sir John on the floor of a vast hall of a cabin while Goodere complacently looks on.[58]

In reality this was a clumsily executed murder in a room barely big enough

A somewhat fanciful depiction of Dineley's murder. Mahony and White tighten a length of rope around their victim's neck while Goodere looks on with sword drawn. From *The Genuine Trial of Samuel Goodere Esq, Matthew Mahony and Charles White* (1741). Bristol Archives, 14754/8

C. The Captain in his Night Gown & a Drawn Sword in his hand at the Cabbin Door, while Mahony Strangles S.ʳ John, and White lies upon his Leggs.

Another illustration of the murder. Once again, Goodere is shown in the room with Mahony and White but he actually stood guard outside while his accomplices strangled Dineley. From *The Genuine Trial of Samuel Goodere Esq, Matthew Mahony and Charles White* (1741). Bristol Libraries, B10146 to swing a cat o'nine tails. Amid the rumpus and pitiful cries of the baronet, it was never clear to anyone outside the room as to who did what. In his own deposition Charles White claimed he was a passive, unwitting witness to the murder. Matt. Mahony murdered Dineley, 'but how and in what manner he cannot say.'[59] Yet this was the confession of a desperate man who felt ensnared by Goodere and the rough-mannered Mahony and hoped for some reprieve from a death sentence.

The most detailed account of the trial suggests Dineley was struggling on a flock bed while one [likely White] held him down and the other [likely Mahony] tightened the rope around his neck.[60] Sir John offered them twenty guineas. 'Must I die? Must I die?' he exclaimed. This brutal course of events, which seems to have lasted twenty minutes or more, awoke people in the cockpit. James Dudgeon heard cries of murder, as did Buchanan from the gunroom.

So, too, did Margaret Jones, the wife of the cooper. She was having a night with her husband in the sloproom, a not altogether unusual course of events for warrant officers when a ship was at anchor.[61] She alerted her husband beside her; he later testified that Dineley 'cried like a Person going out of the World, very low.'[62] He 'kecked' or retched; he gasped for life. 'O my poor life' were purportedly the last words he spoke.[63] While the two men were strangling Sir John, someone tried to come into the cabin, but were rebuffed with the retort 'kept out, you Negro' or 'keep out, you Negar', a very bewildering statement since only the captain was at the door.[64] The Jones couple, who could only have been feet away from the scene of the crime, saw nothing in the pitch-black room until Goodere handed Mahony a candle. Then, through a crack in the partition, they saw someone rifling Sir John's pockets, cursing because he found silver coin before gold. Margaret Jones could not see who it was, but she recognized White's voice. Reluctant to move Sir John for fear of the noise, White struggled to relieve the dead man of his pocket watch. Mahony suggested he pull it from Sir John's waistcoat by the chain.[65]

Captain Goodere was not a witness to the murder. He stood outside the cabin, offering Mahony a candle to ensure the deed was done. Just before 3 am he locked the door to the cabin and recalled the sentry. This detachment was deliberate, for if he was unable to dispose of his brother's body at sea or persuade his crew that Sir John had committed suicide,[66] Goodere intended to set up his assassins as the real culprits. He had them share the money, about £30; he offered Mahony his own silver watch in return for Sir John's. He arranged for their rapid departure from the ship down the hatch-hole, with three weeks' leave and a protection from the press. He then framed the pair as dastardly thieves who killed for money. Earlier he had suggested to the

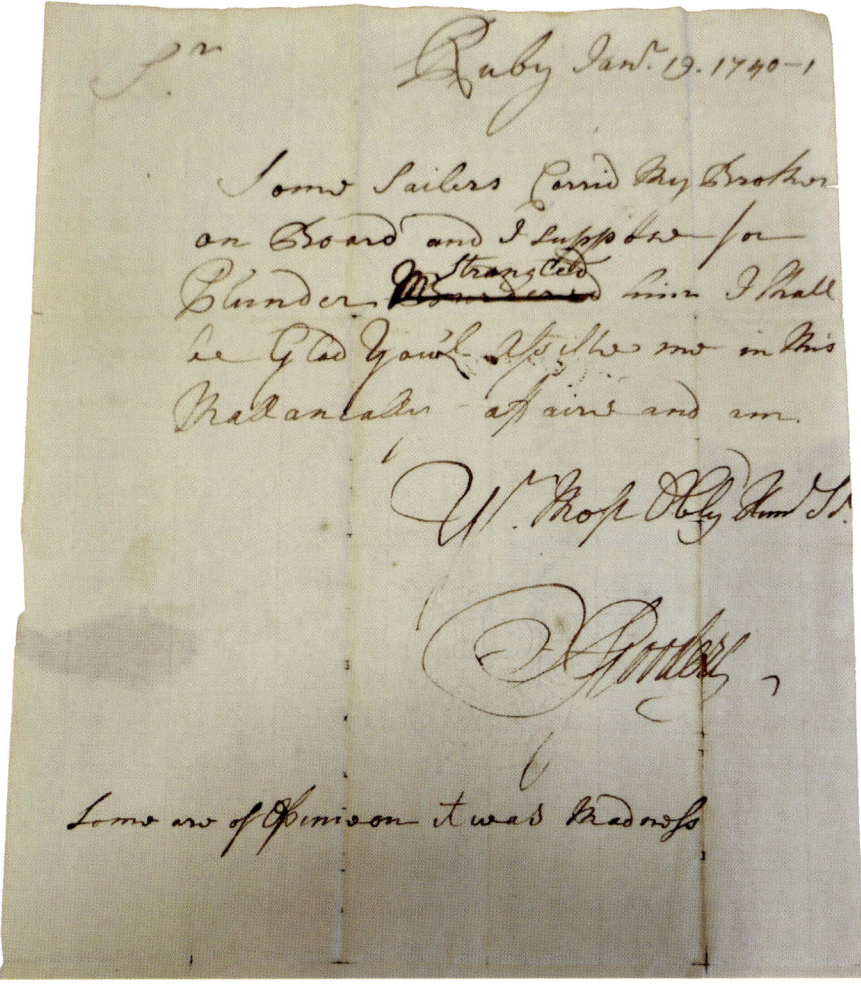

Samuel Goodere's hurriedly written note to Jarrit Smith, sent from the *Ruby* shortly after the discovery of his brother's body. Bristol Archives, AC/JS/50/39

surgeon's mate that an inventory should be taken of his brother's personal effects just in case Sir John was robbed by the crew.[67] Now he accused his hired assassins of that very fact. Captain Goodere wrote a letter to Jarrit Smith to that effect. 'Some sailors Carried my Brother on Board and I suppose for Plunder strangled him. I shall be glad you'll assist me in this Melancholy affaire.' For good measure and to keep his options open, he added in a post script, 'some are of opinion it was Madness'.[68]

It was probably delivered to the early morning yawl along with White and Mahony. It was the explanation he offered on his arrest; in fact, he seems to have echoed the very words he scribbled to Smith. 'What if the Villains have murdered my Brother?' he exclaimed when first confronted with Sir John's death. 'Can I help it? I know nothing of it.' Once again he speculated 'plunder' as a motive and appealed to his inquisitors, just as he had to Smith, 'I shall be glad you'll assist me in this Melancholy Affaire'.[69]

The captain's explanation was unconvincing for a number of reasons. To begin with, he stood sentry during the crucial hour of his brother's death. He was in the cockpit when the cry of murder went up, and he shooed Buchanan away when he came down with a candle from the gunroom, a gesture the seaman made when the captain passed his own to Mahony inside the purser's cabin. These actions raised the suspicion that he was an accomplice. So, too, did the fact that he authorized the departure of Mahony and White when the yawl was sent off early in the morning to collect and deliver the mail. That very morning Captain Goodere had also tried to persuade the master of the *Ruby*, Theodore Court, to sail down the Channel as far as the Holmes, where there was no anchorage and only 'foul ground' for a ship of its size. And to do so without a pilot to guide them.[70] It was an odd request from a captain who should have known the hazards. What was it he wanted to hide?

Edward Jones and James Dudgeon, the cooper and the surgeon's mate, were convinced a 'hellish cabal' had been at work that night. Dudgeon advised Jones to make sure that Dineley was dead before reporting the incident to the second lieutenant. Jones removed the scuttle, a small rectangular hole used to ventilate and communicate between decks, and then prodded the corpse to ensure there were no signs of life.[71] Then the two of them, along with sentry Duncan Buchanan, approached second lieutenant William Perry.

Samuel Goodere was allegedly a popular captain with the crew, even though he had assumed command but two months earlier, in November 1740. Even Williams, who testified against him, sang his praises as a captain. 'Never did a more worthy gentleman bear a Commission under his Majesty', he is said to have declared. Hyperbole aside, he was certainly an improvement on the former commander, Captain Robert Fytche, a deranged man who four months earlier had committed suicide by blowing his brains out while throwing himself out of the starboard gallery window.[72] Not surprisingly, Perry was incredulous about what he heard, and very loath to act against the captain without firm evidence of his guilt. Still, the news that Goodere had permitted Mahony and White to leave the boat so early in the morning was unsettling, particularly in the light of Dineley's death. Jones maintained the ship was in an 'uproar' over it, although precisely who knew remained uncertain.[73] But when he threatened to report the circumstances to the Admiralty Board and the mayor of Bristol, Perry caved in.[74] While he could not detain Mahony and White, he had the carpenter confirm Dineley was dead, and then considered how to act.

A plot was hatched to draw Goodere out of his cabin, on the grounds that Jones' chest had been robbed, and then seize him. How decisively the naval officers moved in that direction is a little unclear, for we have conflicting evidence. The *Ruby*'s logbook suggests that Goodere was confined by the crew at ten in the morning, while the silver oar or civil power arrived at four in the afternoon. Lieutenant Parry's logbook relates that he acted swiftly once Dineley's murder was confirmed by the carpenter, who broke down the door to the purser's cabin. Yet some of the trial testimony suggests Perry and company had not arrested Goodere when John Chamberlayne, the water bailiff, came on board.[75] James Dudgeon, the surgeon's mate, for example, claimed that he and lieutenant Perry had been invited to breakfast with the captain on the morning of the 19th and that 'soon after' the silver oar approached. When the bailiff entered the captain's cabin, Chamberlayne was told by Perry that they were 'about to seize' Goodere. Edward Jones, by contrast, implied that he and others had already taken Captain Goodere into custody, noting that Perry had dragged his feet on the matter.[76] The discrepancy might be resolved by reports that the water bailiff sent for reinforcements to take Captain Goodere back to Bristol. At least one printed account endorses this narrative.[77] If this were true then Goodere was captured early in the morning, soon after the silver oar arrived, but he was not taken off the boat until later that afternoon. Lieutenant Perry initially seems to have been reluctant to release Goodere into the hands of the water bailiff, on the grounds that the case should be tried in the High Court of Admiralty, but he was eventually persuaded to do so.[78]

James Dudgeon ensured that Dineley's body lay undisturbed on the flock bed. The corpse revealed signs of struggle: an awkwardly articulated right leg; severe scratches about the neck; blood emissions from the nose and mouth.[79] It did not take the coroner's inquest long to pronounce that Dineley had been murdered and to point the finger at Goodere, Mahony and White.[80] The jury, which included a freeholder and distiller from Temple parish, a yeoman from St John's, and a variety of artisans from other central parishes, were in no doubt who was responsible.[81] Mahony and White were considered the direct perpetrators of the deed, while Goodere was deemed to be 'present, aiding, abetting, comforting and maintaining' them.[82] This verdict formed the substance of the indictments against the three men.

By the time the coroner's verdict was delivered, the two assassins had been arrested. White was secured at the *Bell* in Marsh Street 'very much in liquor'.

He pretended that he was flush because his mother had sent him money.[83] Mahony had tried to extract some back wages from his former captain, James Mervin, a skipper who worked in the Mediterranean and Baltic trades, but Mervin was now in Newgate because a merchant had called in a debt of £400 which he could not repay.[84] Mahony then spent some time at the *Brockweir Boat* on the Back; perhaps trying to fence Goodere's watch, for when the constables came to investigate the matter, the landlord's wife tossed it in the privy to conceal its whereabouts.[85] He was secured on higher ground, in a private house opposite the *Ship* on St Michael's Hill. Like White, he was very drunk when he was taken, and he was still wearing a bloody neckerchief, a predicament that would have damned him in a forensic age. Both men were sober enough the following morning to make a full confession in Bridewell. Each accused the other of the actual deed, but it didn't really matter who strangled Sir John and who assisted. Both were found guilty by the coroner's inquest, along with Sir John's brother, Captain Samuel Goodere. What protestations of innocence he made at the Council House fell on deaf ears.

CHAPTER FOUR

The Trial

Fratricides were newsworthy. Murder was 'abominable' in 'the Sight of God and Man', exclaimed one pamphleteer, but 'if we descend to Aggravations and consider it as dissolving the Ties of Kindred and Consanguinity, it will raise in us a greater Degree of Horror. When a Brother rises up against a Brother, and murders him in cold Blood, the very Thought is so shocking that Nature itself is hardly able to support it.'[1] So began the first tract to come off the press on the Dineley murder. In biblical terms, the murder had the mark of Cain; it was 'the blackest of crimes', the primal murder whose 'passions of anger and jealousy' had only multiplied since that event.[2] In literary terms, the pamphlet had the mark of modernity. Priced at 4d. a copy, it was expected to reach a broad audience, for there was a surge in readership by the 1740s. The annual circulation of newspapers tripled between 1713 and 1750, from 2.4 million to 7.3 million, and at the onset of the War of Jenkins Ear readers scrambled to read the latest 'advices' on the confrontation with Spain in the Caribbean.[3] Admiral Vernon was news; the navy was news; and a murder at sea in a vessel designated to raise recruits for war was bound to attract public attention. Especially if it involved one brother killing another.

The author of *The Bristol Fratricide* did not bother to wait for the trial. He knew he had a story to tell. Details in London and regional newspapers had unfolded in late January. The *Daily Post* and *London Evening Post* had the bare bones of the story by 22 January from 'various letters from Bristol', but could name no suspects, for 'the City magistrates are closely employ'd in discovering the perpetrators'. Early reports indicated 'a considerable part of a Man o' War's crew let into the secret', a story so 'ill-concerted' that 'it could not gain credit were not all the Bristol letters of yesterday full of the narrative'. But the suspects were known and named soon enough. The *Gloucester Journal*, for example, drew on the coroner's report and bluntly registered Captain Goodere's complicity in his brother's murder. Other newspapers quickly picked up the story and within a week, readers were being invited to savour the details in a tract, 'collected from Affidavits and other Authentic vouchers.'[4] These referred to depositions sworn at the coroner's inquest and before mayor Henry Combe on 19 and 20 January 1741,[5] and beyond that, to the

THE
Briſtol Fratricide:

Being an Exact and Impartial

NARRATIVE

Of the Horrid and Dreadful

CATASTROPHE
OF

Sir *John Dineley Goodere*, Bart.

Perpetrated by the
Contrivance, Aſſiſtance, and Encourage-
ment of his Brother

Samuel Goodere, Eſq;

Commander of the *Ruby* Man of War,

And Executed by

Matthew Mahony and *Charles White*,

Now in Cuſtody for the ſame.

In which is contained

Some ACCOUNT of the Life of the De-
ceaſed Sir *John Dineley Goodere*, Bart.

The whole being a faithful Account of this Tragical Affair.

Collected from Affidavits and other authentick Vouchers.

LONDON: Printed by J. HART in *Poppins-
Alley, Fleet-Street.* 1741.

The front cover of *The Bristol Fratricide* (1741), the first pamphlet account of the murder to be published. Although it clearly names the three defendants as perpetrators and executors, the pamphlet appeared for sale some three months before the opening of their trial. Bristol Libraries, 9532 gossip of the quay and the *Ruby*. The author of *The Bristol Fratricide* could also rely on the accounts that circulated in the provinces. The *Newcastle Courant*, for example, featured a letter from Bristol misleadingly dated 17 January 1741, which reported Sir John's abduction and murder by 'a couple of Desperate Fellows' who had been bribed by the captain. 'The Magistrates were very busy in taking Informations on this Unhappy Affair', it continued, and believed one of the assassins had already been taken up.[6] More details of the murder unfolded in subsequent weeks, allowing writers to create a dramatic narrative. Although some historians have ventured that eighteenth-century crime was reported in an impersonal way, this was certainly not true of the Dineley murder.[7] The abduction of Dineley and the report of the coroner, Nicholas King, quickly shaped the narrative.[8]

On the abduction, the author of *The Bristol Fratricide* had good information about the hiring of men from the Vernon privateer and the manner in which Sir John was whisked along the quay to the awaiting barge. On the actual killing there was some embroidery, since the confessions of Mahony and White were rather vague about who did what, each incriminating the other. In the pamphlet they were cast as 'two inhuman villains' who strangled Sir John by each pulling on the rope; and they did it for large sums, £150 and £200, a lot larger than they actually received from a conspiring captain. Their brutal murder, moreover, was observed by the peeping toms, Edward and Margaret Jones, who 'saw the whole transaction'.[9] In this version of the murder, Mahony and White were as guilty as hell, and so too, was the duplicitous captain whose quarrels with his brother and support of his flighty wife, Lady Mary Dineley-Goodere, were savoured and sketched. Clearly someone had dug deep into the muckraking details of the acrimonious divorce, with Lady Mary purportedly caught *in flagrante* with Sir Robert Jason in a hayrick. And they delved into the property disputes that had brought the brothers to such acrimony. Like the newspapers, the author of the *Bristol Fratricide* had picked up much of the gossip that flowed about compromised fortunes and broken entails in the Goodere family; although one wonders whether Samuel Foote, the nephew of the brothers who was in debtors' prison in London but anxious to profit from the family scandal, traded information in return for details of the unfolding events in Bristol, or even traded information for money to abet his own release from the Fleet.[10]

In a modern context these pre-trial revelations would have compromised the case against the captain, particularly so because the author of *The Bristol Fratricide* advocated no mercy, and charged that any concession to the captain would raise a 'just jealousy in the Vulgar' who were severely punished for

Thomas Rowbotham, *Bristol Guildhall* (1825), the scene of the trial. Bristol Culture: Bristol Museums and Archives, M2437

crimes of property which often stemmed from poverty.[11] The issue of whether the jury was not already influenced by the barrage of news about the murder was raised at the trial. Goodere complained that the newspapers were 'full of reflecting false Expressions to prejudice the People against him'.[12] One of his counsel, Mr Frederick, specifically cited *The Bristol Fratricide*. But the prosecution brushed off the objection, and the jurymen duly swore 'they had never seen any such Pamphlet or Papers', a very improbable assertion.[13] The presiding judge, the Bristol Recorder, Sir Michael Foster, did not press the issue. He did, however, entertain the notion that the prosecuting witnesses should be examined separately, out of earshot of the others; on the grounds that otherwise they might echo each other's opinion. Mr Vernon, who led the case for the Crown, objected that the defence was trying to slur the character of prosecution witnesses, who 'attend here on the public service (and some of them persons of figure)'. It was a strategy, Vernon suggested, 'casting a sort of blemish on their credit'. Jarrit Smith, appearing as both Crown solicitor and prosecution witness, backed him up. Was he to leave the room as well? Foster confirmed Smith could stay, but although the request was a little irregular, he allowed the other witnesses to withdraw to a private room.

Whether this had been a deliberate attempt by the defence to nobble Smith's handling of the trial is impossible to say. We know the Bristol lawyer systematically marshalled the witnesses for the trial. He summoned Thomas Chamberlayne to show Goodere had approached him to arrange a meeting with his brother; Morris Hobbs and midshipman Thomas Williams to detail the plans for the seizure; six witnesses to reveal how Dineley was forced along St Augustine's Back. Thomas Williams was again called to prove that the privateers were disembarked at the Redcliff Glasshouse and to recall the conversations of the brothers on the barge; a further six to relate how and where Sir John was confined once on board the *Ruby*; and the Jones couple, James Dudgeon and Duncan Buchanan 'to prove the Murder, what was said and what happened at that time'.[14] Smith also had witnesses to show Mahony and White were smuggled on shore and that Mahony had Goodere's watch in his possession prior to its recovery from the *Brockweir Boat* bog-house. Smith himself detailed Goodere's duplicitous moves to reconcile with his brother, the nature of their disagreement, and the captain's insistence that he knew nothing of his brother's death upon committal in Bristol.

By any standards Jarrit Smith laid the groundwork for a pretty tight case, made tighter by the fact that Mahony and White had both signed confessions implicating Goodere, although they could not incriminate themselves and were not therefore called to the stand. There was no opportunity for the captain or his lawyer to play on the inconsistencies of their evidence and maintain they were villainous liars. In a modern era, legal pundits would have highlighted Jarrit Smith's compromised position as solicitor for the prosecution, witness, and creditor of the murdered man. But this does not seem to have bothered the presiding judge, Sergeant Michael Foster, or the jury. It did not even merit a comment in the press.

This left Captain Goodere and his counsel with few options when mounting a defence. His barristers successfully parried an attempt to revisit the quarrel between Goodere and Dineley over Burghope House on the death of their father. They also succeeded in eliminating the broken entail as a plausible motive for murder. Jarrit Smith had hoped he could press this issue; indeed, his notes on the brief reflected that 'it ought to begin a history of the long-standing dispute between the brothers; with the declaration by Goodere that nothing Sir John could do would deprive him of his estate.'[15] But Justice Foster rejected it as evidence even though it was contextually vital to the story.

Still, it was a small victory for the defence. In the light of the confessions, the abduction, and the witnesses around the purser's room, Goodere's counsel,

Messrs. Frederick and Shephard, faced an uphill battle. The battle was made more formidable by the fact that Goodere could not muster his witnesses from the *Ruby*. On 16 February 1741, just under a month after his arrest, Goodere wrote to the Admiralty requesting the presence of Lieutenant Parry and two midshipmen as witnesses for his trial. The Admiralty agreed to do this, promising to deliver them after their cruise off Lundy hunting for seamen, but the cruise dragged on and the *Ruby* did not anchor in Kingroad until 30 March, four days after the trial resumed on account of Goodere's poor health.[16] Did the Admiralty deliberately delay the witnesses? Did the Board really care? Why didn't Goodere's counsel ask for a second adjournment as the *Ruby* made its way back from Milford Haven? Did Goodere himself have second thoughts about bringing these three men forward? Especially Parry, who as we have seen, eventually collaborated in the captain's arrest.

One thing is clear. Goodere's counsel did not protest their absence at the beginning of the trial. While they launched a defence on procedural grounds, they made no mention of the Admiralty's broken promise. Their first line of attack was to argue that the Bristol general sessions of oyer and terminer had no right to try the case, on the grounds that it occurred outside the city jurisdiction.[17] Goodere or his friends had applied for a habeas corpus to remove the case to the High Court of Admiralty in London, maintaining that the *Ruby* was anchored in the open waters of the Bristol Channel.

Goodere was taking a chance doing this. There was no guarantee that the Court of Admiralty would treat him any differently. Capital punishments at Execution Dock were if anything harsher, because the gallows rope was sometimes shortened to prolong death by asphyxiation and have the condemned convulse in the wind. Admiralty executions dictated that the bodies of the condemned should be washed by three tides, and it was not unknown for guilty captains to be gibbetted on the Thames.[18] Presumably Captain Goodere felt that as a regulating officer in Bristol responsible for recruiting in a popular war, he could call in favours and escape the noose. Certainly, his authority as the commander of the *Ruby* would command more respect in a naval court than in Bristol, although the possibility of 'dancing' at Execution dock and dangling in chains on the banks of the Thames was not so remote as to presume a naval trial would give him a safe passage.

The Admiralty considered the jurisdictional issue in late January. The advocate general, Dr Paul, and the admiralty advocate, Sir Edmund Isham, both thought Goodere had a case and recommended that the trial take place in London. Indeed, a writ of habeas corpus was issued to have Goodere delivered to London Newgate and on 5 February the war office ordered the commanding officer of Colonel Blakeney's regiment in Bristol to have a party accompany him to the metropolis.[19] Yet on 2 February the Admiralty Board had decided to ask for a second opinion on the jurisdiction of the case and ordered the Admiralty Solicitor to request the opinion of Sir Dudley Ryder and Sir John Strange, the Attorney and Solicitor General.[20]

From the biography of Sir Michael Foster, it is clear that Ryder consulted the Recorder. He argued that Bristol had jurisdiction in Kingroad and even if the Admiralty had some concurrent claim to try the case, the coroner's inquest anchored the case in Bristol. Sir Edward Coke's reading of 15 Richard II confirmed this. A Bristol case was in any case cheaper and would be in the interests of 'public justice.' The power of the magistrates would be compromised if this trial was taken out of their hands, Foster added, 'and the esteem of the people is you know in great measure the support of all government.'[21] Ryder and Strange found these arguments compelling and consequently challenged the Admiralty counsel. The evidence that Bristol's jurisdiction extended to Kingroad at the estuary of the Avon was overwhelming, they insisted, and they therefore urged the Admiralty to allow the case to proceed in Bristol. This was agreed upon in the second week of February, but it did not prevent the newspapers reporting that soldiers travelled down to Bristol to bring the three defendants back to London for trial.[22] Troops may have marched along the Great West Road, although the war office records reveal no further evidence beyond the original order. Captain Goodere had expected them in the third week of January, for according to the keeper of Bristol Newgate, Abel Dagge, he destroyed the record of his commitment by the coroner for fear it might compromise his case.[23] He must have been frustrated when he was told he had to stay put.

Some newspapers suggested Captain Goodere changed his mind and decided to stand trial in Bristol; others that the writ of habeas corpus came too late to be implemented, presumably because news of the Admiralty's decision not to proceed with a trial had already reached Bristol.[24] Whatever the case, Goodere would not let go of the issue. At his trial, he taxed the master, Theodore Court, on whether the *Ruby* had drifted into the Severn, asking him whether the ship was moored east or west of an imaginary line drawn between Posset Point [Portishead] and Denny Island. It was his biggest personal intervention in the whole trial. On such arcane matters the prosecuting counsel was derisory. It was well known that the city authorities executed writs in Kingroad, averred Mr Vernon, which had long been 'allowed to be within the local Limits of the City and County of Bristol.' This was the *lex loci*, underwritten by the Bristol charter. In the circumstances, he should be sorry 'to find the Jurisdiction of a City…shaken by a Side-wind.'[25]

There were other points of law on which Goodere and his counsel hoped to cobble the prosecution's case. One was to dispute whether Sir John was appropriately named on the indictment, whether he should have been described as Sir John Dineley-Goodere, Baronet, as he was in some of the evidence.[26] Modern readers might regard this as a legal quibble, but cases had been decided on such picayune matters in the eighteenth century. It forced the prosecuting counsel to expatiate on the history of the baronetcy, one of James I's revenue-raising ventures, and to cite a statute of 12 Henry V which stated that full titles were only necessary in cases of outlawry. Goodere's counsel turned up the heat by demanding that the letter patent of the baronetcy be produced in court. Sir Michael Foster waved the demand aside. He thought the question of whether Sir John was a baronet or not was immaterial to the case. 'I would not deny the Prisoners any advantage they are by Law intitled to,' he declared, 'but I cannot admit of Evidence which can only serve to amuse.'[27]

Once these attempts to halt the case were lost, Goodere's counsel had little strategic alternative but to concentrate their efforts on the cross examination of prosecution witnesses. Given the strength of the prosecution case, this was largely an exercise in damage limitation, its urgency demonstrated by counsels' intervention when Foster asked Goodere if he would like to ask any questions of Jarrit Smith. Shephard jumped in before his client could answer, requesting permission to ask the questions himself, rather than risk allowing Goodere to do it. In fact, the right of defendants' counsel to cross-examine witnesses remained something of a grey area in 1741. Traditionally, questions would be put to witnesses on behalf of a defendant by the judge who, in theory at least, looked after their interests in court. But, as Shephard pointed out, it had recently become 'every day's practice at the courts of Westminster, Old Bailey and in the Circuit', for defence counsel to take on the responsibility. Vernon raised an immediate objection and Foster seemed insufficiently sure of himself to make a ruling, so the cross examination proceeded with both Shephard and Goodere addressing witnesses.[28]

Shephard raised the question on whether the captain had really abetted the crime. The captain's first line of defence, expressed in that hastily scrawled note to Jarrit Smith shortly after the murder was discovered, had been that he was surprised as anyone at the death of his brother by two villainous seamen but this had been compromised by the coroner's verdict and the confessions of Mahony and White. His second was that he had not been present when the murder was committed; he did not see it. Was he therefore guilty? Mr Vernon responded by saying that if a person stood watch to a room where the murder was committed, he was 'as much a Principal in it as the rest…it is not necessary he should be *in conspectu* [in view] if near enough at hand to embolden his accomplices in the Murder.'[29] He went on to cite a 1541 case where Lord Dacre was found guilty for abetting a murder in a deer park even though he did not witness it, and also the well-known murder of Sir Edmund Bury Godfrey during the Popish Plot of 1678, in which the porter of Somerset House, Henry Berry, allegedly stood watch while the magistrate was murdered.[30] The law was clear enough, and Edward Jones' recollection that he saw a 'white hand' on Dineley's throat added substance to the notion that the captain was very much an accomplice.[31] Sailors had calloused weather-beaten hands; captains rarely so, or certainly not to the same degree.

The issue then rested on whether Goodere intended to kill his brother, whether it was *malice prepense,* malice aforethought. On this issue the prosecution marshalled a host of evidence to show the captain had deliberately abducted his brother for that purpose and then stood sentry when the crime was committed. Goodere tried to sustain his own version of the events by insisting his brother was insane and that he had simply confined his brother to protect him from himself. After all, the *Ruby*'s boatswain had already confirmed, in evidence for the prosecution, that Goodere instructed the crew 'that we need not mind [Dineley] because he was mad and that he was brought on board on purpose to prevent his making himself away.'[32] Dineley had then either been robbed and murdered by sailors or else somehow strangled himself 'in a fit of the Phrenzy'.[33] This argument, the best in fact that Goodere was able to muster, deserves some consideration. He produced servants to highlight Sir John's mental instability and dementia. Bridget King swore Dineley would 'call his Servants up' in the middle of the night and 'fall a singing, and then he would go to bed again'. He 'hath been quite raving mad.' Mary Stafford testified that at Tockington Sir John would ring for her services at all hours, for no reason whatsoever. 'He would take a Knife, Fork, Glass-Bottle, or any thing that came in his way to throw at us', she recalled, 'asking of us, what did we come to rob him?'[34] A salt officer professed that at Charlton he had seen Sir John 'do several Acts of Lunacy as a Mad-man.' But the prosecution countered these claims by producing several gentlemen who declared Sir John to be a good neighbour, and *compos mentis*, perfectly capable of writing his own will. In the face of this testimony, where gentlemen were generally considered to be more creditable witnesses than servants, there was little Goodere could do to press his version of events. Moreover, as Michael Hay and Roy Porter have noted, 'for the propertied classes, magistrates typically set the behavioural hurdle high before they would judge a party to be of unsound mind'.[35] Eccentricities of character, in other words, were only to be expected in men of Dineley's class.

Perhaps Goodere's brightest hope was the Rev Mr Watkins. As vicar of Cropthorne a mile from Charlton, Watkins was a family friend, willing to testify that he had told Goodere of the changes made to Dineley's will several months before the murder. Goodere could therefore argue that he had nothing to gain by murdering Dineley; on the contrary, his only realistic recourse was to persuade his brother to change his mind. Here, the issue of Dineley's insanity might become more material; enough perhaps not only to invalidate the revised will but to justify Goodere's need to secure and confine Dineley while coaxing him into compliance. It might then be possible to argue that Dineley had thrown a fit on board the *Ruby*, struggled with his captors and lost his life through misadventure. However, the impact of Watkins' evidence was overshadowed by Vernon's smart cross examination. Watkins must surely have become very familiar with Sir John over the years, asserted Vernon; did he consider Dineley mad? Not in the least, replied Watkins. In fact, Dineley's character had been 'very much misrepresented to the world'. After that disappointment, Goodere let his witness go, and Vernon successfully repeated the tactic with Ashfield, one of the character witnesses.[36] Although he had not intended the issue of his brother's insanity to be his only line of defence, he had certainly meant it to frame an explanation for his behaviour. Was there really any prospect of success?

In murder trials of the period, insanity was occasionally admitted as a defence, but it was usually the defendant's, not the victim's state of mind, that formed the subject of inquiry. The key question, moreover, concerned a person's mental capacity at the time a salient act was committed, not his or her susceptibility to occasional acts of lunacy. As the Solicitor General would later put it at the conclusion of the trial of Earl Ferrers for shooting his factor in 1760, 'If there be a total permanent want of reason, it will acquit the prisoner. If there be a total temporary want of it when the offence was committed, it will acquit the prisoner: but if there be only a partial degree of insanity, mixed with a partial degree of reason…the judgement of the law must take place'. What was therefore required, whether it be the madness of the defendant or the victim that was being questioned, was clear evidence that a person had lost the ability to 'distinguish the nature of (their) actions', to 'discern the differences between moral good and evil' or to exercise self-restraint. In other words, if Goodere was unable to establish that Dineley was perpetually insane, he would need at least to prove insanity at the time the will was revised and again at the time of Dineley's abduction and confinement on the *Ruby*.[37]

Insanity was by no means easy to prove, however, partly because there was no common agreement, even in the law courts, over its precise definition. Between 1740 and 1749, a total of 24 defendants at the Old Bailey tried to excuse their actions by reason of insanity, only eight of them successfully. Medical expertise was rarely called upon; indeed, Ferrers' trial in 1760 was probably the first in which the judgement of a renowned 'mad doctor', John Monro of the Bethlem asylum, was consulted on behalf of a defendant.[38] What counted in court was not expertise but public perception, and Goodere may have been encouraged by precedents in which madness was conceived in sufficiently loose language either to reduce a charge against a defendant or discredit a prosecution witness.[39] In 1727, for instance, Thomas Nash, arraigned for the murder of his wife, and 'troubled in mind on occasion of his being cheated of an estate by his brother', was found unfit for trial on entirely anecdotal testimony. Par for the course was a witness who 'had known him for some Years to be a very Crazy Person, not taking his natural Rest, but magotting and rambling like a Mad-man'.[40] A year earlier, William Atkinson had his case reduced to manslaughter after his wife took the stand to question the reliability of the principal prosecution witness, a woman who 'used to go about the Streets like a Mad Woman, with her Hair loose, and Patches upon her Face, and that she had been 3 Years in Bedlam'.[41]

There had been instances, too, in which murder case defendants successfully evaded conviction by alleging the insanity of the deceased. Peter Noakes, for example, was charged with shooting his friend, William Turner, through the head in the private room of a London Inn in 1731. Noakes denied it, claiming Turner's death was suicide brought on by an occasional insanity. 'Did you not observe Mr Turner walking in a melancholy-mad Posture?' Noakes asked an inn servant during the trial. The servant wasn't sure. 'When I first went in, he was walking gravely', he replied, 'and the second time he was singing'. As evidence of suicidal intent, it was thin, but Noakes was acquitted nevertheless.[42]

Defendants were not always so fortunate. That same year, Robert Hallam tried something similar when called to account for the death of his wife. The prosecution held that Hallam pushed his wife out of an upstairs window, that they had frequently been heard quarrelling, and that his wife had been heard screaming 'murder' shortly before she died. Hallam denied it. His wife had thought herself possessed by the Devil, he said, and had thrown herself from the window in a frenzy of madness. And he had witnesses. 'She was sitting

Mahony and White in a cell at Bristol's Newgate gaol, awaiting trial for Dineley's murder. From *The Trials of Samuel Goodere, Matthew Mahony and Charles White*, broadside (1741), Bristol Libraries, B10146

on the Settle by the Fire-side, rubbing her Hands, in a very melancholy Mood', recalled one. 'What's the Matter, says I? Why, says she, the Devil's got into me, and I believe he will never leave me till I have made away with myself'. Be that as it may, Hallam was convicted and hanged, though he denied murder to the last.[43] He was a labouring man; Noakes and Turner were gentlemen.

Even so, it would take more than his superior social class to save Goodere from the inevitable judgement of the court, and the testimonials he had gathered to his own good character were simply no match for the weight of evidence pointing to his premeditated malevolence. In the end, he rather pathetically claimed his illness in Newgate had prevented him from organising a better defence, and that the Admiralty had not allowed the timely release of supporting witnesses from the *Ruby*.[44]

After a trial of nine hours the jury, drawn once again from the central Bristol parishes but also from the sprawling northern parish of St James,[45] found him guilty, as they did Matthew Mahony. Unlike Goodere, who had two barristers defending him, the latter was unrepresented at the trial and according to the judge did not 'say anything by way of [a] proper Defence.'[46] He simply pleaded he was a 'poor press'd Servant', drunk when he made the confession, and 'frightened out of [his] Wit'.[47] After these verdicts, which took the jury only fifteen minutes to decide, it was a foregone conclusion that Charles White would be found guilty the following day. Soon after, on 28 March, 1741, the three men were brought before the court to hear their sentence: death by hanging on the public gallows. As for the privateers, three of them were tried on a misdemeanour for abducting Dineley at College Green. They were fined 40 shillings and sentenced to one year's imprisonment.[48]

After the sentence Captain Goodere put on a brave face. He walked back to Newgate in a scarlet cloak, a mark of his new, temporary baronetcy however infamously inherited, and doffed his hat to passers-by.[49] He was a proud man with a coat of arms, for whom honour and outward civility mattered. Privately he smouldered. Rumours of his desperation circulated the press. In January one of his servants had been found with files and razors in his pocket. Now it was feared the captain had hired the Kingswood colliers to swarm the jail and rescue him. The threat was taken seriously because Mahony had confessed that a party of 'stout fellows' had offered to rescue them before the trials began. As a result, the door to Goodere's cell was reinforced, the keeper's room was secured, and arms were brought in to give the coalminers 'a warm reception.'[50]

Mahony and White were put in irons in the condemned hold; White's irons were increased when he had the audacity to complain to Jarrit Smith that the

Newgate jailer, Abel Dagge, had pocketed his pay ticket for £23 that he had hoped to use to clear some outstanding debts. Dagge's son told him 'were it ten times worse than before it [the irons] should not come off.'[51] Goodere, by contrast, had a cell to himself with a writing desk and paper. And write he did, for he tried to call in some favours. He allegedly wrote to two MPs requesting their help.[52] He reminded the government he had mobilized his seamen to return Sir George Oxenden as MP for Sandwich, an Admiralty borough. This type of solicitation was typical of Goodere's dealings with government. He also wrote to Admiral Sir Charles Wager, a cabinet minister and close associate of Sir Robert Walpole, asking for a reprieve, 'wch will be of the utmost advantage to my distressed innocent Children.'[53] He floated the rumour that he was the victim of a partisan plot in Bristol, attributing his misfortunes to civic hostility to the press gang and to the revengeful spirit of Jarrit Smith 'a notorious Tory of this City', a coded way of suggesting Smith was a damned Jacobite. He persisted with his claim that he should have been tried at the High Court of Admiralty.

In the mid-to-late nineteenth century public opinion could influence the government's decision to reprieve murderers, but in the eighteenth century these matters were still handled discreetly, within the prevailing corridors of power.[54] Goodere's wife, Elizabeth petitioned the crown, requesting that her husband be sentenced to transportation for life 'or whatever His Majesty thought proper.'[55] So, apparently, did some of his friends. When these overtures failed, Goodere became more composed. On 8 April, as a momento mori, his coffin was carried into his jail room with the inscription 'Samuel Goodere, aged 53 years, who departed this life, April 15, 1741.' At this point he still persisted in his innocence, professing he had not intended to kill his brother. He only sought to 'bring him from those Measures he was pursuing, so highly injurious to the Family.'[56]

Eventually, under the entreaties of the Reverend John Penrose,[57] he broke down and confessed to the murder, yet insisted that it was only in the early hours of 19 January that he resolved to carry out the deed. He resisted the notion that his efforts to reconcile with his brother at Jarrit Smith's house were duplicitous, as the prosecution had claimed. In his written confession to Penrose, he insisted his brother's murder 'was not the effect of premeditated malice' despite the fact that Sir John had provoked him by cutting off the entail to Charlton and stripping him of his birthright. 'All I wanted was to frighten him into a compliance of recalling what he had done; how I fell suddenly into the design of dispatching him is what I cannot account for myself.'[58] To the end he maintained that the murder of his brother was the result of an 'irregular passion' that did not accord with his reputation as an honourable gentleman and paternal captain. It was an explanation that emphasized impulsive killing rather than rational forethought, fuelled by matters of honour and fraternal respect as much as money. In the light of Goodere's felicitous marriage to a relatively prosperous Welsh widow, it was not an implausible plea; although judging from Elizabeth Goodere's will, where she talked of resolving her husband's debts before devising her estate to four of her children, it would seem that Sir John had seriously run down the Burghope estate, leaving Samuel with a pitiful inheritance.[59] Honour and fraternity were not the explanations advanced by the prosecution, who sought to unmask how Goodere had maliciously masterminded the murder and deployed a company of privateers and crewmen to abduct and strangle his brother aboard the *Ruby*.[60]

In a separate letter Captain Goodere thanked Jarrit Smith for his efforts to bring about a family reconciliation, and entreated him to assist him with his prayers, for Smith now beheld 'a miserable object wretch who was once accounted a Man of probity and Honour, plunged into perdition by his own folly and rashness' for a 'crime which must fill all with the utmost abhorrence and indignation.'[61] Samuel Goodere thus fulfilled some of the expectations of a contrite confession before execution while trying to maintain a slim measure of honour for his wartime services. We say 'some' because Goodere did not venture verbally to confess his guilt to the public at the gallows, although he did apparently submit his written statement to Rev. Mr Penrose on his knees. His nephew believed, from the reports he had heard, that he died with a 'becoming decency and the tranquillity of a sensible man and a true penitent'.[62]

Captain Goodere took communion with his wife on the evening of 13 April, just thirty-odd hours before he was executed. He did not see any of his children, although later reports believed his eldest daughter visited him.[63] During his time in jail and in his journey to his execution, he exercised the privileges of a gentleman. He had better accommodation in Newgate than his fellow malefactors; he had visitors. He travelled the final journey to St Michael's Hill in a coach, accompanied by the Reverend Mr Penrose. There had been some criticism of this indulgence on the grounds that it shielded the rich malefactor from the open judgment of the public. In the case of Captain John Jeane, hanged at Execution Dock, London, in 1726 for the brutal murder of his cabin boy, a coach was denied him on the grounds that his crime was too grotesque to merit the concession. It was predicted that henceforth coaches would no longer be permitted on the path to the gallows, save in the most extraordinary of circumstances.[64] Such optimism proved illusory. Judges and jurists might proclaim equality before the law, but money still mattered when it came to prison and processional privileges.

The other malefactors to be hanged that day, Mahony, White, and a young woman named Jane Williams, stood in a tumbril with halters round their necks. Williams was a 22-year-old seamstress who had been seduced by a young man under promises of marriage. When she became visibly pregnant, she lost her job, and was at a loss what to do, being unable to rely on the help of her fatherless family. She thought of putting her child into parish care but cringed at the prospect of destitution or bridewell while her application was being processed. She considered committing suicide but was persuaded by her lover to smother the baby. As a result, she was indicted under a 1624 act for 'concealing the birth' of her child, a statute which specifically targeted children born out of wedlock in an attempt to curb the illicit sexuality of women. Under the statute the mother was guilty unless she could prove her innocence, a predicament that jurists like Blackstone increasingly felt to be severe. In fact, the trend in infanticide trials at the time of Williams' committal was towards greater leniency. Forty-six of the 61 cases that came before the Old Bailey in the mid-century decades resulted in an acquittal. In the month before Jane Williams was hanged, the judges on the Home circuit reprieved a Mary Rolfe for the same offence.[65]

There is no evidence to suggest poor young women in Bristol inspired similar acts of leniency, although there had been relatively few comparable cases in the city in recent years. Sarah Benbow was hanged in 1723 after her newborn child was found dead in a neighbour's vault, 'its mouth stuffed full of paper and cinders'. She insisted she had only wrapped the child in a petticoat and left it for her neighbour to find in her washroom, but judge and jury were unmoved. Martha Morgan suffered the same fate in 1734 for 'strangling her infant with a small cord and throwing it into a Bog House'. She confessed to the crime beneath the gallows. What became of the 'unhappy young woman' who confessed to drowning her child in a horse pond at the bottom end of Milk Street a few days after its birth in 1736 is unrecorded.[66] Jane Williams then, was no more fortunate, written into anonymity by a press that could find only harsh words for her. There she appeared an ignorant wretch, godless, unable to recite the Lord's Prayer.[67] Actually, she had received the rudiments of Christianity from her parents and was thought by the Newgate chaplain to be 'naturally of a mild and easy temper.'[68] It was more likely that the trauma of her ordeal rendered her catatonic.

Eight people had been condemned to hang at the Bristol sessions of March 1741, four of them for burglaries and felonies, including one fifteen-year-old girl named Mary Harding. These four thieves had their sentences commuted to fourteen years' transportation.[69] This was not unusual. A high proportion of men and women sentenced to death in English courts at this time could expect to be spared the noose, either by the presiding judge at the end of the session or on appeal to the Crown shortly afterwards. Plenty of people still went to the gallows of course. In the same month that Goodere was hanged, as many as twenty-one men and women were executed at London's Tyburn from a total of twenty-three capital sentences delivered by the jury in the January and February sessions.[70] Execution, in other words, was not determined solely by the letter of the law, but by the discretion of its interpreters. Quite how these decisions were made is not always clear. Sir Michael Foster, the Bristol Recorder, was normally quite punctilious in his recommendations to the Secretary of State for some commutation of sentence, but his application for March 1741 is curiously missing from the state papers.[71] We can assume perhaps that since four of the eight condemned were murderers and the other four thieves, it was a relatively simple allocation to make, assuming he intended to spare about half of them. Foster may have felt that eight hangings in a session for such a variety of offences would reduce the impact of the 'awful lesson' of the law on spectators, whose attention would in any case be focussed primarily on Goodere and his accomplices. Large numbers were certainly anticipated. As one newspaper reported, 'So shocking a scene as four hanged for murder [Williams for infanticide] drew vast crowds from some miles around the country, which together with the city residents made the concourse exceedingly great.'[72] These were key crimes that fascinated spectators, the very people whom the authorities hoped would draw the appropriate lessons. Public executions were exemplary. They were designed to deter as much as punish.

On Wednesday 15 April, around noon, the four malefactors began their ascent to St Michael's Hill. The procession took almost an hour. Many years later Richard Smith suggested that the crowd cried 'shame' at the differential treatment accorded the condemned as they trundled up the cobble slope, although contemporary reports do not confirm this.[73] The three men were said to be resigned to their fate and did not shed a tear. They confessed their crimes in writing, but we do not know whether the sailors' confessions, known for some time, were converted into broadsheets and hawked around the gallows.[74] Only White addressed the crowd, urging the assembly not to be ensnared by malicious people such as he had been by the captain. After reciting some prayers and singing a short psalm they were tied up, Goodere first. White slung his halter round his neck in preparation of the hanging. The men kissed

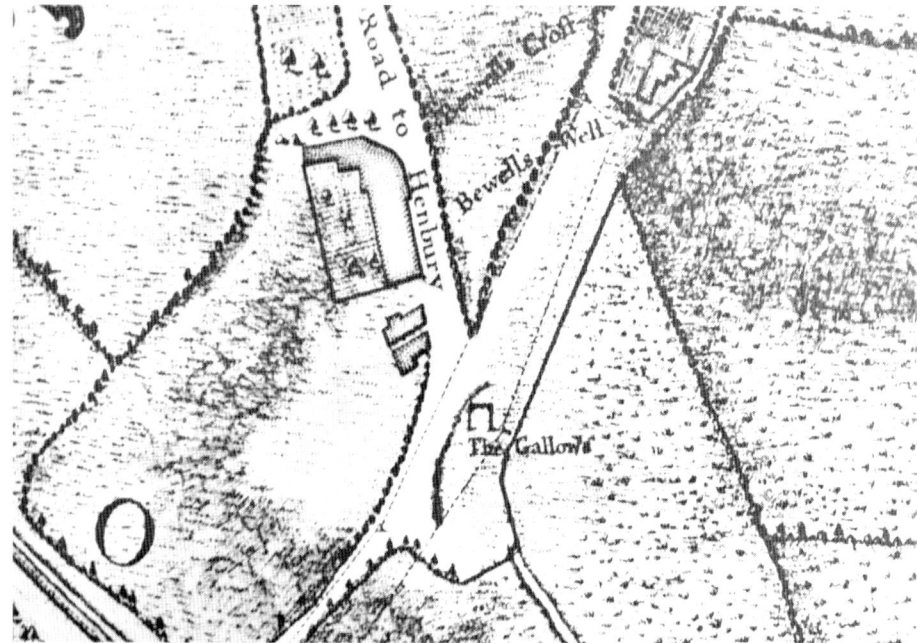

The site of Bristol's gallows at the top of St Michael's Hill; still open country when Goodere, White and Mahony were hanged here in 1741. Detail from John Rocque, *Plan of the City and Suburbs of Bristol* (1742), Bristol Archives 07770/1

each other. White and Mahony, who continued to claim they were 'spirited up' to killing Dineley 'by threats, promises and liquor',[75] finally forgave the captain for manipulating them. When the captain dropped a white handkerchief, the four were turned off the cart. How long they twisted on the gallows is unclear; some reports suggested twenty minutes, others as much as an hour.

News of the deaths of Dineley's killers travelled fast. Printing presses sprung quickly into action as grub street hacks competed to get the story out first. 'To prevent impositions', cautioned an advert in the *London Daily Post* on 20 April, 'this morning will be published, price only 6d, printed at Bristol and sent up by the flying coach...the genuine dying speeches', of the three men.[76] No such attention was paid to poor Jane Williams. According to one nineteenth-century account, her body was carried off by 'quondam friends and neighbours' and taken to Broad Quay near Marsh Street, where she had lodged. The coffin was set on a bench, opened, and passers-by were asked to contribute to a wake, a mass, and a decent funeral. How successful these solicitations were for this poor seamstress is uncertain.[77] What happened to the bodies of the three men is the subject of our next chapter.

CHAPTER FIVE

The Gibbet

> See'st thou that pole upon that isle of mud
> That looks as if full many a year the flood
> Had washed its base? From whence the carrion crow
> Watches the River AVON's ebb and flow?
> Why was it placed there? Does some legend tell
> What spot it marks, and what near it befell?
> There is no legend – you the truth may see
> In the Rev. SAMUEL SAYER'S History…

So goes Richard Smith's *The Fratricide*, a rambling poetic interpretation of the Goodere murder, on the final resting place of Matthew Mahony almost a century earlier. Smith was a well-known and colourful character, often seen running around Bristol in a rough camlet cloak, with a white dog trailing his gig. As a proprietor of the *Bristol Mirror*, he was able to first publish his poem in the paper in three successive instalments in 1839, and we'll examine the tone and content of his verse more fully in our final chapter. But Smith was first and foremost neither a journalist nor a poet but a prominent member of the city's medical establishment. He entered the Bristol Infirmary as a junior sawbones when still a young man in 1796, but had risen by 1812 to become senior surgeon, curator and instigator of the institution's museum of medical curios, and a member of Bristol's reformed Council from 1836 until his death in 1843. 'Among his peculiarities', it was noted in *Notes and Queries* some years later, 'Mr Smith had almost a morbid curiosity in criminal cases, a trait of character that may be veiled as a love of forensic medicine. This was well seen in his museum.'[1]

He was well connected in Bristol society and able to trace his pedigree back to the sixteenth-century alderman who founded the Red Maids school. His grandfather was the well-known parson Alexander Catcott, the rector of St Stephen's, who had championed Bristol as a modern Tyre, 'the crowning city whose merchants are princes and whose traffickers are the honourable of the Earth', a judgment that flattered Bristol's social elite while conveniently ignoring its trafficking in enslaved Africans. His connections enabled him to move effortlessly within Bristol's upper crust, following his father as a president of the Dolphin Society, hosting a dinner of the St Stephen's ringers in place of Tory alderman John Haythorne in 1832, and serving as a councillor for St Augustine's ward for the last seven years of his life. Indeed, Smith won only five fewer votes than Thomas Daniel, the city's undisputed Tory 'king', in the year he was first elected to municipal office. His fascination with the Goodere case, and the fate of Mahony in particular would shape the later fate of both the gibbet cage and the 'pole upon that isle of mud'; indeed, it played a key role in restoring public interest in the story in the Victorian city. Of the three convicts, only Mahony was sentenced to be gibbeted however, so we shall deal first with the bodies of the other two convicts.

Surgeons from the Infirmary, hoping to grab at least one of the trio for the dissecting table, evidently made a move for White as he was taken down from the gallows and he 'by some means or other was got into (their) clutches,' but the Sheriffs stepped in and ordered his release. According to Smith, once White's body was safely in the arms of his friends and family, it was taken directly to St James's Churchyard and buried beside the central footpath leading to Barton Alley.[2] Why was White saved from the dissecting table? Had the sheriffs already promised Goodere to the surgeons? There was nothing exceptional about sending the bodies of the hanged to infirmaries for public dissection in 1741, but allocation was in the gift of the sheriffs. Surgeons were expected to have made a close study of anatomy as part of their training and to have practiced on human corpses so, given an obliging judiciary, claiming them wherever possible from the gallows was a practicable way of doing it. The city's recently completed Infirmary building lay conveniently close to the bottom of St Michael's Hill, at the junction of Marlborough Street and Maudlin Lane. Yet however grave the crime, and regardless of either the advancement of medicine or the punitive requirements of the Law, families were naturally resistant to having the bodies of their loved ones sliced open, hacked into pieces and put on public show.

Historical attention to unseemly struggles beneath the gallows between the friends and families of the condemned and agents acting for the surgeons has usually focussed on the experience of the capital where, as Peter Linebaugh has shown of the 1740s, they were frequently hard fought. But provincial centres were not immune, even if hanging days were less common than in London where eight times every year the Old Bailey sessions condemned defendants to death. At Bristol and elsewhere, sheriffs were left having to balance the legitimate interests of the surgeons against the risk of serious crowd disorder at the conclusion of an execution ritual designed to be both awful and solemn.[3] And the extent to which they could ever consider themselves fully in control of the execution process at Bristol was moot. In 1738 Thomas Boon went to his death on the hill but used his time beneath the gallows to publicly name his conniving mistress as the cause of his misfortunes. Rather than take the lesson intended for them by the authorities, the crowd took Boon's side and spent two days besieging the woman's house, breaking the doors, windows and fittings and defying the mayor's reading of the Riot Act. 'We think it justice to serve her so', ran an anonymous threatening letter tossed over the railings of the Mansion House, 'and your worship worse if you doth not hold your peace'.[4]

Understandably then, sheriffs were not always in a position to guarantee the surrender of criminal bodies to the surgeon's knife. There had been just ten executions on the St Michael's Hill gallows in the previous ten years.[5] Given that this was the first and last time four executions for murder would take place in Bristol on a single hanging day, the city surgeons will certainly have been hopeful of securing at least one of them. But past experience may not have filled them with confidence. Twice in recent years, the Infirmary had been denied the bodies of the condemned by crowd action that left the sheriffs' authority in tatters. In 1734, the body of Thomas Kitchingham, a soldier in Colonel Montague's regiment hanged for murder, was 'taken care of' by his comrades in arms, who took it to St James churchyard and buried it themselves, adding quicklime and water to the hastily dug grave, 'to prevent the surgeons stealing the body'.[6] Then, two years later, the body of John Vernham was carried away from the gallows by a party of Lightermen, placed in a small boat and rowed down river to be 'buried in the sands at Kingroad, secure from the surgeons'.[7]

The sheriffs' difficulties were not restricted to questions of crowd control however, for the hanging process itself had been no better managed in recent years, making the smooth execution of such a high profile hanging as Goodere's all the more important. Vernham and the man hanged with him, Joshua Harding, had been taken down from the gallows too early and both were found to be still alive an hour or so later. Vernham's recovery lasted only a few hours, but Harding survived to become, briefly, the talk of the town. The sheriffs managed to secure him in a cell once again where surgeons were sent for to bleed him. At first it was proposed that he be taken back and hanged a second time but several contemporary sources suggest he was pardoned or reprieved instead.[8] As Elizabeth Hurren has shown, recovery was not unusual in an age where hanging was anything but a precise science and a reprieve followed by transportation for life a surprisingly common consequence. Indeed, it was a surgeon's first task when sent a criminal corpse to cut, to determine whether medical death had taken place (a process known as anatomisation) and only once satisfied of it to perform a dissection (the post-execution punishment).[9] Nevertheless, the Corporation's political opponents had a field day over Vernham and Harding. The Jacobite *Fog's Weekly Journal* cast blame not only on the shoulders of the Sheriffs but on the Walpolean Recorder, Sir John Scrope, who had already been dumped from his parliamentary seat for the city by a Tory victory at the election in 1734. 'A certain great man in the Law is like to lose his place which he holds for the City for some bungling work in the execution of his office', the paper speculated.[10] Scrope kept his place, but there was further bungling in 1739 when the Sheriffs were obliged to hang John Kimmerly four times because 'three several ropes broke…whereby his neck was much hurt and his body bruised by the falls so that his shirt was stained with blood.'[11] The Kimmerly debacle had come hot on the heels of the controversy over the management of the execution of the Scottish soldier, David Reid, condemned for sodomy in 1738, as outlined in our second chapter. Ultimately, Reid escaped the noose only because an eleventh-hour reprieve arrived during a 24-hour postponement imposed by the Corporation to avoid a clash with the annual mayor-making ceremony. As far as the Bristol crowd were concerned, Reid's evasion from justice was entirely the fault of the Corporation.[12]

This pattern of ineptitude, established over the past five or so years, may be said to mark the context in which the Goodere executions were staged in 1741 and in which decisions would have to be made about the disposal of the bodies. Mahony, already reserved for the gibbet, was not therefore a candidate for dissection. But given the experience of a hostile soldiery at Kitchingham's hanging, the sheriffs would also have been anxious to avoid confrontation with any sailors in the crowd sympathetic to White. There had already been those rumours of colliers and 'stout fellows' ready to rescue the threesome from Newgate to consider. And White, after all, was a seaman whose previous good character had been clearly attested in court, who had been made drunk by Goodere and Mahony immediately before the murder, and whose 'malice aforethought' was unproven at best, casting doubt over the justice of his conviction. Moreover, White had used the opportunity to address the assembled crowd before the gallows to remind them that he had been 'ensared out of his life by the intrigues of the Captain'. If anyone was to be put to the knife in the Infirmary then, the most likely candidate was not seaman White but the murder's 'unnatural' instigator, Captain Goodere, whatever his social class.[13]

What actually happened to Goodere's body after death is not completely clear. His final resting place was a prepared plot in the family estate at Burghope, but in some accounts it went first to be publicly dissected.

One of these texts was Richard Smith's *Fratricide* which imagines the public slicing of Goodere's body by the Infirmary's surgeons. They cut him, removed his heart and held it up so that the assembled crowd could see that it was truly black, then replaced it and sewed him back up. In his own notes, Smith identified his first mentor at the Infirmary, the senior surgeon Godfrey Lowe, as his source for this story. 'The corpse of the fratricide was brought down from the gallows to the Infirmary,' Lowe allegedly told Smith, 'where the surgeons, Thornhill and Page, in the presence of many persons, made with a scalpel a crucial incision upon the thorax and abdomen'. However, Lowe had been dead since 1806 and was only a year old when Goodere was hanged. A more likely source was the Rev. Samuel Seyer, a contemporary of Smith's, who published the story in his *Memoirs, Historical and Topographical of Bristol and its Neighbourhood*, in 1823. Seyer's account was later reprinted more or less verbatim by George Munro Smith, in his *History of the Bristol Royal Infirmary* (1917):

> After the execution, the body of the fratricide was brought by the Under-Sheriff, followed by an immense crowd, to the Infirmary, where a receipt was given for it by Messrs. Thornhill and Page who were in waiting for it. The subject was then paced on a Tressle, and Mr Thornhill, taking a scalpel, made a crucial incision. In this state it was exposed to the populace until evening when it was delivered to his friends.[14]

Seyer's hand may also be detected in Latimer's unreferenced claim that 'a surgeon stuck a scalpel into the breast. In this state it was exposed to the populace until the evening and then despatched to Herefordshire and buried'. It is a trail that is picked up by Lawrence Stone in *Uncertain Unions & Broken Lives,* and it leads logically and unsurprisingly to Ian Kelly's greatly embroidered retelling of the incident in *Mr Foote's Other Leg*.[15] Credibility is certainly lent by the naming in some accounts of Thornhill and Page as the principal surgeons, for they were amongst the most eminent men at the Infirmary in Lowe's day. We labour these points because the dissection story, produced in print for the first time a century after the events it describes, will not be found in any of the contemporary accounts of the trial and execution, either in the newspaper press or in the pamphlet literature. On the contrary, several state that Goodere's body was taken from the gallows, not to the Infirmary, but back to Newgate and kept there overnight before its release to his family, by order of the magistrates, 'in order to prevent any art being made use of to bring him to life'.[16] If, *en route* to the gaol, Goodere's corpse had been admitted to the Infirmary to have its heart cut out, concerns about his later resuscitation are unlikely to have been entertained for long.

If Goodere's body was indeed subjected only to the brief formality of a single scalpel cut and then despatched for burial, he was a good deal more fortunate than Charlotte Bobbett and Maria Davis half a century later. Bobbett and Davis were hanged on St Michael's Hill in 1802 for the murder of Davis's infant son, then taken back down the hill to the Infirmary, 'followed by an immense rabble' and there publicly opened up, displayed and completely dismembered over a period of three days by four surgeons. Richard Smith, still relatively junior, looked on, delivered a lecture to the crowd on criminal anatomy, and made copious notes. After a group of medical students had finished the job by cutting up the muscles, Davis and Bobbett's bones were sent to London for maceration and articulation, then returned for public display in a specially prepared glass and mahogany case for Smith's Infirmary Museum. Indeed, they remained on display until 2017 when they were finally removed and incinerated.[17] Unlike Goodere, neither Bobbett nor Davis belonged to the propertied classes and had not a scrap of social influence to mediate their evisceration. Whatever Samuel Goodere's fate, sensational murders and trials such as these are rarely lost to public memory in essence, but in their detail they may become confused over time. As we shall see in the final chapter, by the dawn of the following century, and until well into the Victorian era, any number of muddled retellings of the Bristol fratricide were published for the popular market. In several of these, all three condemned men were taken to Hotwells to be hanged, 'in sight of the place where the ship lay when the murder was committed'. This version of events, carefully copied and circulated, originated in the misreporting of the *Tyburn Chronicle* in 1768.[18] Of Richard Smith, a man who may have read any number of conflicting accounts before penning the *Fratricide*, we shall hear more in due course, but first we must return to Matthew Mahony.

If, from our Western twenty-first century standpoint, being slowly hanged in public appears punishment enough for even the most grievous offence, the concept of post-execution punishment may be difficult to comprehend. But in a less secular age, the exploitation of popular fears about the destination of the soul and a proper respect for physical remains after bodily death, made sense on its own terms and the terrors it represented to the condemned were real enough. Anatomisation and dissection were one option, but more horrifying still, not only for the felon but for his family and friends, was the

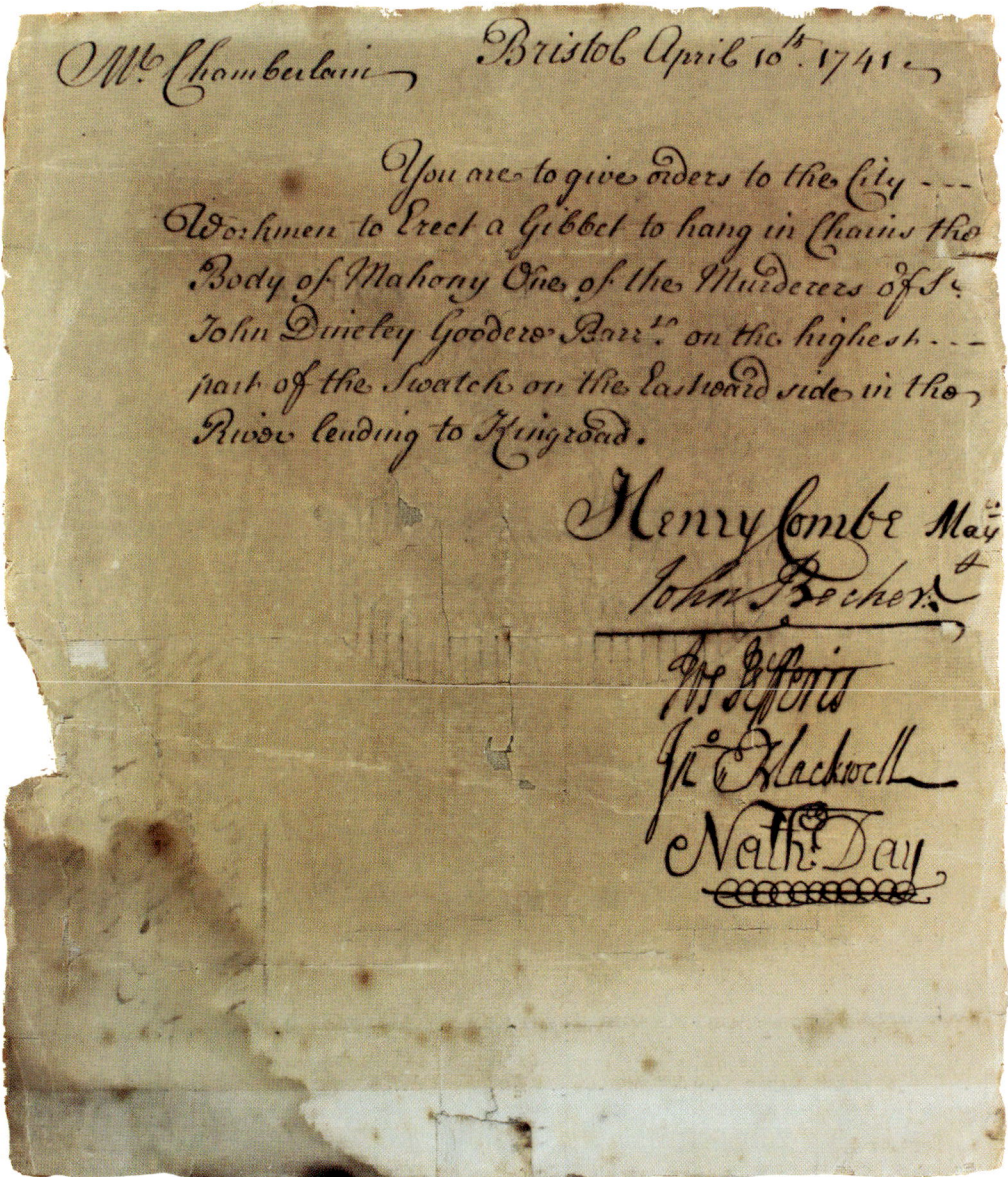

The notice from the mayor and magistrates ordering the city Chamberlain to erect a gibbet pole for Matthew Mahony 'on the highest part of the Swatch on the Eastward side in the river leading to Kingroad'. Bristol Archives, 11373/2

gibbet, or 'hanging in chains' as it was more colloquially known. A gibbeting might either be ordered by the judge during sentencing or by the High Sheriff in the days following. In either case, the condemned man (and it was only ever men) would be visited by a blacksmith in his cell and carefully measured. An iron frame would then be made to encase his body and a pole and cross-piece ordered from which to suspend him, often some thirty feet from the ground so that his remains were beyond the reach of anyone standing below. A location at a good vantage point, preferably in close proximity to the scene of his crime would be selected and the pole dug well in. Nails might be banged into the base as an impediment to climbers. After being cut from the gallows, the body would usually be brushed with tar to help hold it together against inclement weather, then carted to the pole and hoisted to the top. Some efforts might be made to render the corpse relatively decent, or at least to minimise grotesquery; the covering of the face with a cloth, for example. When a black servant and a soldier, were hung in chains at Shepherds Bush on the outskirts of London in 1737, it was reported, 'The black hangs in a very indecent manner, having nothing over his face but quite exposed, with his mouth wide open and his swell'd tongue hanging out, which looks very frightful. He is hung in his green livery but without shoes or stockings. The soldier has a white cloth over his face and hangs more decent.'[19]

In theory, the gibbet cage and its pole would stand until they fell from the ravages of the weather; sometimes a period of several years but more often they stood until removed and clandestinely buried, whether by common consent or sabotage.[20] Jenkin Prothero, gibbeted for murder on Durdham Down in 1783, did not remain there for long if Richard Smith is to be believed. 'I remember well going to see it', he recalled in later life, '…It remained standing about a month, when in the night the gibbet was sawed off and the body bundled, irons and all, into a hole dug for that purpose'. Smith would have been just 11 years old at the time. Nevertheless, some poles and cages remained in place for many years and became familiar marks on the landscape. Shortly after the Goodere executions, the bodies of two more Irishmen, Henry Payne and Andrew Burnett, hanged for robbing and murdering a man on Durham Down in 1744, were gibbeted close to the edge of the Avon Gorge on a spot that 'commanded a view of the river in order to be a terror to the Irish who passed up and down the river'. Within days, the cages had been pulled down by their friends and hidden in the rocks of a quarry below, but they were quickly discovered by the authorities, retrieved and re-erected, this time more securely fixed. The bony remains were evidently still in place five years later when another murderer, Joseph Abseny, was sent to join them on the same apparatus. Any lingering doubts about the impact of post-execution punishments on the sensibilities of the condemned may be safely dispensed with by Abseny's address to the crowd gathered at the foot of the scaffold, for he 'expressed a great concern at being hanged in chains and said he did not care if they quartered his body, so that it was not hung up in the air as prey to the birds'. How long this pole remained a landscape feature on Durdham Down is unknown, but the discovery of two skeletons in a shallow grave close to the site in 1843 prompted a correspondent of the *Bristol Mercury* to recollect seeing it still standing in his own lifetime.[21]

This then, was the fate of Matthew Mahony and we may yet wonder at his selection for it rather than Goodere, the man who commanded him. Since relatively few upper-class men were hanged for any offence during the eighteenth century, the number making themselves available for gibbetting can never have been great. Hanging in chains was a punishment usually reserved for the most violent murders, smuggling affrays and highway robberies, the placing of gibbets designed as a warning to others of their own class and criminal persuasion. The underlying assumption that the gibbet's victims tended to reflect the social status of those most likely to commit the brutal crimes it was designed to punish meant that elite perpetrators might appear anomalous. If as Tarlow says, gibbeting was a means by which 'the Establishment intended to enforce social conformity in respect of law', its over-use on elite bodies would be, quite simply, a waste of the sheriff's money.[22] Not so the body of Matthew Mahony. The mayor ordered a gibbet to be erected on the Swash (or Swatch) a tidal mudbank at the mouth of the Avon, and Mahony's body was accordingly rowed down the river and hoisted up in full view of any vessel making its way into Bristol, a dreadful warning to all who passed by. As Joseph Leech melodramatically put it in his own graphic retelling of the tale in 1862, Mahony's 'ghastly and gibbeted corpse dangled in the wind and swung wildly about in the storm, frightening many a Jack-Tar (whom nothing else could frighten) as his ship lay at anchor off the spot, and he kept the night watch on board.'[23]

Quite possibly, Mahony was suspended over the bones of John Vernham, who it will be remembered, was secretly buried in a Kingroad sandbank by Lightermen five years earlier. The Swash was as close to the scene of Dineley's murder as it was possible to plant the gibbet pole, and the site had the added advantage of being fairly inaccessible to rescuers and souvenir hunters, and sufficiently distant from any settlement to avoid complaints about the smell. The Swash lay at the meeting point of two opposing currents, its parameters constantly shifting with the tide and demanding careful navigation by shipping

Samuel Griffiths Tovey, *Mahony's Gibbet* (1842). Bristol Culture: Bristol Museums and Archives, M1366. The pole and cage had collapsed into the sand by 1784 and by the time Griffiths made this drawing, all that remained was a stump. The actual pole would have been much taller than this, probably 26-30 feet in height and more sturdily fixed into the ground

looking for the narrow and curving deep water channel that gave access to the river. It was a treacherous place, hazardous for landing and quite capable of claiming the lives of inexperienced boatmen who ran aground on it.[24]

The Bristol courts did not make a habit of hanging felons in chains. Between 1740 and 1784, ten men were hung from gibbets close to the city, and these were the first since an isolated case in 1714. However, only two of the eleven were sentenced by Bristol's own court and Mahony was the first of them. The other nine were sent by order of the county assizes in Gloucestershire to the north and Somerset to the south, one to Brislington Common, one to Totterdown, two to Bedminster Down and five to Durdham Down. After Mahony, the only man to be hung in chains by order of the Bristol courts was yet another Irishman, Patrick Ward, in 1761. Ward was a marine from the *Devonshire* tender, fooling around with a loaded pistol beside the river at Shirehampton. When a local man told him to be careful with it, Ward shot him dead. Judged to have committed the crime within the city jurisdiction, Ward was hanged on St Michael's Hill and gibbeted beside the river on Shirehampton Common, bringing the total number of gibbet poles visible from the river to three. One reason for the punishment's relative rarity was its cost. No final account for hanging Mahony in chains has survived, but the city Chamberlain's bill for gibbetting Patrick Ward ran to £12 19s 10d, about £1300 in today's money. By the time the Sheriffs submitted their annual expenses (or 'cravings') to the Exchequer office at the end of the year however, even this very considerable sum had doubled to £24 6s. As well as the bespoke iron cage, it included a prodigious amount of solid oak timbering, haulage, horse hire and accommodation, and between one and four days labour costs for at least twelve men. To put these expenses into comparative perspective, the cost of hanging Patrick Dillon for sodomy on St Michael's Hill that same year, but *without* gibbetting his body, was just £7 7s.[25]

For all these reasons, and notwithstanding the sensational nature of the murder for which he was hanged, Mahony's gibbeting could hardly have failed to capture public attention in Bristol. And if Bristolians had been offered few prior opportunities to actually witness a hanging in chains first hand, they will certainly have heard about them for they rarely passed without comment in the newspaper and pamphlet press even when staged at a distance from the city. Nationwide, in the ten years preceding Mahony's gibbeting, 43 separate sentences had been handed down across the country, roughly half of them from the Old Bailey and destined for the approach roads to the capital, but the rest from a broad range of assize circuits at the rate of four or five a year.[26] Some of these cases had resonances for Bristol moreover, despite being resolved elsewhere. On the Gold Coast in 1737 the crew of the *Tewksbury*, a Bristol merchantman trading for Africans, mutinied and murdered the captain. The ship was retaken a day later and the mutineers hauled before the Admiralty court where five of them were sentenced to hang in chains.[27] A day after Goodere, White and Mahony were sentenced in Bristol, an Irishman named Bryan Connell, a fugitive from justice for two years since murdering one Brimley, a farmer, as he returned home from Daventry Market, was hung in chains at Weedon, Northants. The provincial press picked up the news and energetically circulated a story that some lines of doggerel verse were to be fixed to Connell's gibbet pole. It must surely have made comforting reading for Mahony as he sat in his cell awaiting the same end:

> Ye travellers that pass along this road
> Stand still and know the dreadful cries of blood,
> Poor Brimley's shrieks and loud expiring groan
> With calls for vengeance fled before God's throne
> Tho' fleeting month and circuling years run round

> In God's own time, the murtherer is found
> Vain all attempts to hide from Heaven's eyes
> By wondrous steps, black crimes to light shall rise
> Tho' secrecy be sworn and darkness veil the skies
> Justice, incensed, steps from behind the scenes,
> When least expected, loads the wretch with chains…
> Learn hence, long punishments great sins attend,
> Behold, the cursed murtherer and his end.[28]

The gibbeting of the soldiers, Cornelius York and John Millard, close to the city's southern boundaries a year earlier was a well-publicised example much closer to home. Together with a third soldier, George Masters, and armed with swords and pistols, these two men had committed a string of violent robberies in Bedminster, Brislington and Durdham Down as well as in the city itself. Finally apprehended in Somerset however, all three were condemned to death at the Bridgwater assize and sentenced to be hung in chains on the same day, one on Brislington Common and two on Bedminster Down. Masters died in prison but the sentence was carried out on the other two, and a fourth member of the gang, William Rowe, was tried at Bristol and hanged on St Michael's Hill a short time afterwards.[29]

Mahony's gibbet stood on the Swash, without interference, for many years. It became a noted navigational landmark for shipping, helpfully marking the Swash at high tide just as Ward's marked the Avon's southern bank a few hundred yards further up river after 1761. Their positioning was intended to make an impression on anyone heading to Bristol on the water and so it did, as an account of one ship's arrival in 1772 illustrates: 'Before we came up to Cookes extraordinary tower, just as we had nearly approached ye mouth of ye river ye Ladies were not a little alarmd at two very disagreeable objects viz a couple of gibbets on ye left hand whereon Captn Goodere and a foot solider had been formerly suspended. The first for murdering his uncle ye latter a farener. When past these the rest of ye way was made more agreeable, sailing thro verdant groves and glowery gardens till we arrived at ye Hotwells'.[30] If this account is correct, both gibbets were empty by this date, and Mahony's cage had certainly fallen by 1784 but their infrastructure stood firm. Seyer confirmed that 'the stump of the (Mahony's) gibbet is now standing' as late as 1829, a guidebook to the area noted it in 1843, and the 25-inch First Edition Ordnance Survey map was still marking a 'Remains of Gibbet Pole' as late as 1872. The final traces were probably only eradicated by the construction of the new Avonmouth docks between 1869 and 1877 which required the removal of the Swash.[31]

Until Richard Smith intervened in the 1840s, Mahony looked set to disappear without trace from popular memory. There is no record of the number of people who trooped out to witness the hoisting of the cage but the chosen location was relatively inaccessible by land. Until the modern town of Avonmouth grew up in the shadow of the new docks, the mouth of the river was marked by a long stretch of salt marsh and a scattering of farms. As one commentator put it (albeit inaccurately) in 1830, 'Many has heard that Captain Goodyere of the navy, who murdered his brother, was hung in chains, but that sight could only be seen by going to the sea shore some miles off from the city. And of those who had seen it, not one, I believed, now remained alive'. The area was so notoriously desolate and uninviting that some early twentieth century commentators were impressed that anyone should have thought it worthy of dock development, for who would want to want to visit it otherwise? As one early-twentieth-century commentator put it,

> When the Port and Pier railway line was constructed from Hotwells close to the river bank, its destination was a flat mud-bank, of vast expanse and appalling loneliness. On a bleak, gloomy day, a shivery mortal, looking over the low-lying shore of the channel, might have been impressed but it would have been by rather a dismal spirit, and the discovery on the map that out near the Severn shore there stood the gibbet would fit in well with the sombre character of the scene.[32]

Before the growth of Avonmouth in the 1870s, the entire terrain was 'a dreary waste of flat, swampy land and long reaches of mud', the remains of the gibbet pole 'the only feature of interest… set in olden times to act as a warning to evil doers who saw it from the sea'. It would scarcely be seen, in other words, from the land.[33]

The Durdham Down gibbets, more frequently encountered, were much more likely to impress themselves on local memory and become the subjects of folklore. Jenkin Prothero, hung in chains on the Downs in 1783 was one of these, for 'a report arose that every night, as the clock struck twelve, he descended from the gibbet and walked through the village. Not a family could send a servant out with a message after twelve at night, so sure were they of meeting Jenkin Prothero'.[34] Prothero's gibbet was initially sited at the top of what is now Pembroke Road, close to a number of private houses, and a petition to have it taken down or relocated was sent to the Crown within three weeks of its erection. The appeal was successful and the pole moved, possibly to a site close to the Ostrich Inn, deeper into the Down. As we have seen, Richard Smith believed Jenkins' body remained publicly exposed there for no more than a matter of weeks before it was cut down and surreptitiously buried on the spot by local consent. Nevertheless, Prothero's gibbeting continued to hold its place in popular memory. In 1905, childhood memories of doggerel rhymes ('Old Shenkin Prothero; One leg longer than t'other oh' was one) still persisted and the hanged man's restless spirit was said still to be haunting the marshes at Hallen as late as 1934.[35] Mahony's gibbet, more geographically remote, was perhaps a less likely cause of lasting conversation or local legend, but it continued to do its memory work in some quarters at least. In 1857, a Bristolian contributor to *Fraser's Magazine* penned an essay on ravens in which he recalled watching the birds soaring over the hills at Blaise Castle:

> In the days of our youth, well do we remember watching a pair soaring and weaving high over Giant Goram's chair and listening to that deep and solemn note which they often at such times intone (and which Welsh Williams, the under-gardener – whose head was full of corpse candles and tollochs – declared with a shudder was the cry of *corph, corph*), not without thinking that they might have had a taste of Mahony.[36]

Mahony's resurrection was a consequence of the public interest rekindled by Richard Smith's *Fratricide*. Always on the lookout for fresh acquisitions to his museum in the Infirmary, he was contacted in 1840 by a maker of mathematical instruments called Richard Rowland and asked if he would like to see the original gibbet irons. Smith will have been aware that the cage had long since fallen victim to the ravages of the weather but its actual whereabouts was then unknown. He accepted at once, for Mahony's remains would be a perfect addition to a collection that already included the skeletons of Maria Davis, Charlotte Bobbett and John Horwood, all dissected at the Infirmary after execution. Smith had been principal surgeon at Horwood's dissection in 1821. He had ornate cases made for each skeleton and fashioned a book of press cuttings, broadsides and phrenological charts and diagrams on Horwood, bound in the young man's carefully flayed and tanned skin. Rowland told Smith that he, his brother Sam and two friends had rowed out to the end of the Avon as long ago as 1784 for a jaunt, but their boat ran aground on the Swash and they were forced to wait several hours for the next high tide to float free. With nothing better to do while they waited, they waded onto firmer land to inspect the stump of the gibbet pole. A minimal amount

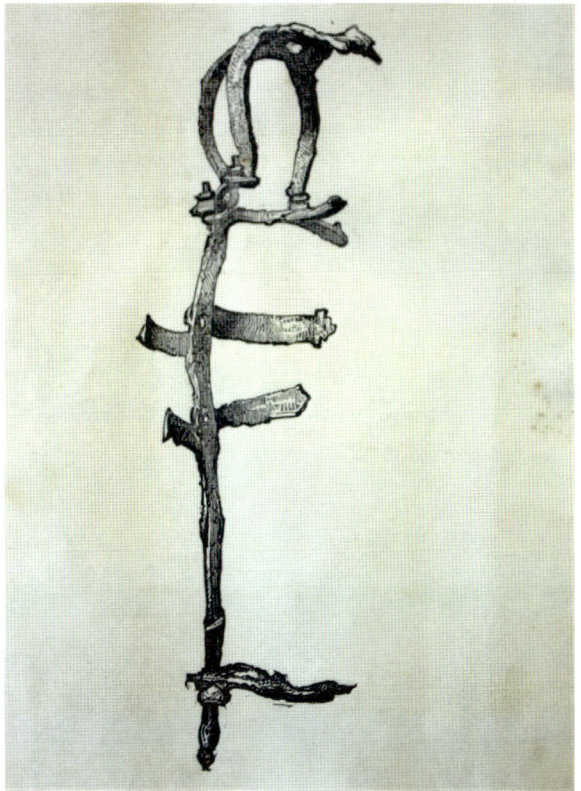

Richard Smith's drawing of the remains of Mahony's gibbet cage, as retrieved for display at the Infirmary museum. Bristol Archives, 35893/36/t

of digging revealed the rusting and buckled remains of the iron cage beneath, now buried in the mud. The Rowland bothers dragged the irons onto the boat, rowed back to Bristol on the next tide, and stashed them in the cellar of Sam's house on the Quay. They remained there until Sam Rowland was reminded of them by *The Fratricide*, and alerted Smith to their existence. He permitted the surgeon to remove the remains to the museum to join the skeletons of Bobbett, Davis and Horwood.

Rowland next confided the whereabouts of the pole, the larger part of which had toppled onto the mud during a storm in 1838 and been retrieved by a pilot from Pill. Smith went straight to Pill and found a twelve-foot section of it in a wood yard, 'studded with thousands of nails at the very bottom'. This, too, was claimed for the museum and transported back to Bristol. He was disappointed to discover that the pole had already been damaged by the Pill men, and parts of it cut up to make 'snuff boxes for the curious in relics', including a section in which 'MM 1741' had been inscribed in nails.[37] But disappointment did not prevent Smith from pursuing a similar course and within weeks he had begun cutting fragments from the remains of the cage, and chips of timber from the pole. These he fastened to cards with cotton thread before endorsing each relic set with his signature:

> 'A veritable piece of the gibbet and irons of Matt. Mahony,
> executed on the 15 of April 1741,
> witness thereunto Richard Smith on the 15 April 1841.
> NB Beware of counterfeits. None are genuine unless attested as above'.

How many of these Smith made, and to whom they were given or sold it is impossible to say, but at least five have survived in the public collections of the city.[38]

In November 1842, Richard Rowland's son contacted Smith and told him that it was not just the cage the brothers had brought back from the Swash but some body parts too. Nobody had mentioned them to Smith before because neither Richard nor Sam could find them, but the son had come across them while clearing out the cellar. Smith collected the remains and added them to his collection. 'They are the arm bone or humerus', he recorded, 'and the two bones of the lower arm; also a thumb and finger and a few bones of the wrist. These have now joined the other relics in my museum at the Infirmary'.[39]

Smith's papers recording all this activity appear to have found their way, in dribs and drabs, into the city library after his death. By 1850, at least one of Smith's relic cards had been gifted by the City Chamberlain to Joseph Leech, maverick editor of the *Bristol Times and Mirror*, along with a small bundle of associated notes and cuttings about the case. Leech confessed himself a little disturbed by these 'gallows-like relics and I could hardly touch them without disgust, especially the iron in which I knew rotted away, high up in the air, the remains of a terrible murderer', but as we have seen, it didn't stop him publishing his own imaginative account of the Goodere case in 1862. He donated the remains to the city Library where they were joined by two more of Smith's relic cards in 1900, again via the *Times and Mirror*, through the gift of 'a lady'.[40] As Nikita Marryat and Peter King have pointed out, the preservation and display of gibbeted relics in museums and libraries, hundreds of years after they were first set up, has effectively extended the shame of post execution punishment far beyond the original intention and long after the repeal of the Murder Act.[41] The removal from public display of Horwood's skeleton and its subsequent burial in 2011 at the request of his descendants should certainly be seen in this context.[42] Matthew Mahony had no family to plead on behalf of his corpse when Smith acquired his bone

To mark the centenary of Mahony's gibbeting, Richard Smith produced a series of cards like these, each with small pieces of the pole and the cage stitched to them and carrying a signed authentication from Smith himself. Whether he was selling them as souvenirs or giving them away to interested friends is unknown. Several examples survive today in the collections of Bristol Public Library and Bristol Archives. Bristol Archives, 9733/3 and 35893/36/t fragments in 1842. If Smith's intention was to ensure Mahony's gibbet remained in the city's collective memory *in perpetua*, he cannot have been disappointed, though the feelings it inspired were as likely to be moved by levity as horror. At a meeting of the Bristol Board of Guardians, called in 1886 to discuss parochial responsibility for the disposal of unidentified bodies washed up on the Swash, 'Mr Wintle remarked that he believed there was a gibbet on the island. They hung fellows there – for not voting right at elections (laughter)'.[43]

What ultimately became of Mahony's relics is something of a mystery. In 1905, the Infirmary's 'honorary pathologist' confirmed that the gibbet irons were still on display in the museum, beneath the original manuscript order from the mayor to the chamberlain to construct the gibbet on the Swash. That document is now in Bristol Archives, but the irons have disappeared. They were certainly photographed at some stage because a copy was reproduced in Munro Smith's history of the Infirmary in 1917. Of the pole there is no sign either. Despite Smith's insistence that he had placed it in the museum, the honorary pathologist had never seen it and he 'feared that someone, not knowing that it was anything but a piece of apparently useless timber, has had it removed'.

If the last resting place of Mahony's shattered skeleton remains unclear, some sought to make a mystery of Dineley's fate too. Richard Smith penned a letter to the press in 1842:

> It is very singular that not the slightest notice is taken in any record which I have seen respecting the body of the murdered Baronet. The veil of oblivion seems to have been at once cast over it and has never been removed. Did the Captain throw it overboard in the night?... As Sir Dineley was wealthy, had he been deposited in any church or chapel, we would have heard of it, but all is profound silence.[44]

As Smith was surely aware, however much the Captain may have hoped to throw Dineley's body overboard, he cannot have done so or there could never have been an inquest. In fact, it was quite certainly buried as discreetly as his brother's, in the family vault at Cropthorne on 6 February 1741.[45]

As to the inheritance at the root of the case, so keenly fought over by Goodere and Dineley, that too was quickly buried. The baronetcy passed first to Goodere's eldest son, Edward, who never married and died insane in 1761. It then passed in turn to Edward's younger brother, John, who began his enjoyment of it with the claim that he was owed £8000 in backdated rents on the family's Worcestershire estates. The money ought to have been paid to his brother Edward, the legal beneficiary of his grandfather's will for the last twenty years, he asserted, but his rights had been denied by a 'Conspiracy' that now threatened to deprive John as well. In Lawrence Stone's charitable verdict, John was not quite as mad as his brother had been but 'was certainly mentally unbalanced'. Like Edward, John never married and, financially insolvent, had sold off what was left of the Burghope estate by 1776. Heirless and penniless, he lived out his final days as one of the Poor Knights of Windsor, offering open invitations of marriage to every passing wealthy heiress, which is where we first met him in Chapter One. He died in 1808 and the baronetcy died with him.[46]

CHAPTER SIX

The Dineley Murder as Parricide

In George Lillo's play *The London Merchant*, the villain George Barwell reflects at the end of act 3 that 'Murder is the worst of crimes and Parricide the worst of Murders.'[1] It was a contrite moment when he paused to consider his own stabbing of his uncle, and then to cite some of the notorious parricides in history: Cain, for killing his brother; Nero his mother. As Lillo made clear to his audience, parricide meant killing any close relative, breaking the trust, the bonds of duty and companionship that should normally develop within a household. In its most denotative sense, parricide meant killing a father or head of the household; a figure to whom one owed duty and obedience.[2] In this context, as Samuel Johnson explained, it could encompass the murder of a patron, or the assassination of a head of state. In *The Crisis,* a virulently anti-ministerial weekly of the American war, its meaning was extended to include political traitors bent on undermining libertarian values and the integrity of the empire. But as Ephraim Chambers noted in his *Cyclopaedia*, it could be extended 'to the murder of any near relation.'[3]

In this chapter we consider the Dineley murder as a parricide, within the context of four others in close temporal proximity, from 1726 to 1751. They feature the murder of a husband by a wife and two accomplices in 1726. They also involve the murders of two fathers, that of Charles John Drew in 1740 and Francis Blandy in 1751, both of whom were well-known attorneys. And finally, they include Joseph Jefferies, a wealthy retired London butcher, who was shot in the face in July 1751 by his servant, with the complicity of his ward, niece and heir. All of these acts were considered outrageous crimes that affronted patriarchal authority and the legitimate governance of households. They severed the ties of blood and family that were seen to be a fundamental source of social stability in the eighteenth century. They flouted religious faith and obligation and the natural power of family. They were abominable crimes that prompted publicity, censure and potentially aggravated forms of punishment. Consequently, they offer some interesting comparisons to the murder of Sir John Dineley by his brother Captain Goodere, and a context to Recorder Michael Foster's judgement, 'Tis true, murders of this kind are not very frequent, and less so in this nation than in any other.'[4]

The most savage of these crimes involved Catherine Hayes and two lodgers who slew, beheaded and dismembered her husband John on 1 March 1726. The actual circumstances of Hayes' death are reasonably clear, having been revealed in the confessions of the two men, Thomas Billings and Thomas Wood.[5] Apparently, Hayes was party to a wager that he could drink half a guinea's worth of liquor without getting drunk, and once he was inebriated and sleeping on a bed, the two men dispatched him with blows to the head. Then, in conjunction with Catherine Hayes, they tried to conceal the body by dismembering it. The head of John Hayes was smuggled out of the house on Tyburn Road and taken to Millbank, or the Horse Ferry, Westminster, where it was thrown in the Thames. The limbs were wrapped in a blanket and taken to a pond or ditch in Marylebone fields the following night. The head was discovered on a sandbank by some Thames watermen, and once in the hands of the local authorities, placed on a pike at St Margaret's church, Westminster.[6] Later it was put in a jarful of spirits so it would not decompose. For about a week, speculations ran high as to whose head it was, but eventually several people identified it as that of John Hayes, who was well-known in the area as a pawnbroker and moneylender. People had become suspicious about Hayes' absence and taxed his wife about it. She offered unconvincing explanations as to why he was away, and once she identified the head in the jar as her husband's and his limbs were dredged from the Marylebone pond, it was only a matter of time before she and her two lodgers were arrested for murder. The three suspects were committed to different jails and questioned separately; the two men confessed to the murder in their interrogations. Catherine Hayes tried to maintain her innocence a little longer, but the confessions and the corroborating evidence of an upstairs lodger, a Mrs Springate, weighed heavily against her.[7]

The enormity of the homicide, and indeed, the enormity of the offence for Catherine Hayes, which in her case was petty treason, meant she faced the worst possible punishment, execution by burning. Although there were still commentators who thought there were no provocations that might extenuate this particular crime, which was considered a rebellion against domestic order, there had been a shift away from the strict terms of the statute legislating petty treason to allow for mitigating circumstances.[8] Catherine Hayes certainly sought to include some, for she complained to visitors at Newgate that she had been brutally beaten and miscarried at the hands of her husband on at least two occasions. She also claimed she had been 'three-parts starved' during the marriage.[9] Yet it was very difficult for women to enter a plea of self-defence against violent men because of the conventions of husbandly rule, particularly in Catherine's case where there was no immediate and legally visible provocation.[10] It was far easier to portray Catherine as a restless, ambitious, conniving woman with a voracious sexual appetite. According to the narratives that circulated about her life, she had one child out of wedlock, had seduced Hayes into a clandestine marriage, had quarrelled with his parents, and had subsequently forced him to abandon a middling farm in Warwickshire for more dubious fortunes in the metropolis.[11] To be sure, on his own admission John Hayes was a violent drunk and wife-beater, but Catherine was hardly a respectable foil to his behaviour, for she was accused by one JP of having an affair with Tom Billings, who turned out to be her son.[12] Incest, it was claimed, compounded the sin of her parricide. Together with the stories of her wild youth with army officers at Ombersley before she was married and her sexual transgressions thereafter, it nullified her claims of grievous domestic abuse. Had those claims had been genuine, claimed 'Philalethes' in *Mist's Weekly Journal,* why had Catherine tolerated 20 years of such behaviour? Besides, the writer continued, the fact that Catherine Hayes spent six weeks agitating for her husband's death and enticed her own son to commit the deed was 'hideous'; and indeed 'monstrous' if Hayes was Billings' father, as was sometimes claimed, and if the perpetrator was her lover to boot.[13]

Catherine Hayes had to face a horrific death by burning, without even the extenuating circumstance of being strangled before the flames consumed her, for the executioner was unable to pull the rope around her neck by virtue of the heat and rage of the fire. Some papers even insinuated it was an indulgence she had not deserved.[14] As for the two men, both were sentenced to be hanged and gibbeted, a fate they wriggled to avoid. Tom Wood avoided it simply because he died of jail fever two or three days before the execution.[15] Billings' corpse swung in the wind on the Paddington Road, near the pond where Hayes' limbs were thrown.

Catherine Hayes and her associates received the full rigour of the law. The same possibility loomed large in the trial of Charles Drew for the murder of his father in February 1740. Drew was the only son of a respected and well-connected attorney in Long Melford, Suffolk. His father, who had a fortune of roughly £60,000, but had five daughters to attend to, kept his son on a relatively tight rein, granting him an annual income of £100 and the full run of the hounds.[16] This did not satisfy Charles Drew junior, whose gentlemanly pretensions and profligacy demanded more money than his father was prepared to give him. Drew racked up debts, ran with a disreputable crowd of smugglers and poachers including one William Mace, alias Captain Rat, and appears to have had a demanding mistress in widow Elizabeth Boyer, the housekeeper to a Mr Richardson at nearby Liston Hall.[17] His infatuation with Mrs Boyer, who cozened him to marry her, prompted him to consider doing away with his father, from whom he had become increasingly estranged. Drew also feared his inheritance was imperilled by the marital discord in his family, by the preference his father seemed to show to his sisters, even the possibility that his father might incarcerate his mother in an asylum and eventually remarry. And so he had one of his smuggling companions, Edward Humphries, sound out several blackguards in the neighbourhood about the possibilities of killing his father in return for a £100 reward. Nothing came of this, but Charles Drew certainly entertained the notion that Humphries might assist him and obtained a gun from Mrs Boyer for the task. In the end Humphries backed off, leaving Drew to shoot his father at point black range at the door of his house around midnight on 8 February 1740.[18] Humphreys, who was a spectator to the crime and a possible accessory, was sent to London to lie low, as eventually did Charles Drew who decamped to a bagnio in Leicester Fields, London. As a result of some miscommunications and misdirected letters, the murder was unravelled by Sir Thomas De Veil, who arrested Drew and sent him to Newgate and subsequently to Bury St Edmunds to stand trial at the Suffolk assizes.[19] By the time Drew came to trial the evidence against him was strong. He had been a fugitive from justice; he had tried to bribe a Newgate turnkey to release him; and his alibi that he was at Liston Hall at the time of the crime was flimsy. It also transpired that he had tried to frame Humphries as the killer and a fugitive from justice.[20] After a trial of six hours, it took the jury only a matter of minutes to find Drew guilty, and he was sentenced to be hanged and gibbetted at the scene of the crime. No concessions were made for his father's frosty attitude towards his son or his lack of parental affection. Whether Drew junior was actually gibbetted is a little unclear because some newspapers make no mention of it. One anticipated such a sentence, and another claimed it was carried out, as did the criminal broadsheet *The Unnatural Son*.[21] Sufficient evidence, perhaps, in an era when criminal trials were not comprehensively reported. The broadsheet also acknowledged the large publicity surrounding the case and emphasized that Drew had been indicted for the 'horrid, cruel and unnatural Murder or Parricide' of his father, a crime that merited the seizure of the Long Melton estate for the crown. Even with the help of insiders such as Lord Hervey, the vice-chamberlain of the Household, it took three-and-a-half years' lobbying to retrieve it for the family.[22]

Drew's murder made 'no small notice in the World', remarked *The Unnatural Son*. Many planned to make the trip from London to Bury St Edmunds to witness his 'Behavior and Exit'.[23] According to newspaper accounts, a 'great crowd' assembled to see Drew die, one only surpassed in the Suffolk town by the execution of barrister Arundel Coke and his labourer, John Woodburn, for the attempted murder of Coke's brother-in-law, Edward Crispe, in 1722.[24] The Drew affair thus seems to have been something of a provincial event in much the same way as Goodere, although it did not receive the same press coverage and penetration as its West-Country counterpart.

Neither of these murder trials, however, attracted quite as much publicity as those of Mary Blandy and Elizabeth Jefferies in 1752. Coming on the crest of a crime wave and panic about social order at the end of the war of Austrian Succession,[25] these two trials resonated with the public because they suggested there was no sanctuary from social danger, that crime lurked everywhere: on the highway, in the park, on the street, and in the household itself. As the prosecuting counsel argued in his opening remarks on the Jefferies trial,

> What a shudder must human Nature receive when it recollects there is no Place where Security might be depended upon, but at the same time Persons are barring their Doors from Thieves from without, they are inclosing worse Enemies within. Nay, the nearest ties of Kindred are no security.[26]

Both the Blandy and Jefferies murders were very much household dramas, and they emerged at a time when there was a renewed debate about clandestine marriages and the appropriate exercise of patriarchal authority over propertied unions that eventually resulted in Hardwicke's Marriage Act of 1753.[27] They spoke, in effect, to the sexual politics of the age, and as such offered telling commentaries on contemporary courtships, love and money, parental tyranny and vice.

Let us explore some of these issues by beginning with Mary Blandy, the Henley murderess accused of poisoning her father. Parricide was considered to be particularly reprehensible in her case, because she had been liberally and generously educated to be a lady of fine accomplishments, able to move in select circles, a regular visitor to the Reading assembly rooms. Her family was said to have expended £15,000 on this endeavour and her father seemed devoted to her.[28] According to several accounts, Francis Blandy openly doted on his daughter and ultimately forgave her for poisoning him, provided she would prosecute the man who was really responsible, Lieutenant William Henry Cranstoun, because he provided her with the materials for his demise.

Miss Blandy had met the Scottish lieutenant when he visited his uncle, Lord Mark Ker, at Henley in the summer of 1746. He was then on a recruiting mission for the Marines after the Jacobite rebellion, and he returned again the following summer and struck up a more intimate friendship with the young lady. At the time, Miss Blandy was engaged to another army officer, although a match seemed increasingly unlikely. Cranstoun took the opportunity to press his interest, although he made it clear that he needed to relinquish another relationship before he could seek her father's consent to marry. Mary consented to this arrangement and rather quickly, so did her parents; particularly her mother, who seems to have taken a shine to the Scottish lieutenant, a scion of the Scottish aristocracy, and related to some of the best families in that land, including the Campbells, the Homes, and the Lothians.

Cranstoun's desire to marry Mary Blandy nonetheless ran into more difficulties than he imagined. Although he never cared to admit it, he was already married to one Anne Murray, the daughter of a Leith merchant, by whom he had one daughter. The child was baptized by a minister of the kirk in the presence of members from both families, a ceremony that certainly made the union appear public and consensual. Cranstoun hoped he could extricate himself from this marriage because it was contracted privately without the official sanction of church or kirk. He tried to get Anne to disown it on the grounds that a match with a Catholic family linked firmly to the Jacobites was disastrous for an army officer in King George's service. As far as Cranstoun was concerned, it didn't help that Anne's brother, Sir David Murray, was in jail awaiting trial for participating in the 1745 rebellion, and that her nephew was none other than John Murray of Broughton, the secretary to the Pretender to the British throne, Prince Charles Stuart. The connection, he argued, was ruining his chances of promotion, as well as casting aspersions on his own family, which over the course of the seventeenth century had made the transition from Stuart to Hanoverian loyalties very smoothly. Anne initially agreed to a dissolution, but then quickly relented and in October 1746 took Cranstoun to court to have their marriage officially recognized. Under Scottish law, a private marriage was legal if it had been acknowledged in some manner, as Cranstoun's clearly had been. The Commissary Court in Edinburgh upheld this fact. In March 1748 it ordered Cranstoun to pay his wife and child an annuity of £50 for life.[29] This decision completely frustrated Cranstoun's potential match with Blandy. To marry her would technically be bigamy.

Cranstoun still believed he could extricate himself from this predicament although quite how remains a mystery. His belief that a formal English marriage would trump an irregular one was presumptuous, and it was very doubtful that his connections to the Scottish aristocracy could avail him of a solution. He had however won the favour of Mary's mother, and her father had always been a flunky for title, so for a time he remained in their good graces. He had even managed to reconcile Mary to his past infidelities and to the disclosure that he had an illegitimate child by another woman in 1745. But after the death of Mary's mother, the attitude of her father Francis hardened, and heeding friends' advice, he banned Cranstoun from the household and ordered Mary to refrain from corresponding with him. Mary, however, was besotted. At the time of separation from her lover, she was 31 years of age, with declining prospects for a future match. She bitterly resented her father's decision, cursed him for a 'toothless old rogue', and conspired with Cranstoun to poison her father's gruel with arsenic, a strategy that resulted in the poor man's death.[30]

The other murder, that of Joseph Jefferies, was more dramatic and brutal. He was twice shot in the face at close range while in bed. The shots were ineffectually executed because the balls of the pistol had been crudely cut to fit the barrel. They rendered Joseph Jefferies speechless after the blast and unable to identify his assailants in the eighteen hours left to him.[31] The murder was also ineffectually planned. Jefferies' niece, Elizabeth Jefferies, conspired with her then lover, the servant John Swan, to kill her guardian because he threatened to cut her out of his will, or at the very least severely reduce her legacy if she persisted in seeing Swan. Elizabeth persuaded Swan, a poor widower and former bricklayer, to commit the crime on the promise of marrying him and reaping the benefits of the Jefferies' property, a small fortune accrued from Joseph's successful butcher's business in the city. Swan was reluctant to do this without a third party and so he and Elizabeth approached a seaman cum harvest labourer named Thomas Matthews to help them, promising him the huge sum of £700 on the successful completion of the deed. It was a reckless offer, because Matthews had only worked in the Jefferies household for a week or so, and there really was no knowing what his reaction might be; whether he would be complicit with the murder or blow the whistle on it. Matthews tentatively agreed to be a party to the crime, but it was an uneasy and tense collaboration from the beginning.[32] While in London to purchase the pistols they would use, Swan and Matthews became rowdily drunk at the *Green Man and Bell* in Whitechapel, and the landlord, suspecting them to be highwaymen on account of the pistols, had them brought before a JP, Sir Samuel Gower, who committed them to Clerkenwell Bridewell. Elizabeth had to come into London from Walthamstow to bail them out, raising suspicions of what they were up to. The incident only increased Matthews' aversion to the plan and when it came time to execute it in July 1751 he backed down, leaving Swan to commit the murder, and

Elizabeth Jefferies to fake a robbery with violence.

Jefferies and Swan were first indicted for the murder of the Walthamstow butcher in the summer of 1751, but the prosecution asked to delay a trial because Matthews was still at large. Consequently, both the Jefferies and Blandy trials came up at the same time, in the spring of 1752. In the Jefferies' case the prosecution had a material witness in Matthews, who had been complicit in the murder of the butcher and had turned king's evidence. The one hurdle counsel faced was that Elizabeth Jefferies had been originally indicted as a principal to the murder whereas in fact she was strictly speaking an accessory. The defence tried to block a new prosecution but the presiding judge, Sir Michael Foster, allowed it. Thereafter it was plain sailing. Within two hours Jefferies and Swan were found guilty of murder and petty treason respectively, and sentenced to be executed by public hanging, with Swan to be gibbetted near the scene of the crime.

The Blandy trial was more tortuous. More depended on circumstantial evidence, on the poisonous qualities of the gruel, and on Mary's efforts to burn her correspondence with Cranstoun, who once Mary had been arrested, quickly disappeared to escape arrest.

To the end Mary Blandy claimed she was innocent, that the powders she administered on Cranstoun's orders were merely love philtres to bring her father round to the prospect of their union.[33] In an age of quack potions and medicines, such charms were not unknown, even though educated opinion was leery about their efficacy. George Colman noted an advertisement for 'a most efficacious lover powder by which a despairing lover might create affection in the bosom of the most cruel mistress.' 'Lovers', he reflected, 'have indeed always been fond of enchantment',[34] and enchantment, certainly, was part of Mary's defence. She claimed she was tricked into administering poison by her lover and was innocent of maliciously plotting her father's death. Cranstoun, she asserted, had put some of the powder in Mr Blandy's tea before he left for Scotland in the summer of 1750, and because her father suffered no obvious symptoms from the dosage, she thought it harmless. In her eyes she had been treacherously deceived by her lover and made an awful agent of her father's death.

Did the public believe her version of the events? 'Guilty or Guiltless, who can surely tell?' ran one couplet from the prologue of *The Fair Parricide,* 'A spotless Angel or a Fiend of Hell?' While in prison Mary wrote a vindication of her position, one, as literary historians have noted, that was novelistic in tone.[35] It was strangely redolent of a novel of a love-sick young woman, driven to despair by mercenary parents, and the darkest intrigues of a libertine, who

The execution of Mary Blandy. *The New and Complete Newgate Calendar* (1795)

is the ultimate source of her ruin. The novel was by Samuel Richardson. Entitled *Clarissa Harlowe,* it was a very popular book in 1748, when Mary's relationship with Cranstoun was in full cry. Although the stories of Clarissa and Mary were not strictly comparable, they were both familial melodramas, and their tropological similarities as domestic tragedies may help explain why some members of the 5000-strong crowd cried when a seemingly demure, dignified, Mary Blandy, dressed in sober black, went to the scaffold. Although there was one unsent, hastily scribbled note to Cranstoun that betrayed her complicity in the murder,[36] many regarded Mary as a victim of the Scottish suitor, a lying rogue who, to the consternation of the authorities in London, eluded arrest in Scotland, escaped to the continent, and died there in late 1752 without ever coming to trial.

The Blandy affair thus had some of the qualities of a 'sentimental murder'.[37] In the eyes of 'Axylus' in the *Covent Garden Journal,* Miss Blandy was the victim of a heartless army officer who thought nothing of destroying the virtue of a 'thoughtless girl', an act that was often deemed a 'victory' in the officers' mess.[38] Despite a social environment that looked with horror on patricide, Mary Blandy managed to win some sympathy as the duped lover of an unscrupulous libertine, and perhaps even as the victim of a marriage market that discounted love and affection for interest and money. She could appear trapped by parental snobbery and the artifices of gallantry and deceit. A symbol of her father's success as a Henley lawyer and conveyancer, she was offered up as a £10,000 prize to a suitor, although bizarrely without the conventional portion that accompanied propertied marriages.

Elizabeth Jefferies won no such sympathy, even though she deserved it. She was the niece and ward of Joseph Jefferies, whom he had brought into his household at the age of five at the behest of his boat-building relatives in Bridgnorth, Shropshire. But Joseph had raped his ward when she was fifteen and had lived incestuously with her for several years after the death of his wife; a relationship that resulted in two pregnancies, an abortion and a miscarriage. Joseph eventually dumped Elizabeth for a maid servant, so it was reported, but the evidence from the trial revealed that he still resented the favours she showed other men and threatened to remove her from his will. It was the retired butcher's malice, cruelty and brutality that drove Elizabeth to such desperate straits. This part of the narrative only emerged when Elizabeth Jefferies broke down and confessed to the whole affair in Chelmsford gaol, but parenthetically, for, while acknowledged in the press, it did not form part of the printed text of her confession and was sidelined as a factor in the murder.[39] Indeed, because Jefferies' defending counsel was only allowed to cross-examine witnesses and barred from framing a narrative that might establish motives of provocation, sexual abuse was not offered as a mitigating factor in the trial, or in any petition for a pardon or respite of sentence. Indeed, in the wake of her trial, it was rumoured that parricide might be reconstituted as petit treason.[40]

So how does the Dineley murder shape up in the light on these other parricides? It is worth emphasizing that the term 'parricide' was never used in conjunction with the killing of Sir John Dineley even though a fratricide technically fell within its ambit. Certainly the homicide was regarded as a 'deed of darkness', a 'black crime' a 'black and frightful murder'. Indeed, Mr

Vernon, the prosecuting counsel, went out of his way to emphasize that Samuel Goodere was 'the unnatural author and contriver' of 'a shocking piece of Cruelty,' and that unlike the brutal assassins who actually strangled Dineley, he had this 'black characteristic, that he was the Brother of the Deceased, and as such, bound by ties of Blood and Nature, to have preserved his Person from Violence.'[41] Goodere's crime was thus a violation of natural law in ways that White and Mahony's was not. To be sure, his fratricide lacked the political import of a mariticide [husband-killing] or a patricide, particularly those carried out by female perpetrators, whose actions fragrantly defied the hierarchical order of eighteenth-century households. Nonetheless, Goodere's murder flouted ties of consanguinity that were still seen as the bedrock of civil society. A 1702 sermon classified fratricide along with patricide and matricide as the 'blackest of crimes.'[42]

The enormity of Goodere's crime was amplified by the very premeditated manner in which it was carried out. The abduction of Sir John Dineley by hired privateers and members of Goodere's own crew and his forced march along the ropewalk was bold, brazen and risky. It was an action that could hardly escape detection, even in Bristol by twilight, and it narrowed Goodere's options to either bullying his brother into submission over the changed entail or, short of murder, fabricating Sir John's death as the suicide of a deranged man. Goodere's plan was not well co-ordinated beyond getting his brother on board the *Ruby,* but then nor were some of the other parricides of that era. Drew's efforts to have his father murdered by proxy were clumsy; Elizabeth Jefferies' plot to shoot her uncle was similarly flawed, dependent upon one newcomer of dubious loyalty, and compounded by a poorly executed charade of a fatal break-in. Even the plan to kill John Hayes was crudely improvised, hastily organised around the drinking wager and very vulnerable to detection in a lodging house with thin walls.[43] The reckless way in which John Hayes' head was thrown into the Thames and his body parts dumped in a pond did not bode well for the guilty parties, who were unable to keep their actions secret from at least one of the upstairs lodgers. Only perhaps in the case of the poisoning was the plan reasonably hatched, and even there Mary Blandy panicked once a servant fell ill from an untoward dose of the arsenic. Overall, the common denominator in all of these parricides was the desperation with which they were carried out. In three of the five cases some of the conspirators turned king's evidence before the trials began. And all carried a burden of circumstantial evidence that made the guilty parties very vulnerable to detection.

Legal imperatives ensured that the principal issue in all these trials was whether the accused were guilty or not of premeditated murder. This meant that the main focus was on the immediate circumstances of the crime, not on the large social contexts in which they took place. In a regular trial, where there was no defence counsel, this was very much the case, because judges acted as interlocutor and inquisitor and dominated the proceedings. But even in the cases under discussion, where there was some representation of the accused, the role of defence counsel was limited to cross-examining prosecuting witnesses and producing their own. In this mid-century era, the defence could not present their full version of the case, at least not directly. This might only emerge in the criminal literature that grew up around the case, not so much in the 'official' trial transcript, if such existed in printed form, as in the genuine accounts and narratives that accompanied it. These were hybrid productions, part trial, part biography, part advocacy, that potentially allowed for some heteroglossia, for different voices to coexist in the same text. It is often through these accounts that one can create credible narratives that situate the criminal within his or her history, asking why they committed the acts they did rather than addressing the question that dominated the trial transcript, which was how and when the crime was committed, and by whom.

In all these murder trials there were counter-narratives that offered some mitigating circumstances for the accused. Catherine Hayes had been beaten and refused proper medical attention at childbirth, a fact about which she complained bitterly. Charles Drew, born just before the breakup of his parents' marriage, had been neglected by his father, who failed to provide him with a suitable education and simply tried to control him financially.[44] Elizabeth Jefferies was sexually abused; Mary Blandy was arguably exploited as a conduit of social mobility by her parents; as one contemporary put it, 'cryed up for a fortune'.[45] Samuel Goodere was deprived of his rightful inheritance by a malicious brother who could not tolerate Samuel's support for his estranged wife. Even so, these circumstances were not allowed seriously to mitigate the enormity of the crime, still less affect the sentence. The only exception was Mary Blandy, who plausibly argued she had been duped by her Scottish lover, a matter that troubled the Duke of Newcastle and the Scottish judiciary.[46] Lord Justice Areskine even believed Cranstoun was the 'principal author and contriver' of the murder on the basis of Mary Blandy's examination and moved strenuously to have him arrested before he left Scotland. Even so, Mary was denied the pardon she softly solicited in her prison reflections, although she did win sympathy at the gallows and generated intense speculation as to her innocence or culpability. Her trial and execution spawned

30 productions including a play *The Fair Parricide*.[47]

Coming at a moment when the claims of parental authority were about to be debated in the Commons, the trials of Blandy and Jefferies did generate more general reflections about the use and abuse of parental power. Dr. Samuel Johnson in *The Rambler* reflected on the potential tyranny of parental power, however necessary it might be to social stability. 'The cruelties which are often exercised in private Families under the venerable sanction of parental Authority,' Johnson declared, might 'trample the Bounds of Right with innumerable Transgressions before Duty and Piety will dare to seek Redress;' a redress, he darkly hinted, where parricide might well be a form of self-defense.[48] John Campbell believed that the deaths of Blandy and Jeffries were lessons in why parents should not irresponsibly or arrogantly dominate or corrupt the sexual lives of their kin. Their murders were surely 'sufficient to convince Parents, Guardians and Relatives of the Unjustifiableness of endeavouring to oppose the Inclinations of Lovers, or to use any sinister means whereby to withdraw their Affections from the real Objects of their Love.' However unjustifiable the actions of these women were, 'yet the Conduct of the Parent to the Daughter and the Uncle to the Niece might prove sufficient to stifle the Calumnies of the Publick (tho' not the Sentence of the Law)'.[49] The uncle, Joseph Jefferies, had abused his trust: he had reared his ward 'as little better than a housekeeper without any education so that he could more easily conquer her Virtue…Had she dispatch'd him when he first villainously attempted her Virtue, O what a glorious Conquest this would have been! All laws, both Divine and Human, would have extoll'd her Magnanimity, and her Virtue would have been transmitted to Posterity as a Pattern for her Sex.' But, Campbell continued, in a chauvinist mode not out of step with the age, she basely yielded to the temptation and received the reward for her 'demerits'.[50] Mr Jefferies eventually tired of her, took another woman and raised his niece's resentment. He, rather than his niece, proved 'the instrument of the whole melancholy and tragical scene.'

The Goodere trial, by contrast, offered few comparable reflections on the use and abuse of propertied power in gentry families or on the obligations an eldest son might have to his younger siblings. At the time of the murder in 1741 there were muted complaints about primogeniture. Ephraim Chambers in his *Cyclopaedia* made it clear that primogeniture was an 'unjust prerogative and contrary to natural right.' In this, he echoed John Locke who tartly remarked that primogeniture had no 'pretense to a Right of solely inheriting either Property or Power', a statement that might facilitate a discussion of how estate wealth could be consolidated without cutting out younger siblings from the fortune.[51] Yet primogeniture was not really the issue in the Goodere case, because Samuel accepted his maternal grandfather's will regarding the settlement of the Charlton estates in which he was next in line after Sir John and his heirs. Nonetheless Samuel was certainly taken aback by the hostility John evinced to his inheritance of the Herefordshire estate. He was also troubled by the audacity and malice of his brother in disinheriting his own son and then barring him from his rightful inheritance at Charlton. It was a matter of family honour and trust as much as money that threw him into such a murderous rage. As Lawrence Stone rightly notes, the Goodere story 'highlights the great importance in the generation of family feuds of any violation of traditional norms for the transmission of property.'[52]

In essentials, the Dineley-Goodere story offered an intriguing narrative of gentry rivalry, bitter divorce, and fraternal perfidy. Aspects of this narrative were accented by Harry Lushington Stephen, a lawyer and future high court judge in Calcutta, in his edition of the *State Trials* in 1899.[53] He played up Jarrit Smith's testimony about the broken entail and downplayed the jurisdictional disputes about the place of the crime and the status of the victim. Yet by and large the sociological aspects of the Dineley-Goodere story were assigned to the shadows. There were no harsh reflections on Dineley for the brutality towards his wife or compassion for her vulnerability. That sort of criticism was possible in the Victorian era, for men were sometimes taken to task for not protecting their wives in a chivalric manner. Yet it was very rarely applied to Lady Mary because her wifely virtues were suspect.[54] More often than not, Mary is cast as a flibbertigibbet who plagues her husband and cuckolds him. Sir John then emerges as the victim of marital disharmony and fraternal malevolence; a sickly man whisked away by villains and condemned to a sordid death by hired killers. To be sure, there are occasions when Sir John is stigmatised as a boorish brute, but generally it is his vulnerability, even eccentricity, that comes to the fore. All in all, he is more of a floating signifier than his brother, whose malevolent murderous intentions anchor him in the narrative. In making this judgment writers simply followed the central evidence of the trial. Samuel Goodere masterminds the murder. He is a man whose rage is unbounded, a captain who bribes vulnerable seamen to commit a vile act and then frames them for it.

CHAPTER SEVEN

Fictions and Fratricides

This chapter begins with the proposition that the social construction of murder, the manner in which it is construed and remembered, is as important as what actually happened. It is not a new notion. In *A Sentimental Murder,* John Brewer spent more space discussing the afterlife of Martha Ray, the ways in which the story of her death were reconfigured over time, than he did on her slaying outside a London theatre. His shifting narrative told us much about how this murder of passion and delusion was perceived. In a slightly different vein, historians of Victorian England have studied murder in the context of new communicative practices and anxieties about domestic stability, sexual danger and urban order.[1] They have been fascinated by Victorian noir, the staple of penny-dreadful literature, and the ways in which murderers, and especially murderesses, became celebrities.

In the Victorian era, executions were almost exclusively related to murder, but in the period in which Captain Goodere killed his brother, murder was not the only crime for which you could be hanged. In the sixty years before the Dineley murder, and for almost a century afterwards, capital felonies overwhelmingly involved theft, not homicide. At the Old Bailey, London's central criminal court, indictments for theft exceeded homicides by a proportion of 15 to 1 in the years 1680-1740.[2] Even violent thefts involving highway robbery, smuggling affrays and breaking and entering exceeded homicides by a proportion of 7 to 6. Correspondingly more people were hanged for theft than murder, even allowing for the introduction of transportation in 1717. During the period 1680-1740, 237 men and women were sentenced to death for homicide at London's Old Bailey; the number for theft was 1605, more than six times higher.

At the turn of the eighteenth century a noteworthy number of homicides involved matters of honour or slights to one's reputation. The number of cases in which individuals were run through by a 'rapier' exceeded one hundred, about ten per cent of all homicides. These were often cases where a gentleman's brittle sense of honour was affronted and ended in duels or tavern brawls. Some involved roistering upper-class men who would not brook an arrest from the watch or local constable and stabbed or 'pricked' them in a drunken confrontation in the streets. The libertine Earl of Rochester was involved in one of these affrays in 1676. In the period 1680-1740, 'rapier crime' was in fact larger than family-related homicide, by a proportion of five to three. And by far the largest proportion of family-related homicide involved husbands and wives; often, sadly, the product of wife-beating.

In a sample of 700 homicides at the Old Bailey, 1680-1740, we have sixty [8.6%] that involved members of biological families, and of these sixty, we found only four cases where one sibling killed another.[3] One included a clearly mentally unstable youngster, Mary Tame of Harrow-on-the-hill, who was assigned the task of caring for her infant sister and let her drown while washing her face in a pond. Another featured two brothers whose drunken revels around the Exchange led to a night-time quarrel about the bill and a fatal wounding in the street.[4] The third involved a family quarrel in which the father reprimanded his son for late-night revelling, and in the tussle that ensued, a brother tried to intervene and was inadvertently stabbed with a penknife. The fourth, and the only case that led to a hanging, concerned two brothers who had been drinking and teasing one another all night. Their rivalry escalated when a female friend arrived and urged George Bayley, the brother in bed, to eject his sibling from the room. David Bayley, described as a gentleman of St Martin-in-the-fields, did not take kindly to this suggestion and attacked the woman, one Mary Anderson, stabbing her in the arm and head with his sword. When George tried to intervene, he too was stabbed in the back and belly, wounds from which he died two days later.[5]

None of these cases involved pre-meditated murder, except possibly that of David Bayley. A few outside of England certainly did. One concerned Thomas Ogilvie of Eastmiln, near Forfar in Scotland, who was poisoned by his brother Patrick, and his own wife, Catherine Nairn. Together they committed what the *London Evening Post* described as the 'worst of crimes, incest, fratricide and murder.'[6] Apparently, Lieutenant Patrick Ogilvie came to reside with his brother when convalescing from service in the East India Company. According to servants, Patrick was seen lying 'carnally together' with Catherine on a number of occasions, she moaning with amorous delight.[7] This infatuation led to the poisoning of the cuckold brother. Another featured a squireen from Fingal in Ireland, a Rev Mr Tanner of Holt Patrick, who was fatally beaten on the road to Loughshinny in May 1741 by a fisherman named John Cappogue. He committed the crime on the orders of Tanner's brother, William. As in the Dineley case, a disputed inheritance was the issue, with William fearing that his brother's recent marriage to a lower-class woman would produce children that would frustrate his entitlement to a small property of £80 a year.⁸ The *Daily Gazetteer* devoted half a column to this case because fratricide was very rare, and premeditated fratricide even rarer.

If the Tanner murder was intriguing, the Dineley-Goodere story was even more so, for while it also involved a disputed inheritance, it became entangled in a bitter divorce that swept through the courts and even reached the Lords. The background to the Dineley-Goodere rivalry was lurid and heavy. It was tailor-made theatre for the forms of criminal literature that came into commercial prominence in the eighteenth century when literacy was on the rise, stretching down to artisans and shopkeepers in a city the size of Bristol. These featured the last confessions of the condemned, criminal biographies constructed by the prison curate, and trial transcripts where the details of the crime and the drama of the case unfolded in the testimony and cross-examinations. It also involved the 'breaking news' of the papers, which gave the public the first taste of the crime and prepared the ground for more detailed narratives. Cumulatively these productions narrowed the narrative distance between the reader and the represented events.⁹

The Dineley murder as pre-trial sensation

The social drama of the fratricide was most visibly displayed in the broadside produced by Thomas Harris of the *Looking Glass and Bible* on London Bridge. Printed on Royal paper 'fitted to be framed', it offered a pictorial representation of the abduction and murder of Dineley and portraits of the three villains in prison, all for the price of sixpence.¹⁰ Before that broadside appeared in May 1741 there were detailed accounts of the crime in the newspapers, embellished by rumours circulating on the affair. These were an advance on the moralizing pamphlets and plays that detailed notorious murders in the seventeenth century when a criminal literature first emerged.¹¹ Readers were more readily drawn into the immediacy or near-immediacy of real crime and real criminals; allowing, of course, for a newspaper press that generally specialized in weekly or tri-weekly productions.

In the London papers the story of Sir John Dineley's murder broke in late January, a week after Captain Goodere's arrest. The *London Evening Post* remarked that a considerable part of the crew had been let into the secret of the murder, to a point that it would not have gained 'Credit were not all the Bristol Letters of yesterday full of the Narrative.'¹² In the following issue, a Bristol correspondent laid out the circumstances of the crime in roughly one column of print.¹³ Although the letter had been written just one day after Captain Goodere's arrest, the author had clearly obtained access to the coroner's report and to Mahony and White's confessions, as well as to some information passed on from Sir John's friend and financier, Jarrit Smith. The picture painted was one of fraternal perfidy, a seemingly friendly rapprochement of the brothers followed by the swift abduction of Sir John and a plot to murder him. It was masterminded by Captain Goodere, who prevailed on vulnerable seamen, Mahony and then White, to commit the deed. The account left no doubt all three were guilty, and approvingly cited the coroner's verdict of wilful murder. It shrugged off Goodere's allegations of innocence. It noted that the captain deviously behaved with 'much Chearfulness and Unconcern' when he was committed to Newgate because he had tried to give his story evidential authenticity by writing to Jarrit Smith and proclaiming his innocence beforehand. Once in Newgate, however, thoughts of escaping justice predominated, for files were found on his manservant which revealed the captain hoped to break out of jail.

The drama of the case was highlighted in various ways. The writer devoted considerable space to the violence of the abduction and Dineley's desperate efforts to attract attention:

> Sir John making a Noise, the Enquiry of the People as they hurry'd him along (he loudly crying out Murder! Murder!) was stopp'd by the Ruffians telling them *He was mad and a Thief and a Murderer*; and so [they] convey'd him down the River, while his Brother stopp'd his Mouth and cover'd him over with his Scarlet Cloak, in order to deaden the Cry of Murder which Sir John still made.

This account, or ones very close to it, crop up in at least four London newspapers and reached Gloucester, the Midlands, the North and the East coast by way of the *Gloucester Journal, Derby Mercury*, the *Leeds Mercury* and the *Ipswich Journal*.[14] Within a few months it had reached the coast of America.[15] The narrative continued with Goodere telling the 'Irish papist' Mahony 'That he must murder his Brother, for he was mad, and should not live till Four in the Morning.' The murder was carried out clumsily by Mahony and White 'under the direction of their Commander', a strangulation with hands and rope that lasted thirty minutes. In this narrative Mahony is cast as an Irish Catholic villain whose conscience is assuaged by religious absolution; Goodere as a cold blooded, calculating brother whose vengeful spirit is boundless. In some accounts the enormity of his crime was revealed as soon as the cooper inveigles his way into the captain's cabin on the pretense of reporting a theft. When the lieutenant and 'several stout Sailors' rushed in and seized Goodere once he had opened his cabin door, 'to their Horror and Surprize [they] saw the dead body of Sir John…and by evident Tokens that he had been murder'd by the violent Means of Strangling.'[16] The fact that Goodere was arrested in his own cabin, not the purser's, where the corpse of Sir John lay, was by the by. The more dramatic the revelation, the darker the conspiracy, the better the crime news.

Within the next week further particulars spilled out about the crime. The cooper was identified as a key witness to the crime through a peephole in an adjacent room. The motive for the murder was attributed to critical changes in the entail on the Charlton estate by which Captain Goodere was excluded in favour of Sir John's nephews. It was also alleged that Mahony and White so bungled the initial strangling of Sir John that Goodere had to supply a rope from his own 'scrutore' [escritoire] or writing desk. The captain's participation in the crime was thus confirmed, and the premeditation of his crime was consolidated by the purported revelation that he ordered a watch with the dial 'Death Dineley' as early as November 1739, fourteen months before the deed was committed.[17] We say 'purported' because it seems that this particular watch-face was a journalistic embellishment to the story. Had there been such a watch with an incriminating dial, the prosecution would surely have seized on it in the trial. But it didn't, and nothing was made of the silver watch given Mahony by Goodere, beyond the fact that he tried subsequently to hide it in the privy. So, by the time the *Bristol Fratricide* hit the booksellers, the Dineley murder was there for the 'fabulating' or fictionalizing; that is to say, for building a narrative around the known and fanciful facts.

The *Bristol Fratricide* amplified the story in important ways. It stuck to the central script that all three men were guilty of murdering Dineley and continued to characterise Goodere as a perfidious captain who coldheartedly sought to revenge himself on his elder brother for breaking the entail on the Charlton estate.[18] The premeditated nature of this revenge was underscored by the revelation that Goodere planned the abduction from the White Hart alehouse and hired privateers for the purpose. The number of abductors was inflated, and Mahony and White were confusingly cast among the 'gang of villains' that swept Sir John to the barge, despite the fact that White was recruited later.[19] The details of the murder were also misrepresented. The cooper and wife were now direct witnesses to the crime, despite the fact that, strictly speaking, they were listeners who fleetingly glimpsed the rifling of the corpse when the adjoining cabin was illuminated by candlelight. Equally inaccurately, Lieutenant Perry [Berry in the tract] was now a principal witness to the crime, observing Goodere at the door of the purser's cabin. He was also allegedly resistant to handing Goodere over to the authorities, on the grounds that the case should come before the Admiralty courts. This was plausible, although it does not accord with details in the logbook and in cooper Jones' testimony. It suggests the author scrambled the testimony of Perry, Jones and Buchanan and changed the chronology of the habeas corpus application in order to get his story out as quickly as possible.

The *Bristol Fratricide* made less of Goodere's efforts to free himself by force and made more of his attempts to mobilize the 'credit and influence' of his friends. The captain reputedly wrote to two MPs, one a distant relation, to appear in his favour, and solicited the support of friends in Herefordshire, where he was on the commission of the peace. These revelations paved the way for a paradox: Goodere had a better public reputation than his brother who was 'hated for the Licentiousness of his Life and his Immorality.' It was the murder that erased the captain's virtues and 'rendered him more infamous to Posterity than the other could ever be by a still greater Number of Vices and Imperfections.'[20]

The notion that Captain Goodere was a creditable public servant darkened the nature of his crime. Yet it also complicates the story, for Sir John Dineley was no longer the vulnerable victim of the weekly prints, but an ex-seaman who was 'more fit for a boatswain than to enjoy the Title of Baronet', a man who lacked the politeness of a gentleman and whose irascible, slovenly ways alienated his wife and his only son. Sir John was no saint. He brutally mistreated his wife, abandoned his son and then manipulated him in his final days to break the entail on his estate and disinherit his brother. This was in retaliation for Samuel's support of Sir John's wife in a very acrimonious and litigious divorce; itself a not exactly disinterested act, since Samuel did not want Sir John to remarry, have new heirs, and deprive him of the chance of inheriting Charlton under their maternal grandfather's will.[21] Whether the author of the *Bristol Fratricide* intended it or not, the story of the brother's bitter rivalry began to unravel as a vicious struggle over property and a relentless prosecution of a flirtatious wife for alleged adultery; alleged because Sir John's successful suit against Sir Robert Jason for a criminal conversation with his wife was secured by bribing a putative tenant to perjure himself. 'The domestic Jarrs in Sir John's Family were fomented to such as Degree some Years ago' remarked the author, 'as laid a Foundation for all the Miseries and Misfortunes which have since occur'd.'[22] Although the writer protested he had no 'Design to rake in the Ashes of the Dead', the disclosures turned a black story of fratricide to various shades of gray. It produced a torsion in the text: a fulmination on the enormity of fratricide but a disavowal of the victim whose life was as scandalous and vicious as his brother's. The Dineley murder was a horrible crime; yet it was problematically tragic, despite being advertised that way.[23]

The *Bristol Fratricide* was published in Fleet Street in mid-February, 1741. It was sold in the metropolis and Bristol and Bath by 'all Booksellers and Pamphleteers of Quality' at the affordable price of sixpence. Within weeks it appeared in Dublin and reached the shores of America in just over two months. The *Boston News-Letter* announced its publication in late April under the title of *The Bristol Tragedy,* obtainable from booksellers Kneeland and Green in Queen Street, near the Boston prison. It revealed that the Dineley case had an international appeal among the literate classes.[24] As we argued earlier, the pamphlet prejudiced Goodere's defence before the trial began. Not that such matters bothered eighteenth-century judges. Pre-trial publicity was hardly an issue until the twentieth century when jurists debated the conflicting claims of a fair trial against the freedom of the press. All that the pamphlet did was to intensify the public's interest in the case, preparing the ground for the trial itself.

The media coverage of Captain Goodere's trial

By our calculations there were at least eight versions of the trials that were held in Bristol in late March 1741; nine if one includes the extensive report in the *London Magazine* which ran for eight pages of two-columned print.[25] These calculations are complicated by the fact that the newspaper advertisements for the trials do not always accord with the actual titles, partly because printers hoped to poach readers from their rivals. 'Genuine', 'authentic' and 'compleat' trials abound, confusing inattentive buyers. Samuel Foote's *Genuine Trial of Samuel Goodere Esquire,* which seems to have appeared on April Fool's Day at sixpence a copy, was followed a week later by the *Authentick Tryal of… Goodere* at only four pence. The price reduction seems to have made a difference, for the *Authentick* announced its fourth edition in less than three weeks. Either that or the printer Edward Hill of Fleet Street deliberately launched short runs to puff his production's popularity. These two tracts were swiftly followed by the *Genuine and Authentick History…of Samuel Goodere* at a further reduced price of two pence. This history of the trial claimed that it had the approval of the principal judge, the Recorder Sir Michael Foster, an unlikely event. It also declared it was 'attested by Persons of Credit and Reputation who were well acquainted with the unfortunate Captain and his Brother', a statement designed to deflate Foote's trumpeting of his Goodere pedigree and his assertion that he had insider information.

The fact is the trials provoked a paper war among the printers for a sizeable slice of the market. The huge interest in the fratricide, in the large number of trial accounts and their geographical scope, calls into question Judith Flanders'

THE GENUINE TRIAL

OF

SAMUEL GOODERE, Esq;

(Late Commander of the *Ruby* Man of War)

MATTHEW MAHONY,

AND

CHARLES WHITE,

AT THE

GENERAL SESSIONS of *OYER* and *TER-MINER* for the City of BRISTOL,

HELD BY

Adjournment on *Thursday* the 26th Day of *March*, 1741, before the Right Worshipful *Henry Combe*, Esq; Mayor, the Worshipful Mr. Serjeant *Forster*, Recorder, the Worshipful the Aldermen, and Justices assign'd to keep the Peace, and deliver the Goal;

FOR THE

Murder of Sir JOHN DINELY GOODERE, Bt.

ON BOARD

His Majesty's Ship the *RUBY* Man of War, then lying at *King-Road*, within the Jurisdiction and Liberties of the said City of *Bristol*.

Taken in Short-Hand by Order and Direction of S. FOOT, of *Worcester-College, Oxford*, Esq; and Nephew to the late Sir JOHN DINELY GOODERE, Bart.

LONDON:

Printed by *H. Goreham*, at the New Printing-Office in *Wine-Office-Court, Fleet-street*, 1741.

(Price Six-pence.)

At least eight accounts of the trial were published in the immediate aftermath. This one, *The Genuine Trial of Samuel Goodere, Esq, Matthew Mahony and Charles White* (1741), commissioned by Dineley and Goodere's nephew, Samuel Foote, and published on 1 April, was the first. Bristol Archives, 14754/8

> THE AUTHENTICK
> # TRYAL
> OF
> Samuel Goodere, Efq; Matthew Mahony, and Charles White,
> AT THE
> ## CITY of BRISTOL,
> On THURSDAY the 26th, and FRIDAY the 27th of March, 1741.
> FOR THE
> # MURDER
> OF
> Sir *JOHN DINELY GOODERE*, Bart.
> On Board the RUBY Man of War, in *King-Road, Briftol*.
>
> LONDON:
> Printed for E. HILL, in, Fleet-Street. 1741. (Price Four-pence.)

The Authentick Tryal of Samuel Goodere, Esq (1741). Bristol Archives, 9733/2

claim that murder as a media event was somehow 'invented' by the Victorians.[26] While we fully accept the proposition that the popular representation of murder is as important as the crime itself, we dispute the notion that this was a nineteenth-century phenomenon. Clearly, Flanders' cases catered to an expanding reading public. Cheaper and faster productions especially those revamped in a melodramatic 'penny-dreadful' format, meant tales of nineteenth-century murders reached well down the social scale. Even so, the Dineley murder attracted a large audience when one considers eighteenth-century levels of literacy and its communicative practices.

It might be more appropriate to track the long term 'publicity' of murder: from royal to public justice in the early modern era; from public justice to media event in the eighteenth century; from media event to full-blown melodrama in the nineteenth.[27] Where the Victorian press differed from the Georgian was in its potential impact upon politicians. Crown officers in the

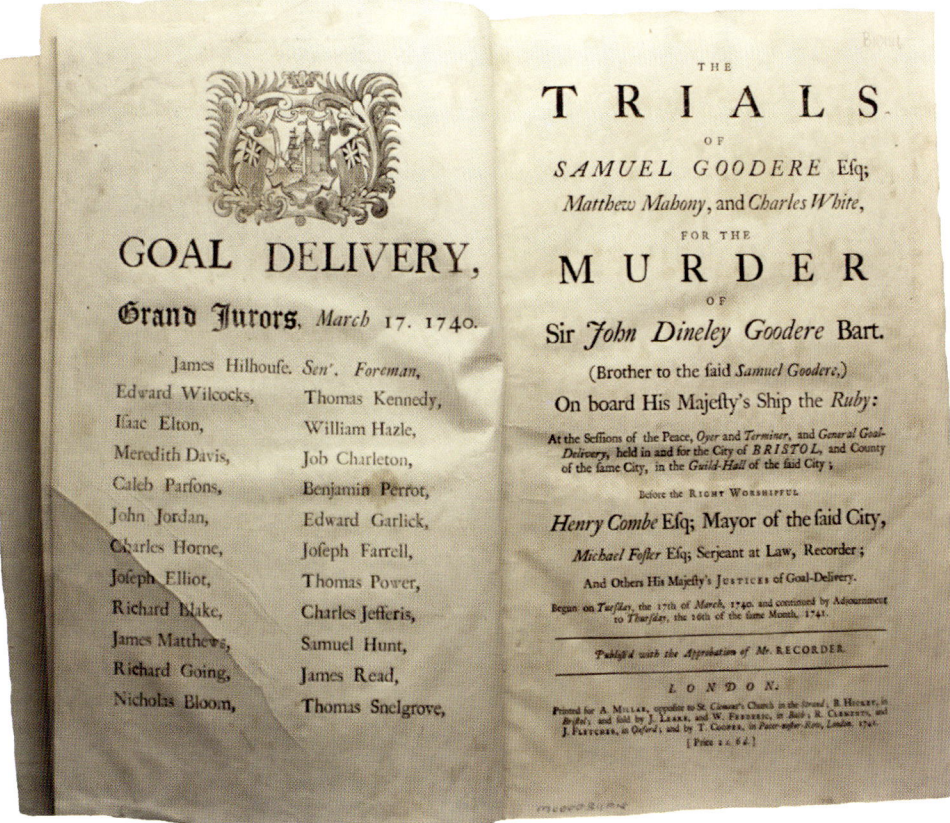

The Trials of Samuel Goodere Esq. Bristol Libraries, B10122. Some published accounts of the trial avoided editorialising, opting for a straight transcript instead. This was one of the fullest. It includes the defence case in full and a separate account of the trial of Charles White

eighteenth century did not have paper clippings on their tables when they considered possible pardons. They simply considered the judgments of judges and influential figures when deliberating on sentences and it was comparatively rare for murderers to escape the gallows unless their offence could be construed as manslaughter. But by the end of the nineteenth century, public opinion as filtered through the press did matter when it came to commuting sentences.[28] So while the Georgian public could register its disapproval of a sentence at the gallows, its ability to influence the course of justice was limited.

Even so, middling audiences were fascinated by the social drama of murder, and in the case of the Goodere trial, the commercial stakes were high for the shorthand writers and printers who hoped to capitalise on the market. Predictably some early versions of the trial trashed rival productions. The *Genuine and Authentick History* declared other accounts of the trial to be 'spurious.' The author of *The Genuine Relation of the Tryal*, which was printed by

Felix Farley and sold in Bristol and London bookshops, declared its rivals to be 'impudent and scandalous libels on the Judicial Authority of the Court.'[29] He deplored the 'barbarous edition' which had Goodere, Mahony and White in the dock at the same time. He accused one pirate edition from Salisbury of misdating the trial and inventing testimony from Lieutenant Perry, when in fact the officer had sailed with the *Ruby* to Milford Haven.[30] The overall impression is that speedy productions – at least five appeared between the end of the trial and the public executions – spawned inaccuracies galore. Particularly noticeable was the melding of evidence from the coroner's inquest and the trials themselves and the drift from the strong circumstantial evidence of the murder to spectator certainty. Edward Jones and his wife never saw the murder; they heard it and glimpsed the rifling of Dineley's body. Lieutenant Perry saw nothing at all, although he was primarily responsible for reporting the crime to the water bailiff and to the coroner. That did not make him a first-hand witness.

The interventions of Samuel Foote
In literary circles the Dineley murder has always attracted a certain notoriety because two of the trial pamphlets were written by his nephew and benefactor, the celebrated comedian Samuel Foote. Ian Kelly has claimed that his two productions attracted more attention than the others by virtue of his family connections. His accounts 'were necessarily privileged within the domain of the various "True Accounts", however vitiated by readers suspicions of a certain self-interest.'[31] In fact, this is far from clear. Foote was not in Bristol at the discovery of the murder or during the legal proceedings, although the *Gloucester Journal* made out that he hastened to the port from Cornwall and attended Sir John's burial at Charlton.[32] He had married Mary Hickes at St Clement Danes on the Strand on 10 January 1741, just a week before the murder, so it was not physically impossible for him to have been there, although his private life was in such disarray it seems highly unlikely. Foote happened to be a scholar of Worcester College, Oxford, whose dons would certainly have disapproved of his marriage as well as his general conduct. In fact, he was ejected from the college in late February 1741 on account of his profligate behaviour and heavy spending. A note in the college's register records that 'Samuel Foote, after a course of many irregularities and lying out of the College' was ordered to appear before the Provost, and after further absences without leave, was deprived of his scholarship.[33] At that point he owed £900 to Alexander Wood, of Brownlow Street, St Giles-in-the-fields, possibly a former sea captain in the Mediterranean trade.[34]

Wood was not the only creditor; there were others, including the Dowager Viscountess Castlecomer, a sister to the Duke of Newcastle, one of the secretaries of state. This was not an enviable position to be placed in. While Foote was able to avail himself of his young wife's dowry, which was worth £50 a year, with an additional annuity of £90 on the death of her mother, it was hardly enough to keep the creditors at bay.[35] And although Samuel Foote was a beneficiary under his uncle John's will, he could not immediately claim a mortgage on the Dineley estate in Tockington and Stapleton. He certainly tried to raise money on his future inheritance, but the family squabbles over who was entitled to what compromised any quick answers. In any case Edward Dineley's last minute will bequeathing his estate to his mother placed the Foote legacy in some doubt.[36] Basically, Foote was too busy fighting off creditors to pay much attention to his uncle's murder even though he could claim insider information into its background. Writing a pamphlet or two on the imbroglio might temporarily keep the wolf from the door, but Sam Foote's debts were too deep to keep him long from prison. Eventually he was forced to enter the Fleet in November 1742, and apart from one brief release, remained there until May 1743.

Foote's collegial status and financial problems forced him to work through intermediaries, including quite possibly Abel Dagge, the keeper of Bristol Newgate.[37] Although the title page of his first production suggests he was in control of his reports – 'Taken in Short-Hand by Order and Direction of S. Foot, of Worcester College, Esquire, and Nephew to the late Sir John Dineley Goodere, Bart.' – it is far from clear that he was, or indeed that he had secured the help of reliable shorthand writers at the trial.[38] In the Jarrit Smith papers in the Bristol Archives, there is a request from Samuel Martin, a prominent businessman in Bristol, to secure a copy of the solicitor's brief and a 'perusal of the part you had in ye Trial.'[39] Martin said he had no other interest in the trial than 'to oblige the public, do justice to ye City and serve a Printer in London who is a faithful good Friend to our Cause.' We have a hunch, no more than that, that the printer was Henry Goreham, who operated out of Wine Office Court off Fleet Street. He was Foote's printer, and Foote's first production, *The Genuine Trial,* is remarkably tilted towards the kind of evidence that Martin solicited.[40] Two-thirds of the pamphlet is devoted to the formal arraignment, the opening remarks of the prosecutor, and Jarrit Smith's own testimony. The rest could have been collected from newspapers and *The Bristol Fratricide,* sources to which Foote had reasonably easy access.

Our second clue that Foote had no reliable reporter in court comes from his assumption that Goodere, Mahony and White all stood trial at the same time. This simply wasn't the case. Charles White was indicted and tried the day after the others. Only a person absent from the scene could have made this mistake. Others followed. Foote states that the defendants asked for pen and ink, but only the captain did because the others were illiterate. Moreover, in Foote's first production, the coverage of the cross-examinations is threadbare. Nothing is said about the White Hart and the plans to kidnap Sir John. Duncan Buchanan, the one witness who was present at the pub, the abduction, the brothers' quarrel on the river, and who spied on the nefarious dealings in the cockpit, is hardly mentioned. He simply appears as the querulous 'sailor' who disputes whether Samuel and Sir John had anything approximating a 'dialogue' on the river.[41] Foote zones in on just a few witnesses who were called to give testimony: the master, but not the surgeon's mate; Edward Jones, the cooper, but only very briefly his wife Mary, who was the one that alerted her husband to the racket next door. The recruitment of Mahony and White is glossed as well, so it is hard to see how readers could have identified with these malefactors and the 'iniquities they all understood', as Kelly asserts.[42]

Once more the cooper becomes a direct spectator to the murder. 'I peeped through an open crevice and saw the fatal tragedy', Jones allegedly declared, and while Goodere stood sentry, ready 'to attack the first person that should oppose…what they were about…White held the deceased hands, whilst Maloney took his handkerchief off, and put it about his [Dineley's] neck, when each pulled as hard as they could in order to strangle him.'[43] Edward Jones saw none of this, and the confessions of Mahony and White dispute who did what. The heavy weight of circumstantial evidence is by-passed in favour of a murderous spectacle. Goodere's rationale for taking Dineley into custody – to prevent him from recklessly squandering his estate – is squarely addressed, although the reader's knowledge of his black crime and his willingness to shunt the full responsibility of his brother's death on his two assassins deepens his duplicity. In Foote's account, the only mitigating factor for his fratricidal uncle seems to be his popularity among the crew; 'he was as gallant and brave a sailor as ever stept between bow and stern of a ship.'[44] There is certainly some hyperbole here, for while it is true a few seamen expressed sympathy for the captain it could hardly be said that 'abundance of sailors appeared on his behalf.'[45] To begin with, Goodere had only assumed command of the *Ruby* some two months before the murder, hardly enough time to establish much rapport with anyone. Second, Goodere complained that he was deprived of character witnesses from HMS *Ruby* at his trial and he blamed the Admiralty for not bringing them back in time from South Wales.

Foote's first essay on the Dineley murder was really a rushed job. It wasn't 'dialogue-heavy' as Ian Kelly has suggested. The *Authentick Tryal* and the Boston *Account* contained a lot more dialogue and were certainly as entertaining.[46] So, too, was the account in the *London Magazine,* which was all dialogue save for the confessions of Mahony and White appended at the end. Foote's distance from the scene of the action and his impecunious condition compromised his efforts to create a court drama that would in retrospect serve as a prototype for his plays. Despite the possibilities of creating a voyeuristic narrative that spanned gentry estates, urban coffee-houses, low-life pubs, and press-gang tenders and culminated in fratricidal fury over broken entails and disinheritance, Foote's first effort fell rather flat.

Samuel Foote's second pamphlet, written a month later, surreptitiously spent a lot of time repairing the mistakes of the first. It printed the confessions of Matt Mahony and Charles White, which added an air of mystery to what actually happened while confirming Goodere's complicity in the murder. It strengthened the drama of the abduction by printing the confessions of the privateers and attending to the evidence of Morris Hobbs, the landlord of the *White Hart*. It also delved into the drama of Sir John's last hours by producing a more credible witness of Edward Jones, who this time hears more than he sees. But Foote's big pitch for fame was publicly to divest the brotherly rivalry of its rumours and caricatures, to bring familial knowledge to bear on the characters of the principal antagonists.

Did he succeed? Did he set the story straight? Foote continues to frame his fratricidal uncle as a Janus-faced villain, open and obliging to his friends, acquaintances and crew, yet privately irascible when his family denied him money to feed his extravagance and malevolent about the privileges his elder brother enjoyed to his exclusion. Sometimes Foote portrays Sam Goodere as a spoilt bully. He disclosed that Samuel robbed his grandfather's house and threatened both his mother and father with pistols when they failed to comply with his demands. From youth, Foote avers, Sam 'learned a contempt for all Laws, both divine and human', a familiar line of argument in the eighteenth-century tracts on crime where human depravity escalates into criminal enormity.[47] Unable to gain a captaincy through his father's influence, Samuel angled to get one by promoting a rival candidate at an Evesham election and later stood against his brother as mayor of the town, turfing him off his privileged pew after election day. This early confrontation with his brother set the stage for bitter rivalries over the Burghope and Charlton estates and a disposition to use violence to achieve his goals. Foote even claims that Captain Goodere tried to bribe and bully a witness to swear that Sir John Dineley forged his son's signature on the deed of recovery; an 'undeniable proof of

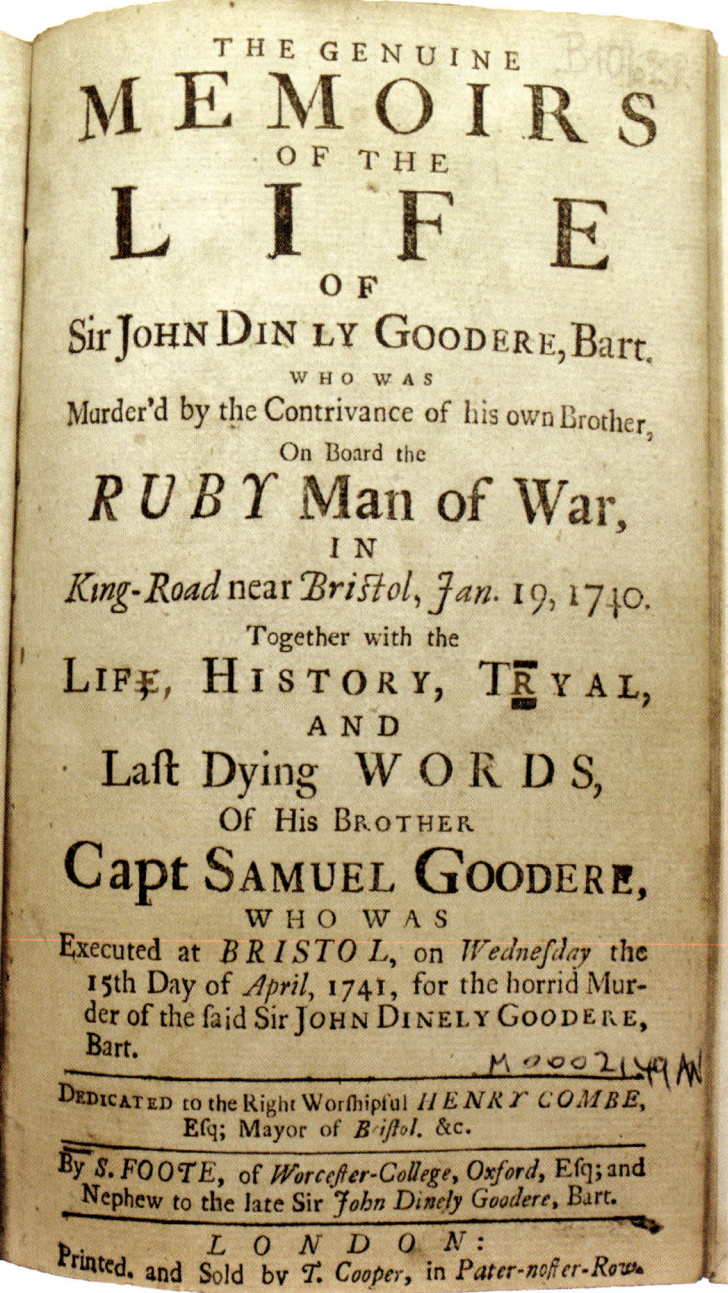

The Genuine Memoirs of the Life of Sir John Dineley Goodere (1741). Bristol Libraries, B10622. Another account from the pen of the dead man's nephew, Samuel Foote, this time a potted biography as well as a resumé of the trial and execution. Sir John, according to Foote, was a 'plain and honest gentleman' with 'a natural goodness of heart' and thus no match for his scheming brother's malicious duplicity.

Captain Goodere's attachment to corruption.'[48] In the end Sam Goodere commits the crime of all crimes and is only redeemed by a gallant exit at the gallows and a recognition of his guilt, to his brother and also to the seamen he had cajoled to commit the murder. According to Foote, his uncle Sam 'was heard to say several Times, *Lord do not reward me according to my Deserts.*'[49]

Sir John Dineley, on the other hand, is cast as a 'plain honest gentleman'[50] whose familial squabbles were explicable without ascribing them to some social pathology or smouldering machismo. His 'natural goodness of heart' allowed his profligate father, Sir Edward Goodere, to take advantage of his generosity, a generosity that was not reciprocated in Sir Edward's will. Educated at sea, and 'not being Philosopher enough to master his Passions', Sir John repays his father's stinginess with a stingy burial, for which he is publicly criticized. Later, when Sir John's marriage to a Stapleton heiress goes sour, the breakdown is attributed to Sir John's gullibility, not to his abuse and misogyny, which even by eighteenth-century standards shocked contemporaries, or to his violent jealousies about his young wife's acquaintances. In Foote's narrative Sir John, his benefactor, is a man misunderstood. His viciousness to his wife is passed over, as it is by other authors,[51] and his willingness to break the entail on the Charlton estate is attributed to the demands of his dissipated son who needed ready cash to pay off his debts, not to his abiding enmity towards his younger brother and his own wife. The signs of pathological instability exhibited by Sir John are explained away as the rough manners of a seaman who never really adjusted to the landed status that was thrust upon him.[52]

Although Foote pretends an air of dispassionate reason in introducing the story, he is clearly partisan. Another indication of this is that in the dedication to the *Genuine Memoirs,* he even exonerates the mayor for failing to act promptly on Jarrit Smith's application for a warrant to arrest the captain, on the grounds that 'honest virtuous Men suspect no Guilt.'[53] In effect, he flatters the judge and the prosecuting solicitor who also happened to be a central witness to the kidnapping. To Foote's credit, he did not go after Lady Mary Dineley, who tried to undermine her husband's recovery of the entail by importuning her son to devolve all his legacies to her. Perhaps he did not wish to alienate her in the future testamentary disputes with his own family. She had challenged his right to Stapleton, on which he had tried to replenish his finances.

Other eighteenth century post-trial productions

How far contemporaries accepted Foote's account of the brothers is uncertain. The Reverend John Penrose, who attended the condemned at Bristol Newgate and hoped to make money selling their confessions, took a more measured line on the brothers, attributing Sir John's defects to his unfortunate upbringing and casting Captain Goodere as a gallant commander who had one fatal flaw, a relentless enmity towards his older brother, 'grounded' on the 'hard usage he had from him'.[54] In Penrose's eyes, Sam Goodere was not the moral monster Foote made him out to be. Others, however, built a counter-narrative around Goodere's sea career and vulnerability as a younger brother. Some saw the murder as a tragedy for Goodere, a courageous commander who had served his country in the assault on San Sebastian and neighbouring Spanish ports in 1719, and whose printed journal served as evidence of his bravery.[55] In this scenario, the captain was a precursor of the contemporary admirals who were contesting the power of the Spanish in Mediterranean and Caribbean waters, despite the regularly omitted fact that his contribution to the 1719 war effort was controversial and resulted in his court martial. So Captain Samuel Goodere entered the slipstream of the bellicose nationalism that broke out after Admiral Vernon's capture of Porto Bello in 1739 and remained high in Bristol even when Vernon's Caribbean ventures faltered.[56] In the light of his public service, perhaps he deserved some sort of reprieve, as his wife and friends pleaded. In the *Genuine and Authentick History,* Goodere was the object of a 'causeless and unjustifiable antipathy' from his brother, a turn of phrase echoed by John Charnock in his *Biographia navalis* later in the century. Sir John disliked the favour Sam enjoyed with his father, who left the Burghope estate to him, leaving the elder brother with only a life interest. Sam was horrified when Sir John gave his father such an undistinguished funeral, one not even fit for a gentleman's servant.[57] When Samuel Goodere sided with his sister-in-law Lady Mary in her marriage dispute, so the narrative ran, Sir John's anger knew no bounds; especially when he helped finance her time in King's Bench prison, expenses that Lady Mary tried to recoup from her husband, on the grounds that he was responsible for her debts.[58] This was the real reason why Dineley broke the entail and deprived Goodere of the Charlton estate on the death of his son.

After the executions, speculations about the motives surrounding the murder of Sir John Dineley died down. The official trial transcripts, those endorsed by the Recorder, appeared in May at a price of 2/6d [12.5 p.] a folio volume. These focussed specifically on the transactions in the court room and the confessions that had been sworn before the mayor. The background stories about the rivalries that plagued the Goodere family were omitted, as they were in the state trials, although they never entirely disappeared from more popular productions. In the formulaic Newgate Calendars or Registers reproduced after 1765, the familial disputes over money and property continued to inform the narrative of why Goodere sought 'the most diabolical means of revenge.'[59] Those invariably involved the broken entail, although Sir John's inability to achieve a clear divorce from Lady Mary, which he blamed on his brother, was often wrapped around it. Indeed, *pace* Lincoln Faller, the Dineley murder did not epitomise a moral etiology of crime, a conviction that the murder was caused by Goodere's innate malevolence, something bred in the bone and nurtured by indulgent parents.[60] That explanation emanated only from Samuel Foote, who in the *Genuine Memoirs of Sir John Dineley* separated the story of his domestic difficulties from those of his murder. In this narrative Sir John was not cast as a brutal misogynist but as a rough-edged baronet misled by rumours of his wife's infidelities; rumours, Foote continued, that were really unfounded. Beyond their domestic 'jarring', the couple's cardinal mistake was to neglect their son, who fell into 'a libertine way of living' and asked his father to redeem his debts and provide him with an annuity in return for breaking the entail. So, in this account, Sir John was not the scheming manipulator of his inheritance, but a father who heeded his desperate son's request.[61] His last-minute 'generosity' made Samuel Goodere's complaints about the recovery seem malevolent, especially when it was alleged that the captain had tried to bribe one of the witnesses to change her story. In Foote's narrative Goodere's actions ran to character; his innumerable slights and threats to the family over the years revealed a depraved man. He stole from his grandfather, physically threatened his father and brother, and showed his enmity towards John Dineley in the Evesham mayoral election of 1734. His rage and malevolence would culminate in a well-planned diabolical murder.

Foote's narrative influenced those that appeared in the Newgate Calendars. They, too, reiterated the notion that the differences between Sir John and Lady Mary were essentially 'domestic jars', although they cited the crim. con. prosecution to confirm the wife's infidelities. They differed, however, in their retelling of the recovery. In their accounts there is no son; Edward has disappeared from the record. Consequently, Sam's rage is not associated with the dubious circumstances surrounding Edward's inheritance, but with Sir John's endeavours to remarry, and failing that, to devise the Charlton estates on his nephews. These calendars admit that Samuel had 'sanguine expectations' of inheriting the estate, but none of them criticise Sir John for breaking the entail, despite the fact that in the eighteenth century, settlement laws were generally rigorously applied. Only a peripheral account in the *Annals of Europe* thought some injustice had been done to the captain because the rules of family inheritance had not been observed.[62]

In the Newgate Calendars, Samuel's revenge was distilled to 'the unjustifiable sin of barbarity founded on covetousness.'[63] This quite conventional account zoned in on the fifth and tenth commandments: thou shall not kill or covet thy neighbour's property. But it still opened the door to a more sociological explanation, for what was it that Goodere coveted? What presumed entitlement eluded him? Consequently, the Dineley murder could still be seen as a narrative about property, money and the predicament of younger sons in an age of primogeniture. It was so in George Borrow's *Celebrated Trials*, although in this case Sir John is misleadingly cast as the direct heir of Burghope, not Charlton.[64] The cruder explanation, that sin and reckless living drove men to terrible crimes was reserved for the common seamen, White and Mahony. Their licentious habits set them up as cruel, cold-blooded assassins. Richard Smith later remarked that Mahony was '"a bold-faced villain", just a proper Pierre in low life, one who seems to have no fear of heaven or man.'[65]

What was distinctly novel about the Newgate registers was the manner and venue of the executions. In these popular renditions of the murder, all three men, Goodere, Mahony and White, were hung in chains north of Hotwells in full view of the scene of their crime.[66] In fact, only Mahony was treated the ignominy of the gibbet after the executions on St Michael's Hill, and then not at Hotwells but seven miles downriver at the Avon's mouth. Quite why so many of the Calendars published after 1768 made this mistake is unclear. Crime scene hangings and gibbetings were actually more unusual in the later years of the century than they had been in Goodere's day, but they had perhaps become more newsworthy when they were used to sensational effect after major incidents of disorder. In London, groups of rioting weavers were hanged at the scene of their crime at Spitalfields in 1768 and so were some of the Gordon rioters in 1780. Perhaps to the Calendar writers, it was simply a way of spicing up the account and insisting that such a black crime as fratricide deserved special forms of punishment. According to Leslie Stephen, Samuel Foote was even introduced in a club as the nephew of a man who was hanged in chains.[67]

A grotesque nineteenth-century woodcut illustration of Dineley's murder, from a later edition of *The Newgate Calendar* (1826)

Oral Memory and Recollection

Memories of the murder lingered. In Herefordshire people believed the ghost of Sir John haunted Burghope House, a story so compelling that by the end of the century the mansion was uninhabitable, used only as a granary. In early nineteenth century Bristol, Samuel Seyer, rector of Filton and chronicler of the city's history, remarked that 'the tale was current within the memory of many persons still living'.[68] As a well-respected parson and schoolmaster with strong local roots we have little reason to doubt his word, although he must have meant people who learnt of the murder from their parents and relatives, for in 1821, when he penned his thoughts, octogenarians were few on the ground.[69] He begins his story in Stapleton, at the entry to the village where the Dineley mansion was situated, no doubt because that site had often prompted recollections of Sir John and his Lawford bride. Nothing is said of their marital strife and legal battles, however, a topic perhaps, that caused him discomfort. It was not the kind of story that the antiquarian and vice-president of the Bristol Library Society would have wanted to recall, let alone commemorate, about his native Bristol. Sir John Dineley is described simply as a gentleman of 'respectable family and fortune', in terms sufficiently anodyne to raise eyebrows even in elite circles. Seyer also expresses surprise that Dineley could be captured in 'broad daylight', forgetting that the incursions of the press gangs were a regular feature of Georgian Bristol, particularly in the twilight hours when the quayside pubs were crawling with sailors. A violent Bristol is not in Seyer's writ; neither are vindictive gentry who would not hesitate to litigate over property entitlements, even within their own families. The enmity between Sir John Dineley and Samuel Goodere is described as long standing; they 'always lived on the worst possible terms, so as to have a perfect hatred of one another'.[70] Yet the reasons for it are kept out of sight by focussing on Goodere's betrayal of both brother and accomplices, a narrative derived from an altogether too literate confession of Matthew Mahony that was purportedly hawked at the gallows. This 'confession' adds an authentic air to a story that evades as much as it informs.

The Fratricide (1839)

One account of the Dineley murder stands outside the conventional modes of criminal literature. This is *The Fratricide,* the rambling poem written by the surgeon Richard Smith in 1839, and which we first encountered in chapter five. Smith himself described the poem as a 'rigmarole', a protracted, diffuse piece of writing in which the Bristol of Goodere is implicitly compared to the city a century later.[71] The subtitle in Gothic print, the *'Right Tragical Historie of Sir John D. Goodere, Bart.'* signals Smith's intention to probe the strange and sheer quirkiness of the past, and the poem begins with a description of the swirling winds and currents of Kingroad with two very different explanations of its turbulence. One takes a providential tack, deriving its inspiration from the Reverend John Conybeare, the Bishop of Bristol from 1750-1755, a known proponent of a polite form of revealed religion. The other is emphatically scientific, based on the ideas of Sir Henry T. De La Beche, a contemporary social reformer, whose report on the heath, sanitation and social ecology of Bristol would emerge six years later.[72] By contrasting these views, Smith imagines Kingroad, the scene of the Dineley murder, as a cauldron of divine or materialist forces. Providential wisdom is juxtaposed to natural science, and the theme of Bristol then and now, 'ancient' and 'modern', forms the axis of which this playful serio-comic poem proceeds.

The Dineley murder and its resolution offered a window into old Bristol

THE FRATRICIDE,
OR
THE MURDERER'S GIBBET;
BEING PART THE SECOND OF THE

Right Tragical Hystorie of Sir John D. Goodere, Bart.

Like a mildew'd ear, blasting his wholesome brother.—HAMLET.

> Let us pursue the trace
> Of light and shade's inconstant pace;
> And wild as cloud, or stream, or gale,
> Flow on, *flow unconfined* my tale!
> W. SCOTT'S *Marmion*, CH. III.

> Exactly opposite the entrance gate
> Of ST. AUGUSTINE'S CHURCH, in low estate,
> Being as its ROWLEY neighbour half as high,
> As you will see if you cast up your eye,
> There stands a dwelling, having, at its top,
> The No. 41—below's the shop

Richard Smith, *The Fratricide or The Murderer's Gibbet* (1839). Bristol Archives, 14754/5c and a different century. Samuel Goodere is characterised as a victim of primogeniture, a younger brother who must 'plough the waves' while the elder lives a life of landed privilege.[73] This ignores the inconvenient fact that John Dineley Goodere was actually the third of six sons and was also put to sea on the assumption that he would have to make his way in the world as well. He came to the inheritance by demographic accident and gentlemanly folly.[74] Smith also considers Goodere a reckless risk-taker whose passion for revenge overwhelms his reason and wonders what the new phrenologists would have made of him had they be able to examine his head.[75] Here one senses Smith would have loved to have obtained a death mask of the captain so he could expatiate on his unusual cranial bumps, just as he had done with John Horwood, a labourer hanged for the murder of Eliza Balsum in 1821, when he disclosed to an astonished audience that Horwood's head had elevated organs of benevolence.[76]

Goodere's accomplice, Matt Mahony, is described as a 'strapper', a rough-edged, tall man who defies heaven and hell and jokes when he is measured for the iron suit in which he will hang for eternity. He is going to die 'game' and tough out a hanging before the drop, a slow strangulation that could last fifteen minutes or more.[77] Once again Smith reveals that the criminal body is a prevailing source of fascination for him, not surprising for a man who collected the articulated skeletons of those he dissected and ventured to advance the 'science of criminology by lecturing about the shape of their heads.'[78] Among other things, he marvels at popular credulities concerning the deceased criminal's therapeutic power. He describes how women forced their way through the crowd to have their scrofula-afflicted children touched by the hand of the condemned. They enchant a silver penny in the same manner, honouring the right of the hangman to the perks of the ritual with a shilling tip.[79] We have no idea if any of this actually happened in 1741. It is very probably Smith's imagination running riot, conjuring up the manifold images of the 'hanging fair' which he could collect from newspapers and critics like Bernard Mandeville and Henry Fielding.[80] By the time Smith composed his 'rigmarole' at the tail end of the 1830s, belief in the magical powers of the criminal corpse was certainly on the wane, but it was not quite extinct and he may have been prompted by a scandalous incident at nearby Gloucester in 1837. There, during an inquiry into the badly managed execution of the murderer, Charles Bartlett, evidence emerged that women were still regularly permitted onto the hanging platform to rub the hand of the condemned despite official disapproval. Moreover, confirmed the turnkey who let them in, 'It has been customary to do so ever since I have been here'.[81]

Woodcut portrait of Captain Samuel Goodere, copied by Richard Smith from an earlier pamphlet and included in his *The Fratricide or the Murderer's Gibbet* (1839). Bristol Archives, 14754/5c

Of particular interest to Smith was the public dissection of criminals, a professional preoccupation for much of his working life but also a topical subject given the furore over the Anatomy Act of 1832. That statute allowed surgeons to use the unclaimed bodies of paupers for medical research, creating a frisson of fear among members of the working class who believed dismemberment would condemn the corpse to linger in everlasting limbo. Bristol had seen such a panic during the cholera outbreak in 1832 when people disinterred bodies from St Peter's hospital to ensure they were buried whole.[82] In Richard Smith's historical scenario, and he had the reputation of being a body-snatcher or resurrectionist in his youth,[83] people seem less bothered when Captain Goodere is put under the knife. They strain their necks to see whether the revengeful brother has a black heart before the sheriffs intervene and tell the surgeons enough is enough.[84] Did this actually happen? Oral memory, what would have been handed down over three generations, plays tricks with the truth. What is clear is that Richard Smith savoured the ghoulish character of eighteenth-century executions and their post-mortem rituals. He wasn't repelled by their barbarity. And as we have seen, this went for Mahony's gibbet as well.

Quite possibly, Smith's interest in the Goodere case was heightened by the looming shadow of another fratricidal gibbeting tale, popularised in print just a few years earlier. This was the story of *Jack White's Gibbet*, first recounted by George C. Dyke in 1833 and reprinted several times in succeeding years. John White's family, so the story ran, had once owned extensive property at Wincanton, Somerset, but was reduced to penury early in the eighteenth century. In 1727, John was working as a lowly inn servant in Castle Cary where he encountered a seafarer recently returned from the wars with Spain. Tempted to robbery by the dubloons the traveller had made free with at the inn, John waylaid him the following day on the road to Wincanton and bludgeoned him to death. The crime was quickly discovered and White was convicted, hanged and gibbeted beside the road at the scene of his crime. Before he died however, White learned that his victim was none other than his own brother William, whom everyone had assumed dead but who was in fact recently returned from war, loaded with prize money. William's intention, according to Dyke, was to restore the good name of the family, repurchase the Wincanton mansion and rescue the wretched John from a pauper's death. Most of Dyke's account, it would later turn out, was fiction, embellished from the case of a man named John White who was hanged and gibbeted beside the road from Castle Cary to Wincanton for murdering Robert Sutton in 1730. This was no fratricide after all, but the story stuck locally and was not convincingly debunked until 1922. Smith must surely have been aware of the legend when he embarked on his own *Fratricide* at Bristol.[85]

Recalling the murder of Sir John Dineley allowed Smith the opportunity to digress into a *vade mecum* of old Bristol. From the gusts and currents of Portishead the surgeon-antiquarian moves to College Green, to his own stomping ground and further back in time, to the White Hart 'pothouse', the rendezvous of Goodere's conspirators, no longer standing when Smith penned *The Fratricide*.[86] He traces the kidnapping through the back streets of College Green to the brick kilns and bank of the Avon where Sir John was forced on to the *Ruby*'s barge, now [in 1839] greatly altered by the floating harbour.[87] Captain Goodere is examined by the mayor and aldermen at the old Council House, demolished and rebuilt by Smith's time, and he is deposited in a loathsome Newgate, which had completely disappeared from the landscape.[88]

The Dineley murder thus conjures up lost sites and memories. Among other things these feature *The Gout* tavern between Baldwin and St Nicholas streets and the *Nag's Head* in Wine Street, from which Jarrit Smith purportedly ordered his Bordeaux claret and champagne. It also includes the five 'straggling houses' between St Augustine's church and the College, now all replaced. One was the scene of another murder in which Richard Smith took an interest, that of Mrs Frances Ruscombe and her servant, Mary Sweet, in 1764. This gruesome act, in which the women had their throats so severely cut that they were nearly decapitated, remained unresolved despite great rewards offered for the discovery of the killer. Interestingly, one of the advertisements about the crime singled out a Jack Tar in a blue sailor's jacket with a 'dirty handkerchief', lurking in the courtyard of the house, the morning of the murder.[89]

According to Smith, Abel Dagge, the keeper of Bristol Newgate in 1741, allowed inquisitive ladies to turn the captain into a 'great puppet show'. The prison was an 'open house' for visitors, subject to the disposition of the keeper, of course. This was in marked contrast to the fearful silences and solitude of the penitentiary of Smith's day, the new institutionally regulated mode of incarceration.[90] The long procession to the gallows – from Wine Street, the Exchange, Broad Street, through St John's Gate, up Christmas Street [now Steps] towards the fatal tree on St Michael's Hill, was on cobbled paths with 'beau traps', loose stones that spurted filthy water on white stockings. It was not a route blessed with modern MacAdam or tarmac, Smith noted. And the crowded streets underscored the public fascination with hangings, and indeed, the possibility of rescue attempts from the rapscallion colliers of Kingswood.[91] Public hangings were still around in surgeon Smith's time, but the last condemned felon to be processed through the streets to St Michael's Hill was the forger, William Carter, in 1816. After that, Bristol's executions took place on top of the entrance gates to the New Gaol on Cumberland Road.[92] The first of these was the hanging of John Horwood, allegedly before a crowd of 40,000 people, although the narrow throughfares in front of the gaol and on either side of the Cut were poorly suited for public audiences.[93]

Smith's poem invited images of a more disorderly, cheek-by-jowl Georgian Bristol with its rough festive conventions, its fountains of Bristol 'milk' [sherry] and satirical poetasters; men like James Thistlethwaite, the 'Whiggish Knave of Trumps' who so lampooned his fellow citizens that he strutted around the streets with 'the butts of pistols parading from his pockets', just in case they turned nasty.[94] In the light of the Bristol riots of 1831, it could hardly be said that the city had changed dramatically in every respect; it still had a venerated tradition of crowd action and plebeian truculence. Yet, while Smith is clearly a modernist, hopeful that scientific inquiry will begin to resolve Bristol's social problems, he has an exuberant nostalgia for the Georgian city and its remembrancers: Barrett, Evans, Seyer and the Virginian planter-cum-antiquarian George Weare Braikenridge.[95] His interest in the Dineley murder becomes one of professional curiosity not of respectable revulsion or post-Reform smugness. It is driven by a passion to master, dissect and analyse the criminal body; to fashion a rudimentary criminology, a quest that had grown exponentially since the publication of Mary Shelley's *Frankenstein,* the experiments of Luigi Galvani and the pseudoscience of phrenology. This fascination with the afterlife of the corpse and its secrets, which billowed in the wake of the notorious Red Barn murder of 1827 and the cholera epidemic of 1832, made Richard Smith's quirkiness quite fashionable.[96] Consequently, the fratricide of 1741 continued to haunt Bristol through its memorabilia, its fragments of gibbet, still visible in the Bristol Archives, and its rusting iron cage. With Richard Smith, the director-general of dissection, the surgeon who bound his own notes in the tanned skin of one of the murderers he dissected, there is a wonderment about the whole affair that never dissolves into melodrama or moral admonition.

> And so will we look around, and take some breath,
> And moralize 'a wee bit' – not on death,
> But on the changes, upon men and things,
> That FATHER TIME inevitably brings

The Fratricide after Smith

Joseph Leech, the eccentric editor of the *Bristol Times and Mirror* and an energetic collector of Bristol ephemera, did his best to reinstate the story in local memory some twenty years after Smith's death. Although the murder and trial had featured in two editions of JKR Wreford's *Curiosities of Bristol* in 1854, Leech maintained his interest was rekindled in 1862 because 'a bundle of pamphlets all written at the time of the occurrence…fell into my hands'. Convinced that few people would recall much about the case beyond a hazy recollection of Smith's briefly popular verse, he penned a lengthy narrative of his own for the paper, loosely based on a digest of the pamphlet and broadside literature. Leech embellished the 'curious' and 'incredible particulars' of 'an extraordinary fratricide, which is another notable proof that truth may be far stranger than fiction', with a few colourful additions of his own. Mary Lawfords' house at Stapleton, inherited by Dineley on their marriage, was an 'old English mansion, picturesque with its gables and old terrace walk', while Dineley was 'dissipated and somewhat eccentric…well known in the streets and coffee houses of Bristol,' where he was considered 'a wicked old rake'.[97]

Equally colourful was a version of the story spun by the minor Victorian novelist, poet and art historian, Walter Thornbury in 1870, first in the periodical, *Belgravia* as 'The Missing Baronet' and then as 'A Real Romance', in *Cassell's Family Magazine*. Thornbury's text, set out in narrative form, adapted phrases taken from contemporary pamphlets and reproduced them as direct speech between the protagonists without straying too far from the trial transcript:

> 'Give me leave, Sir John', said the friendly lawyer Jarrit Smith, pleased at the reconciliation he had effected, 'to drink love and friendship'. 'Aye, with all my heart', agreed Sir John, 'I don't drink wine; nothing but water. Notwithstanding; I wish love and friendship'. Captain Goodere filled a bumper…[98]

A few months later, when the story was picked up by *Alden's Monthly Illustrated Magazine*, fresh license was taken and key scenes breathlessly dramatised. At Dineley's kidnapping, for example,

> A heroine of humble life alone has courage to interfere. 'Are ye men, and stand thus tamely by to witness the butchery of one brother by another? she cries; and with upraised arms, fiercely rushes on the band of miscreants, her child following, clinging to her leader's skirts. The populace take fire. Stones and brickbats begin to fly. Not a moment is to be lost…

Dineley is bundled into the boat and rowed away 'amidst a volley of missiles and curses from those who pursue them to the river's brink'.[99] A less excitable account appeared in the *English Illustrated Magazine* as 'A Famous Fratricide' in 1899, written by the Tudor historian and former editor of the Spanish state papers at the Public Record Office, Major Martin AS Hume. Like some other nineteenth-century retellings of the story, Hume's narrative skips the contextual details of the family feud that brought the murder about and presents Dineley as an eccentric old bachelor, teetotal and largely blameless, while the Captain is 'a callous criminal to the last'.[100]

Mary Mitford, too, was captivated, not just by the bare facts of the case but by the sweeping Romance of the plot and the realism of the dialogue as it was captured in contemporary squibs and the trial transcript. For 'dramatic effect, of incident and of situation which belong properly to romance', she considered, the Goodere story was unparalleled. 'I know none more striking, from the near connexion of the principal characters, the strangeness of the scene, the boldness of the crime, and its most providential discovery'. Once the cooper's 'good wife' had taken the stand and 'followed her husband's evidence in every point with equal clearness and directness', marvelled Mitford, 'witness after witness followed with terrible repetition; a power of simple, honest truth that nothing could shake'.[101] Certainly, few murders of the mid-1740s left such a rich and poignant literary trail to posterity, though for dramatic reconstructions we have to wait until the twentieth century.

In 1933, the radio producer Cyril Wood rediscovered the Goodere story and dramatised one of the trial transcripts with an all-Bristolian cast for BBC radio's Western Region. Judging it 'one of the most famous of all West Country trials', the *Western Daily Press* confided that the production would be 'historically accurate…as far as dramatic considerations allow', but 'the treatment given to certain incidents will designedly be non-realistic', which essentially meant it took liberties with the text. Nevertheless, the programme was eagerly anticipated, for once shorn of its 'drier legal aspects' there would be 'plenty of material for a thrilling play for it has all the elements of a first-class drama'. It was repeated the following year, but judging from the BBC Year-Book, Wood's production proved rather less popular than *The Fall of the House of Usher*, also broadcast that year. Poe's story possessed 'weird and macabre' qualities unmatched by the courtroom exchanges of the Goodere case, in which neither the guilt of the defendant nor the inevitable outcome was ever in question. As one critic put it, 'the constant fading in and out of witness after witness has a fussy if not definitely irritating effect'. In fact, he was surprised the BBC 'thought it worthy of reviving'.[102]

The Dineley murder and Victorian melodrama

The Dineley murder did possess aspects that might have informed a Gothic horror story of the kind Poe would have enjoyed. Dineley was strangled in a small, confined, lugubrious site. The purser's cabin approximated a dungeon in a Gothic castle, a place where hired assassins carried out a dark deed. Dineley's ghost haunted Burhope house, and there was something uncannily talismanic about Mahony's gibbet, even if it was inaccessibly situated at the Swash. Moreover, Dineley's death and imperfect will – he imagined he could ignore his obligations to his wife, whose second husband swooped up the inheritance – set the scene for the fall of the House of Dineley-Goodere. A baronetage on its way to extinction through hate, folly, and insanity was a story that might have appealed to Edgar Allen Poe. Indeed, the Victorian actor, Henry Brodribb Irving, tried to frame his narrative of the story in this manner.[103]

Yet the Dineley story arguably lacked the frisson of a good Victorian murder mystery. It was less adaptable to dramatic representation than the patricide of Mary Blandy, which combined intrigue, lust, gallantry, and insidious murder by poison with the vulnerabilities of well-bred daughters in the genteel marriage market, a theme later exploited by Jane Austen and modern-day scriptwriters ad nauseam.[104] The Dineley-Goodere conflict did not have this kind of traction, even though there was a marital mismatch that generated conspicuous brutality and litigation. It also lacked the air of mystery that surrounded the Blandy affair. Was Mary duped into administering poison to her father by some Svengali-like lieutenant? Was the forensic evidence offered by Dr Anthony Addington, a first in murder cases, satisfactory? These questions continue to intrigue.[105]

Perhaps one other reason why the Dineley-Goodere story lacked broad appeal in the nineteenth century was that while it was a brutal murder, it was insufficiently sanguinary for vulgar Victorian taste. Although Sir John was said to have vomited blood as he was slowly strangled, no one cut his throat. The Ruscombe murders of 1764, where the mistress of the house and her servant had their throats slashed in the broad light of day, had an equally long afterlife, especially since the robber-assassins were never discovered. Despite the fact that this Bristolian story was contextually thin compared to Dineley – it looks like a burglary that turned brutal once the robbers had been detected – it struck a chord. Thomas De Quincey facetiously commended it for its 'originality of design, or boldness or breadth of style.' It was the sort of story that appealed to 'the mob of newspaper readers' who were 'pleased with anything, provided it is bloody enough.'[106] For the same reasons William Makepeace Thackeray toyed with the Catherine Hayes case, transforming it into a burlesque of eighteenth-century depravity.[107] Thackeray tinkered with the theatricality of the story, fully aware of the plebeian public's taste for Shakespeare's bloodier plays, such as *Titus Andronicus*, whose pie-eating scene anticipated Sweeney Todd. Costermongers even told Henry Mayhew they would like Hamlet if it was 'confined to the ghost scenes, and the funeral, and the killing off at the last.' As for *Macbeth*, it would be better liked 'if it was only the witches and the fighting.'[108]

If the Dineley story lacked the spectacle of a gory murder, it also lacked the gruesome mystery of other tales that appealed to popular Victorian taste, tales of the misfortunes of travellers who mysteriously disappear such as the

Bloody Innkeeper of Gloucestershire (1675) or the murder of Sarah Walker by a Kildare innkeeper (1740) who served up the bodies of witless wayfarers as pies for future customers.[109] The Dineley story veered too much towards the social pathology of a newly mobile gentry family. It wasn't quite the stuff of nineteenth-century melodrama. It didn't zone in on the anonymity and social danger of urban crime that undergirded many Victorian murder tales and informed one of the most celebrated, unresolved murder cases in nineteenth-century New York; that of the cigar girl, Mary Rogers, whose body was found drifting in the Hudson at Hoboken, New Jersey. This case caught the attention of Edgar Allen Poe.[110]

One reason why the Dineley murder survived into the Victorian era was because of Samuel Foote's intimate relationship to the case, adding spice to this colourful and witty actor's biography.[111] Another was that middle-class literati found it an ingenious story. Mary Mitford would talk of the boldness of the crime, Leslie Stephen its 'ghastly picturesqueness.' 'The captain was deservedly hanged,' Stephen maintained, 'bequeathing to us that ghastly Rembrandt-like picture of the white hand seen through the crevice by the trembling cooper on the throat of the murdered man.' It was a sublimity that De Quincey would have understood.[112]

Notes

Chapter One: The Chequered Fortunes of the House of Dineley-Goodere

1 Charles Knight, 'Sir John Dinley', *Penny Magazine*, 10 (11 Sept. 1841), 356.
2 *Reading Mercury*, 24 May 1802; *Ipswich Journal*, 21 August 1802.
3 On the mother's death, see *Newcastle Courant*, 29 August 1741; *Derby Mercury*, 3 Sept. 1741.
4 TNA, E112/2042, 198, Exchequer, Worcestershire, 1776.
5 His second uncle by marriage, Samuel Foote, was at one time the mayor of Truro. Charles Dineley-Goodere was mayor of Evesham in 1733 and 1734. The spelling of Goodere and Dineley is erratic. Alternatives include Goodyer, Goodier, Dinley, Dinely.
6 We say the West-Country branch because older branches of the Goodere family, which featured Middlesex JPs, London aldermen and privy councillors, were based in Monken Hadley, Middlesex and Polesworth, Warwickshire. See Frederick Charles Cass, *Monken Hadley* (Westminster 1880), 139-54. Its estates were in disarray by 1640, but employment in the East India Company seems to have revived two branches, one in Herefordshire and the other in Essex.
7 Sir William Foster, *The English Factories in India, 1646-1650* (Oxford, 1914), 295; Foster, *English Factories 1661-1664* (Oxford, 1923), 94, 96, 100, 104, 186, 213, 303, 315.
8 Ramkrishna Mukherjee, *The Rise and Fall of the East India Company* (New York and London, 1973), 93-109, 224-6; Tirthankar Roy, *The East India Company. The World's Most Powerful Corporation* (New Delhi, 2012), 77-80.
9 PJ Marshall, 'British Society in India under the East India Company,' *Modern Asian Studies*, 31/1 (1997), 92-4.
10 John Wells Wilkinson, *The Life and Works of Samuel Foote*, 5 vols (typescript, 1936), 1:49-52, located in the Huntington Library, San Marino, CA. [HM 19996]; John Duncombe & W.H. Cooke, *Collections towards the History and Antiquities of the County of Hereford*, 3 vols. (London, 1802-1882), 2:173-4. See also the biographies of Thomas Prise and Edward Goodere in the *historyofparliamentonline.org* for the House of Commons, 1660-1690 [Prise], and 1690-1714, [Goodere].
11 TNA, C 11/5/22. Samuel Foote v. Edward Goodere, 1714. This document also states that John Goodere's will of 26 August 1696 left the majority of his estate to another John, presumably his first-born son. He must have died, leaving Edward the main beneficiary.
12 She married Theophilus Child, a wealthy London haberdasher. Their son John became president of Bombay in 1682. He was awarded a baronetcy in 1687 and was known for enforcing the East India monopoly against private traders. See IB Watson, 'Sir John Child, baronet, 1637/8-1690' Oxford DNB.
13 Daughter Elizabeth married Charles Somerset of Canon Pyon, Herefordshire, 3rd son of Lord John Somerset. For Pennington, see David Lemmings, 'Spencer Cowper, 1670-1728', Oxford DNB. For Elizabeth, see Treadway Russell Nash, *Collections for the history of Worcestershire*, 2 vols. (London, 1781-2), 1:272.
14 *Genuine and Authentick History of the Life and Character of Samuel Goodere Esq* (London, 1741), 5.
15 GE Cockayne, *Complete Baronetage. Creations 1707-1800* (Exeter, 1906), 5:5-6.
16 TNA, E 112/2042, 193, a schedule of the land is listed here.
17 On Sir Edward Goodere's political career, see the informative minibiography of Stuart Handley, 'Sir Edward Goodere, 1657-1739', in *The History of Parliament. The House of Commons, 1690-1715* ed. Eveline Cruickshank and David Hayden, obtainable through www.historyofparliamentonline.org.
18 William Retlaw Williams, *The Parliamentary History of the County of Hereford* (Brecknock, 1896), 60.
19 'Parishes: Hanley Castle', in *A History of the County of Worcester*, eds. William Page and J W Willis-Bund (London, 1924), 4: 89-101; British History Online, http://www.british-history.ac.uk/vch/worcs/vol4/pp89-101 [accessed 7 October 2019]; Samuel Foote, *(Genuine) Memoirs of the Life and Death of Sir John Dineley Goodere* (London, 1741), 5; *Genuine and Authentick History*, 9.
20 TNA, PROB 11/506/203, 4 February 1709.
21 TNA, C 11/407/6, C11/259/11, C 11/5/22, C 11/1734/32.
22 TNA, C11/1382/18, C 11/407/5, C11/803/9; C 33/381, p. 363, 23 May 1744. Eleanor Foote won her suit for her share of the personal estate of Sir Edward Dineley and was awarded back interest of 6 per cent. It took 39 years in Chancery. Eleanor settled for £4456 and 4 per cent interest on the principal. £1000 plus interest went to Samuel Foote.
23 Anon., *Aristophanes, being a classic collection of Attic wit* (London, 1778), xxxix, 41. Eleanor Foote was in King's Bench for debt and wrote to son Sam for help. 'Dear Sam, I am in prison'. Answer: 'Dear Mother, so am I.'
24 *Remarkable trials and interesting memoirs of the most noted criminals...1740 to 1764*, 2 vols. (London, 1765) 1:65. This rather inaccurate account suggests John was the fourth son, but our reconstruction of the family tree indicates he was the third.

25 Foote, *Memoirs of Sir John Dineley*, 4-5; *Genuine and Authentick History*, 7.
26 *Post-Man*, 30 June-3 July 1716.
27 James Sharpe, *Instruments of Darkness. Witchcraft in Early Modern England* (Philadelphia, 1997), 138, 218-9.
28 *Ipswich Journal*, 20 July 1776; Sharpe, *Instruments of Darkness*, 282.
29 Lawrence Stone, *Uncertain Unions & Broken Lives. Marriage and Divorce in England 1660-1857* (Oxford, 1995), 353, citing the Panshanger MSS D/EP/F154 ff. 60-64v; Norma Landau, *The Justices of the Peace, 1679-1760* (Berkeley & Los Angeles, 1984), 90-1.
30 The mortgages were held by Henry Parsons and Lawford Cole, both Bristol investors. See TNA, C12/1810/20.
31 TNA, C11/1497/13; see also JH Lords 25 (1736-41), 378, where the estate is valued at £20,000.
32 TNA, C11/2554/11.
33 TNA, PROB 11/506/203, see 20n above.
34 See the letter to Miss Bubb published by John Latimer, *Annals of Bristol*, 3 vols. (Bristol, 1887-1903), 2:232. On Mary's 'ruby countenance', see *The cabinet of true Attic wit* (London 1783), 81-2.
35 Wilkinson, *Foote*, 3:649-654; Bristol Reference Library [B10146], *A Letter from Mrs Mary Dinely Goodere to John her Husband* (1730), 2. The latter is bound with *The Trials of Samuel Goodere, Esquire* (1741) in the Braikenridge Collection.
36 Lambeth Palace, Process Book of the Court of Arches, D 601, Dineley v Dineley, (1732) Case no. 2771, 31-2, 154-5; JH Lords 25 (1736-41), 377; Stone, *Uncertain Union & Broken Lives*, 354-5.
37 *Letter from Mrs Mary Dinely*, 3.
38 LPCA, D 601, 35-8, 77-82.
39 Sarah Chapone, *The hardships of the English laws* (Dublin 1735), 50; *A Letter from Mrs Mary Dinely Goodere*, 3.
40 LPCA, D 601, 136-8, 159-60, 190. Mother Redcap was the name given to promiscuous ale-house wives or landladies. See George Cruikshank's print of 1820, BM, 1862,1217.407, 'The Mother Red Cap public house, in opposition to the King's Head.'
41 JH Lords 25 (1736-41), 377; BM, Add Ms. 36,153 ff. 323 et seq.
42 JH Lords 25 (1736-41), 376; Wilkinson, *Foote*, 3:649-54; *A Letter from Mrs Mary Dinely Goodere*, 2.
43 LPCA, D 601:113-4, 184-5, 261.
44 Mary's personal property was subject to her husband's administration, although he could not sell any portion of it without her consent.
45 LPCA, D 601: 42-5, 190-196; Stone, *Uncertain Union & Broken Lives*, 362-3.
46 TNA, C33/357, 83.
47 Wilkinson, *Foote*, 3:349-54; *A Letter from Mrs Mary Dinely Goodere*, 1-2.
48 *Fog's Weekly Journal*, 7 November 1730.
49 TNA, C33/357, 87-8.
50 TNA, C33/357, 141, 150, C33/259, 122.
51 TNA, C 11/1324/25; Stone, *Uncertain Unions & Broken Lives*, 366.
52 LPCA, D 601: 101-11, 179-83, 256-60. Ann Duncox's testimony before the Lords was slightly different. She then implied the sexual activity happened in the morning, when Mary Dineley and Sir Robert Jason were alone in the room. See JH Lords, 25 (1736-41), 377. See also Stone, *Uncertain Union & Broken Lives*, 361.
53 TNA, SP 36/39/3 f.75, December 1736; *The Bristol Fratricide*, (London, 1741), 29-30; JH Lords 25 (1736-41), 386-7.
54 *Gentleman's Magazine* (May, 1732), 772; *Daily Post*, 12 May 1732.
55 Stone, *Uncertain Union & Broken Lives*, 367.
56 JH Lords, 25:387.
57 *Eng. Rep.* 93: 1072, Fowles v. Sir John Dineley; Isaac Espinasse, *A digest of the law of actions and trials at nisi prius.* (Dublin, 1794), 123; *A digest of adjudged cases in the Court of King's Bench* (London, 1775), 220. On the first suit over Mary's debts, brought to Common Pleas in February 1737, see *New York Gazette*, 20 June 1737.
58 BL, Add Ms 36,153, ff. 323-329v.
59 JH Lords, 25: 386-7.
60 BL, Add Ms 36,153 ff. 323 et seq.
61 JH Lords, 25:372, 377, 386-7, 411. Sir John Dineley was not ordered to pay Mary's costs, simply the expenses of her witnesses. Cf. Stone, *Uncertain Unions and Broken Lives*, 369.
62 TNA, SP 36/39/3 f.75, Dec 1736; C 33/357, 141.
63 *London Evening Post*, 31 March -3 April 1739; *Common Sense* 7 April 1739; *Boston Gazette*, 28 May 1739.
64 *Daily Courant*, 17 December 1702.
65 Foote, *Memoirs of Sir John Dineley*, 6-7.
66 Shallops are light open boats.

67 See entry in Oxford DNB and TNA, Adm 1/5271, 24 December 1719. The dismissal is not mentioned in John Charnock, *Biographia navalis*, 6 vols. (London, 1794), 4:241-8. Captain Johnston's letters have survived, but there is only one relating to the siege of San Sebastian and the attack on neighbouring ports, and no mention of Lieutenant Goodere. TNA, Adm 1/1982 (Robert Johnson).
68 Foote, *Memoirs of Sir John Dineley*, 7-9; Peter J. Neville Havins, *Portrait of Worcestershire* (London, 1974), 30. Goodere and Dineley are listed as joint-mayors in 1733, with John continuing as mayor in 1734. See William Tindal, *The history and antiquities of the abbey and borough of Evesham* (Evesham, 1794), 332.
69 *London Evening Post*, 13-15 Nov. 1733.
70 Samuel's first wife, Jane Nicholas, died in 1721. A few years later he married Elizabeth Watts, the widow of James Watts of Monmouth. Her father-in-law had been the archdeacon of Llandaff.
71 *London Gazette*, 15-19 June 1736; *Genuine and Authentick History*, 11-12.
72 On the close relationship between Sir Edward Goodere and Samuel, see Charnock, *Biographia navalis*, 4:245n. For the quote, Wilkinson, *Foote*, 3:649-54 and *A Letter from Mrs Mary Dinely Goodere*, 3.
73 Foote, *Memoirs of Sir John Dineley*, 11.
74 Charnock, *Biographia navalis*, 4: 246n.
75 TNA, PROB 11/695/260, Will of Edward Dinely, Esquire, of Southwark, 6 Jan 1738/9.
76 TNA, E 122/2042/198.
77 Sir John's intention to remarry is mentioned in *Remarkable Trials*, 1:66-7.
78 TNA, E 112/2042/198; E133/58/38.
79 TNA, E112/2042/198.
80 TNA, C 21/2099/23.
81 TNA, C12/1867/10, C12/1810/19, C11/2554/11. For Sir John Dineley's will, dated 27 Feb. 1741, see TNA, PROB 11/707/413.
82 TNA, C11/801/20, 21. C12/1810/20, C12/110/17.
83 TNA, C11/407/6, 1715.
84 *Daily Gazetteer*, 21 May 1741.
85 *Common Sense*, 5 December 1741, reports that Knowles captured a Spanish vessel sailing to Havana worth [presumably with cargo] £200,000.
86 TNA, C11/870, C11/803 and C12/77.
87 Nash *Worcestershire*, 2: 272-3; Wilkinson, *Foote*, 2:871.
88 TNA, C 11/570/15, 19 March 1747.
89 He was James Peachey, who had unsuccessfully contested Hereford in 1754. He died in 1771, one year after the purchase. For Peachey, see www.historyofparliamentonline.org in the 1754-1790 Commons profile.
90 Stone, *Uncertain Unions & Broken Lives*, 378-9; Fitzgerald, *Foote*, 28.
91 Stone, *Uncertain Unions & Broken Lives*, 369.
92 Latimer, *Annals of Bristol*, 2:233-4; it seems Mary fought off the original attempt to discover whether there was a second son. See *Report of cases argued and determined in the High Court of Chancery in the time of Lord Chancellor Hardwicke*, 3 vols. (London 1765-8), 2: 394.
93 Ibid, 2:232.
94 Foote, *Memoirs of Sir John Dineley*, 14.

Chapter Two: Prequel: Bristol at the time of Dineley's Murder

1 For Fytche's reports to the Admiralty, see Nicholas Rogers (ed.), *Manning the Royal Navy in Bristol: Liberty, Impressment and the State, 1739-1815* (Bristol Record Society, Vol. 66, 2014), 3-4.
2 *Weekly Miscellany*, 18 October, 1740.
3 *The Present State of Great Britain and Ireland, in Three Parts* (London, 1738), 73. In a little over two decades of continuous growth, the population within the city liberties had increased from about 23,000 in 1712 to 30,000 in 1735; John Latimer, *Annals of Bristol*, 2:194.
4 Kenneth Morgan, 'Bristol and the Atlantic Trade in the Eighteenth Century', *English Historical Review*, 107/424 (1992), 629.
5 BA, M/BCC/CCP/2/1 Common Council Minute Book 1736-1747, entry dated 13 December 1738; *London Daily Post* 7 July 1738.
6 Steve Poole and Nicholas Rogers, *Bristol From Below: Law, Authority and Protest in a Georgian City* (Woodbridge, 2017), 7.
7 Alexander Pope, *Correspondence*, ed. George Sherburn, 5 vols. (Oxford, 1956), 4: 204-5; *The Complete English Traveller* (1772), 44.
8 AS Catcott, *The Antiquity and Honourableness of the Practice of Merchandize: A Sermon Preached Before the Worshipful Society of Merchants of the City of Bristol* (Bristol, 1744). See also the arguments presented in Andrew Hooke, *Bristollia, or Memoirs of the City of Bristol* (Bristol 1748).
9 BA, 04356/11, based on a review of the apprentice entries, 1735-1740.

10. *A Geometrical Plan of the City and Suburbs of Bristol, Surveyed by John Roque, Land Surveyor* (1750 edition); Nigel Baker, Jonathan Brett and Robert Jones, *Bristol: An Archaeological Assessment, A Worshipful Town and Famous City* (Oxford, 2018), 67; Roger H. Leech, *The Town House in Medieval an Early Modern Bristol* (Swindon, 2014), 44-5; John Varley, 'John Rocque: Engraver, Surveyor, Cartographer and Map Seller', *Imago Mundi*, 5 (1948), 83-91.
11. Ronald H. Quilici, 'Turmoil in a city and an empire: Bristol's factions 1700-1770', PhD, University of New Hampshire (1976), 118-9. The so-called War of Jenkins' Ear between Britain and Spain following tit for tat plundering by privateers in the Caribbean and elsewhere quickly morphed into a wider European conflict as the War of Austrian Succession in 1740. From a British perspective this meant a return to war with France on a number of fronts.
12. *The Craftsman* 7 September 1734; *Daily Journal* 10 September 1734; *London Journal* 14 September 1734.
13. *Daily Post,* 18 July 1738.
14. TNA, SP 36/48, Jefferies to the Duke of Newcastle, 30 June 1739. One of those inconvenienced by the embargo was the poet Richard Savage, lately arrived from London and trying to catch a boat to Swansea. Savage returned to Bristol a few years later, was incarcerated in Newgate for debt, and spent his last days there composing a rambling and hostile panegyric about the city before succumbing to fever. He died in his cell in 1743. Richard Savage, *London and Bristol Compar'd: A Satire Written in Newgate, Bristol* (second edition, London, 1744); Samuel Johnson, *The Poetical Works of Richard Savage, with a Life of the Author* (London, 1777), 48.
15. *Derby Mercury* 28 June, 5 July, 2 August 1739; *Newcastle Courant* 23 February 1739. See also Poole and Rogers, *Bristol from Below*, 218-9.
16. William Hunt, *Historic Towns: Bristol* (London, 1887), 173.
17. *Ipswich Journal* 21 July, 18 August 1739; *Derby Mercury* 22 November 1739. For Bristol shipping losses to Spanish privateers see for example, *Newcastle Courant* 5, 26 July 1740.
18. Evidence derived from TNA, HCA 26/5-12, 30-32; E 190/1195/3, E 190/1214/3, E 190/1215/4; David Richardson, *Bristol, Africa and the Eighteenth-Century Slave Trade to America, volume 2: The Years of Ascendancy, 1730-1745* (Bristol: Bristol Record Society, vol. 39, 1987).
19. *Common Sense,* 23 July 1738.
20. *Sherborne Mercury,* 8 November 1737.
21. For Taylor, see TNA, SP36/11/2, Officers of Lord Molesworth's regiment to Lord Molesworth, 4 May 1729; SP36/14/2, petition of William Taylor, August 1729; SP36/15/1, Lord Molesworth to Sec of State, 3 September 1729; SP36/15/1 Eskersall to (?) 5 September 1729.
22. TNA, SP 36/46, David Reid to Earl of Scarborough, 6 September 1738; David Reid to Duke of Montague, 20 September 1738; petition of David Reid, n.d.
23. *Gloucester Journal,* 28 November 1738.
24. *Sherborne Mercury,* 25 May 1740 & 8 July 1740; *Daily Post,* 19 June 1739.
25. *The New Bristol Guide, Containing its Antiquities Deduced from the Best Authorities,* (Bristol, 1799), 78-9.
26. The *Gloucester Journal* was not unusual in this. For a detailed discussion of early eighteenth-century newspapers and the reporting of crime, see Esther Snell, 'Discourses of criminality in the eighteenth-century press: the presentation of crime in the Kentish Post, 1717-1768', *Continuity and Change*, 22/1 (2007), 13-47.
27. *Gloucester Journal*, 3 June 1723, 24 September 1734, 8 October 1728, 22 November 1737.
28. George Lamoine (ed.), *Bristol Gaol Delivery Fiats 1741-1799* (Bristol Record Society, Vol 40, 1989), ix-xv.
29. *Unparallel'd Cruelty; or the Tryal of Captain Jeane, of Bristol, who was Convicted at the Old Bailey for the Murder of his Cabbin-boy* (London, 1726). Newth's story is told in some detail in *The Political State of Great Britain*, 50 (July-December 1735), 361-5.
30. *London Evening Post,* 8 February 1733. On Rice Harris, see TNA, Adm 1/3673 ff. 175-80; SP 36/29/2, ff. 109-11.
31. *The Tryals of the Seven Pyrates who murdered Capt. Edward Bryan* (Bristol, 1738).
32. *The Cruel Mistress, Being the Genuine Trial of Elizabeth Branch and her own Daughter for the Murder of Jane Butterworth* (London 1740).
33. *Daily Gazetteer*, 28 February, 9 May, 5 September 1738; *Daily Post,* 16 May 1738; Poole and Rogers, *Bristol from Below*, 163-171.
34. *The Colliers of Kings-wood in an Uproar* (Bristol, 1738); *London Evening Post*, 14 October 1738; *London Daily Post*, 17 October 1738; *Daily Gazetteer*, 17 October 1738; TNA SP 36/46, Information of John Abbot, 9 October 1738. To be forced to 'ride the cow-tang' was to be shamed and ridiculed through public exposure, placed on a pole and carried through the streets to a raucous 'musical' accompaniment on horns, drums and other simple instruments.
35. TNA, SP 36/46, William Jefferies to the Duke of Newcastle, 9 and 14 October 1738.
36. *Daily Post*, 7 November 1738; *Daily Gazetteer*, 28 November 1738. The Corporation accounts reveal that £51 was recovered from arrested colliers to compensate property owners for losses sustained during the riots; see Latimer, *Annals of Bristol*, 2:212.
37. *Daily Gazetteer*, 23 January 1739.

38 BA, JQS/D/9 Docket book 1737-1741.
39 Poole and Rogers, *Bristol From Below*, 194-5.
40 *London Evening Post* 23 April 1741.
41 George Randolph, *An Enquiry into the Medicinal Virtues of Bristol Water and the Indications of Cure which it Answers* (Oxford, 1745).
42 Poole and Rogers, *Bristol from Below*, 115, 158-60.
43 *London Evening Post*, 11 November 1738; Latimer, *Annals of Bristol*, 2: 212-4.
44 *The New Bristol Guide*, 80.
45 John Wood, *A Description of the Exchange of Bristol Wherein the Ceremony of Laying the First Stone of the Structure Together with the Opening of the Building for Publick Use is Particularly Recited.* (Bath 1743). The expense incurred by the Corporation in purchasing and demolishing buildings to clear the site was estimated at £20,000. See, *The Bath and Bristol Guide or Tradesman and Traveller's Pocket Companion* (Bath 1753), 34.
46 Madge Dresser, *Slavery Obscured: The Social History of the Slave Trade in an English Provincial Port* (London, 2016), 122; HGM Leighton, 'Country Houses Acquired with Bristol Wealth', *Transactions of the Bristol and Gloucestershire Archaeological Society*,123 (2005), 11-13; 'Richard Combe' in L. Namier and J. Brooke, The History of Parliament: The House of Commons 1754-1790 (London, 1964); *Stamford Mercury* 1 November 1739. Combe fought Edward Southwell for the parliamentary seat vacated by the death of Thomas Coster in 1739.
47 John Wood, *A Description of the Exchange.*

Chapter Three: Murder
1 On the normative reciprocities between landed siblings, see Bernard Capp, *The Ties That Bind: Siblings, Family and Society in Early Modern England* (Oxford, 2018), 103-6.
2 *The Trials of Samuel Goodere, Esq, Matthew Mahony and Charles White for the murder of Sir John Dineley Goodere, Baronet* (London, 1741), 34; *Some account of the trial of Samuel Goodere Esq.* (Boston, 1741), 17.
3 *The Tryals of Capt. Samuel Goodere, Matthew Mahony and Charles White* (Bristol 1741), 47. The five were Charles Bryan, Edward McDaniel, William Hammond, George Comerford, and John McGreary. BA, AC/JS/50/47is. The first three were subsequently indicted for capturing and assaulting Dineley. Some accounts suggest the privateers received as little as a guinea. See *Remarkable Trials*, 1:59.
4 BA, AC/JS/50/42k, deposition of Robert Gibson, apothecary, Redcliff Street; on the alleged financial offer, see *The Bristol Fratricide: Being an Exact and Impartial Narrative of the Horrid and Dreadful Catastrophe of Sir John Dineley Goodere, Bart.* (London, 1741), 10.
5 *Trials*, 14; BA, AC/JS/50/42a.
6 Ibid, 15.
7 *Bristol Fratricide*, 19; *Remarkable Trials and Interesting Memoirs of the most noted Criminals,* 2 vols. (London, 1765) 1:56. Hobbs is said to have thought it odd that tea was ordered, 'it being very uncommon Drink for Jack Tars.' At the trial, Jarrit Smith remarked that he saw a sailor following Sir John Dineley with a bottle in hand. See *Trials*, 10.
8 Percy Fitzgerald, *Samuel Foote. A Biography* (London, 1910), 21; AC/JS/50/38, letter marked 'Sunday morning'.
9 Charnock, *Biographia navalis,* 4:245n. Elizabeth brought at least two medium-sized farms near Llanvetherine into the marriage. See TNA, PROB 11/719/505.
10 See Capp, *Ties That Bind,* 103-6.
11 Samuel left everything to his wife, Elizabeth. She, in turn, paid off his debts before devising her estate to cousin Charles Floyer in trust for four of her children. Curiously the eldest of the twin sons, Edward, is not mentioned in either her or Samuel's will. He died insane in 1761. See TNA, PROB 11/719/505 and PROB 11/719/506.
12 *Trials*, 9.
13 Ibid, 6; *The Trials of Samuel Goodere Esquire*, in *A complete collection of state trials*, 6 vols. (London, 1742), 6:802. [henceforth ST]; BA, AC/JS/50/47i.
14 *Trials*, 5, ST 6:807. BA, AC/JS/50/42l.
15 See the case against the three privateers, BA, AC/JS/50/48. See also *Some account of the trial of Samuel Goodere, Esq.* (Boston, 1741), p. 7, the testimony of Charles Bryant. See also Fitzgerald, *Foote,* 21.
16 *Trials,* 18, evidence of Thomas Charmbury.
17 BA, AC/JS/50/42l. the deposition of Tom Williams reveals where Dineley was taken, and perhaps explains why the journey to the boat was an arduous and frustrating one for Captain Goodere, who at one point urged the gang to 'make pace.'
18 *Trials*, 5.
19 TNA, Adm 36/3140, muster books of the *Ruby*, 1739-1741.
20 TNA, Adm 1/1828 (Samuel Goodere), 22 Dec. 1740; Adm 1780 (Robert Fytche), 3 Sept. 1740. See also Rogers ed. *Manning the Royal Navy in Bristol*, 3-5.

21 *Genuine and Authentick History* , 20.
22 On the hue and cry, see Robert Shoemaker, *The London Mob. Violence and Disorder in Eighteenth-Century England* (London and New York, 2004), 28-30.
23 *Trials,* 16-17. BA, AC/JS/50/42i.
24 See press warrant in TNA, Adm 1/1784 (John Fergusson) 19 July 1756. See also Rogers, *Manning the Royal Navy in Bristol,* xii.
25 *Trials,* 17; ST 6:808; See also H. L. Stephen, ed., *State Trials. Social and Political,* 4 vols. (London, 1899), 2:261.
26 *Trials,* 17, 19.
27 BA, AC/JS/50/42b.
28 *Trials,* 6, 19. See also the deposition of William Dupree and John Ridgeway, a gingerbread baker, BA AC/JS/50/42c.
29 BA, AC/JS/50/47i.
30 The writ is de homine replegiando, cited in the trials. See *Some account of the trial of Samuel Goodere Esq.,* (Boston 1741), 2.
31 *Trials,* 11. Jarrit Smith twice made enquiries whether Sir John Dineley returned to his lodgings, once in the evening and again the following morning. BA, AC/JS/50/47i. Ian Kelly suggests Smith was loath to interfere in this dispute. See Ian Kelly, *Mr Foote's Other Leg. Comedy, Tragedy and Murder in Georgian London* (London, 2013), 50.
32 *Trials,* 6. In bold letters in ST 6:799, see also 6:809 for the conversation. BA, AC/JS/50/42l; In *Remarkable Trials,* 1:58, the words 'this night' are added, making the remark more ominous.
33 *Trials,* 6; *The Genuine Trial of Samuel Goodere, Esquire* (Dublin, 1741)*,* 17.
34 Charnock, *Biographia navalis,* 4:248n.
35 *Trials,* 17. On the westerlies, *Trials,* 21.
36 TNA, Adm 36/3129. 128 men entered from July-September, 1740.
37 Charnock, *Biographia navalis,* 4:247n.
38 This had been suggested on the barge, but humoral readings of mental disorder were losing favour in the professional community. See BA, AC/JS/50/42 l; *Trials,* 6; and Roy Porter, *Flesh in the Age of Reason* (London, 2003), 307.
39 Percy Fitzgerald, *Samuel Foote. A Biography* (London, 1910), 22; *Bristol Fratricide,* 27.
40 *Trials,* 32, 43. In the deposition of midshipman, Tom Williams, this address is described as his 'lodgings' but in fact Sir John had some in Peter street. BA, AC/JS/50/42l.
41 ST 6:810.
42 *London Magazine* 9 (1741), 186.
43 Such as Tom Williams, a foretop man who didn't get on well with the privateers. They resented his questioning why Sir John was to be brought on board the *Ruby,* and at one point threatened to throw him in the river. See *Trials,* 16.
44 *Some account of the trial of Samuel Goodere,* 22.
45 *The Reverend Mr Penrose's Account of the Behaviour, Confession and Last Dying Words of the four Malefactors who were executed on St Michael's Hill at Bristol…15 April 1741,* (Bristol and London, 1741), 8.
46 BA, AC/JS/50/42 k.
47 TNA, Adm 36/3140. See also *Some account of the trial of Samuel Goodere,* 10.
48 *Trials,* 50; Penrose, *Account,* 9-10.
49 Penrose, *Account,* 9-10; TNA, Adm 36/3140. *Trials,* 49, 52-4; ST 6:831; Charnock, *Biographia navalis,* 4:248n.
50 *Trials,* 27.
51 Ibid, 22.
52 *Some account of the trial of Samuel Goodere, Esq.,* 11
53 *Trials,* 24.
54 Charnock, *Biographia navalis,* 4:248n.
55 *Trials,* 7; BA, AC/JS/50/42j.
56 Ibid, 7; BA, AC/JS/50/42j.
57 *Common Sense,* 7 January 1741; BA, AC/JS/50/41.
58 *The True Effigies of Captain Goodere, Mathew Mahony & Charles White* (London, 1741?).
59 BA, AC/JS/50/49.
60 'Likely' because in their confessions, White and Mahony accused each other of strangling Dineley. The *Trials* talk of 'one of them having half throttled him [Dineley] with his hands, they put a Rope about his Neck and at length strangled him.' 7. For Mahony and White's account, *Trials,* 31, 49.
61 Ian Kelly suggests that Mrs Margaret [or Margaret-Ann] Jones was rather coy about being on the ship, although we have found no evidence of this in the trial transcripts. The captain did not apparently know Jones was married, but warrant officers were entitled to bring wives on board. See *Trials,* 21; Kelly, *Mr Foote's Other Leg,* 42-3; David Cordingly, *Heroines and Harlots. Women at sea in the age of sail* (London, 2001), 102-3.

62 *Trials,* 25; ST 6:800, 811-13.
63 Charnock, *Biographia navalis,* 4:249n.
64 *Trials,* 26; *Tryals,* 36.
65 *Trials,* 24, 47-8. BA AC/JS/50/42j.
66 Charnock, *Biographia navalis,* 4:249n.
67 ST 6:615.
68 BA, AC/JS/50/39, dated 19 January 1741.
69 *Trial,* 23; BA, AC/JS/50/47i.
70 Ibid, 20, 40.
71 Ibid, 25, 28. In some accounts this checkup was done at the insistence of Lieutenant Perry. See Stephen ed., *State Trials,* 2:266.
72 *Some Account of the Trial of Samuel Goodere,* 7; TNA, Adm 51/4324, 6 September 1740. The dating is wrong because Robert Fytche was still writing to the Admiralty on 8 September about Spanish prisoners who had small pox. See TNA, Adm 1/1780 f. 318, printed in Rogers, ed. *Manning the Royal Navy in Bristol,* 4.
73 One newspaper thought 'a considerable part' of the crew knew about the murder, but there is no hard evidence for this assertion. *London Evening Post,* 20-22 Jan 1741.
74 *Trials,* 20; ST 6:809, 812.
75 TNA, Adm 52/4324, entry for 19 and 20 Jan 1741. *Trials,* 28. Chamberlayne is cited as the sheriff for 1741-42, taking office several months after the murder. He was a common councilman from September 1740 until his death in 1752. See Alfred Beavan, *Bristol lists: municipal and miscellaneous* (Bristol, 1899), 213, 282. The suggestion that the water bailiff officiated is in *Bristol Fratricide,* 12 and in BA, AC/JS/50/42 d, the depositions of Jones, Sharp and Buchanan. Elsewhere a Mr Chamberlayne is cited.
76 ST 6: 814, 816; BA. AC/JS/50/42d; *Bristol Fratricide,* 12-13.
77 *Remarkable trials,* 1:63-4.
78 *Bristol Fratricide,* 13; Wilkinson, *Foote,* 1:285.
79 *Trials,* 28.
80 TNA, Adm 51/4324, entry 2o January 1741. The inquest jury included a distiller, a tiler, glazier, barber and wigmaker from some of the city's central parishes.
81 We located ten of the jurymen from the 1734 Bristol pollbook.
82 BA, AC/JS/50/41.
83 *Trials,* 27.
84 Ibid, 32. On James Mervin, see *Daily Gazetteer,* 30 August 1739.
85 Ibid, 20, 29.

Chapter Four: The Trial

1 *Bristol Fratricide,* 5.
2 Robert Boyle, *Love and religion demonstrated in the martyrdom of Theodora* (London, 1703), 25; Thomas Cogan, *Letters to William Wilberforce on the doctrine of hereditary depravity* (London, 1799), 64.
3 Jeremy Black, *The English Press in the Eighteenth Century* (Aldershot, 1991), 105; Kathleen Wilson, 'Empire, Trade and Popular Politics in Mid-Hanoverian Britain: The Case of Admiral Vernon', *Past and Present,* 121 (November. 1985), 74-109; Gerald Jordan and Nicholas Rogers, 'Admirals as Heroes: Patriotism and Liberty in Hanoverian England', *Journal of British Studies,* 28/3 (June, 1989), 201-24.
4 *Daily Post,* 22 January 1741; *London Evening Post,* 19-22 January 1741; *Daily Gazetteer,* 13 February 1741; *London Daily Advertiser,* 17 February 1741; *Gloucester Journal,* 27 January 1741.
5 *Bristol Fratricide,* 16, refers to a deposition taken from the apothecary handling Mahony's medical condition. The name is incorrect, it should be a Robert Gibson, not a Mr Ford, but the substance of the conversation is correct. See BA, AC/JS/50/42 k.
6 *Newcastle Courant,* 31 January 1740; also reported in the *Public Register,* 24 January 1740, and the *Derby Mercury,* 29 January 1740.
7 On the impersonality of crime news, see Charles E. Clark, *The Personal Prints. The Newspaper in Anglo-American Culture, 1665-1740* (Oxford, 1994), 51-2.
8 On the development of the coroner's inquest in making murders a matter of 'public justice' and community concern, see Krista Kesselring, *Making Murder Public. Homicide in Early Modern England* (Oxford, 2019), ch. 2.
9 *Bristol Fratricide,* 11.
10 *London Evening Post,* 5-7 February 1741; *Country Journal,* 7 February 1741. The appendix of the *Bristol Fratricide,* 'A Brief Account of the Life of the late Sir John Dineley Goodere, Bart.' appears to contain insider information. *The Genuine Trial* (Dublin, 1741) was said to have been taken down in shorthand on the orders and direction of Samuel Foote of Worcester College, Oxford, Esquire.
11 *Bristol Fratricide,* 24.

12 *Tryal,* 44; *Trial,* 36.
13 *Trial,* 36. The same issue was raised in another fratricide, involving the Kinloch brothers, 1795. See Horace Wyndham, *The Mayfair Calendar. Some Society Causes Celebres* (London, 1925), 191-2.
14 BA, AC/JS/50/47 e-f.
15 *Trials,* 9; BA, AC/JS/50/47a.
16 TNA, Adm 1/1828 (Samuel Goodere), 16 Feb. 1741; Adm 51/4324, 6 April 1741; Adm 36/3140, the general muster book of the *Ruby,* 1741.
17 Bristol's general session of oyer and terminer had the status of an assize, although no circuit judges attended it.
18 Among others: John Jane, 1726; James Lowry, 1752; David Ferguson, 1770; John Sutherland, 1809. On Admiralty executions, see Gregory Durston, *The Admiralty Sessions 1536-1834* (Cambridge, 2017), 150-60.
19 WO 4/36, 290.
20 TNA, Adm 1/1502/611, 2 February 1741 and Adm 1/1502/614, 7 February 1741.
21 Michael Dodson and John Disney, *The Life of Sir Michael Foster, Knt.* (London, 1811), 5-10.
22 *London Evening Post,* 5-7, 7-10 February 1741; *Daily Gazetteer,* 6, 7, February 1741; *Common Sense,* 14 February 1741; *Weekly Miscellany,* 14 February 1741.
23 BA, AC/JS/50/43 c.
24 *London Evening Post,* 12-14, 21-23, February 1741; *Common Sense,* 28 February 1741.
25 *Trials,* 21; ST 6:810-12.
26 *Trials,* 12-13; *Tryals,* 46. A few accounts also suggest the issue also applied to Samuel Goodere, who on the death of his brother, should have been addressed 'Sir Samuel Goodere, Bt.' not 'Samuel Goodere, Esquire.'
27 Ibid, 13.
28 *Trials,* 16. This exchange has been noted by historians as significant in the development of defence advocacy in English law. See John H. Langbein, 'The Criminal Trial Before the Lawyers', *University of Chicago Law Review,* 45/ 2 (1978), 313-4; and 'The Prosecutorial Origins of Defence Counsel in the Eighteenth Century: The Appearance of Solicitors', *The Cambridge Law Journal,* 58/ 2 (1999), 361-2.
29 *Tryals,* 37.
30 Allegedly, because the murder of Sir Edmund Bury Godfrey was essentially unresolved and he was found a long way from the scene of the crime.
31 Ibid, 24-5.
32 *Genuine Trial,* 19.
33 *Authentick Tryal,* 13.
34 Ibid, 33-4.
35 Roy Porter, *Mind-Forg'd Manacles: A History of Madness in England from the Restoration to the Regency* (Athlone, 1987), 38.
36 *Trials,* 36.
37 Nigel Walker, *Crime and Insanity in England. One: The Historical Perspective* (Edinburgh, 1968), 56-62.
38 Ibid, 59, 64.
39 Porter, *Mind-Forg'd Manacles,* 38-9.
40 Old Bailey online, t17270412-21, Thomas Nash, murder, 12 April 1727.
41 Old Bailey online, t172600711-27, William Atkinson, murder, 11 July 1726.
42 Old Bailey online, t17320114-41, Peter Noakes, murder, 14 January 1732. For the neutrality of the medical expert witness in this case see also Stephen Landsman, 'One hundred years of rectitude: medical witnesses at the Old Bailey, 1717-1817', *Law and History Review,* 16/3 (1988).
43 Old Bailey online, t17320114-9, Robert Hallam, murder, 14 January 1732; *Select trials at the Sessions-House in the Old Bailey... To which are added, genuine accounts of the lives, behaviour, confessions, and dying speeches of the most eminent convicts,* 4 vols. (London, 1742) 3, 287-303.
44 Ibid, 34-6; *Tryals,* 43; TNA, Adm 1/1828 (Goodere) 16 February 1741. Goodere asked for Lieutenant Perry, Midshipmen Robert Heathorn and Richard Wilson, John Mandrel and Hugh Driscoll. The Admiralty responded that they would allow their release once the *Ruby* returned from its current cruise.
45 Goodere challenged two candidates for the jury. Of the ten we have been able to locate, five lived in St James, including one mariner, Christopher Lilly. One juryman, William Jones, was an esquire, two were freeholders; others included a sadler, a glover, a staymaker, mason, innholder and baker. Politically they featured both Whigs and Tories.
46 Ibid, 42.
47 Ibid, 36.
48 *Trials,* 43; *Country Journal,* 7 February 1741; BA, AC/JS/50/48. The three were Charles Bryant [sometimes Bryan], Edward McDaniel, and William Hammond [Hammon].
49 *London Daily Post,* 7 April 1741. Samuel Goodere's succession to the baronetcy was never officially

recognized. In the arcane language of heraldry, his coat of arms is described as 'Gules, a fesse between two chevrons vair.'
50 *All Alive and Merry,* 27 April 1741; *London Evening Post,* 23-25 April 1741; *Daily Gazetteer,* 24 April 1741; *Daily Post,* 27 Jan 1741; *London Evening Post,* 24-27 Jan 1741.
51 BA, AC/JS/50/44.
52 *Bristol Fratricide,* 19.
53 TNA, Adm 1/1828 (Goodere), 1, 4 April 1741. On earlier solicitations, this one to Walpole, see TNA, SP 35/43/2 f 93, 18 June 1723. On Jarrit Smith's politics, see Poole and Rogers, *Bristol from Below,* ch. 5.
54 Martin J. Weiner, 'Convicted Murderers and the Victorian Press: Condemnation vs. Sympathy', *Crimes and Misdemeanours: Deviance and the Law in Historical Perspective,* 1/2 (2007), 110-125.
55 *London Evening Post,* 9-11 April 1741.
56 Samuel Foote, *Memoirs of Sir John Dineley,* 34.
57 John Penrose, 1713-1776, was the son of an Exeter tailor, who took holy orders. He was likely related to the Rev. Rumney Penrose, the rector of St Werburgh.
58 Penrose, *Account,* 12.
59 PROB 11/719/505, the will of Elizabeth Goodere, proved 6 July 1742.
60 On the differences between medieval and early modern versions of homicide, see Pieter Spierenburg, 'Long-Term Trends in Homicide: Theoretical Reflections and Dutch Evidence, Fifteenth to Twentieth Centuries', in *The Civilization of Crime. Violence in Town and Country since the Middle Ages,* eds. Eric A. Johnson & Eric H. Monkkonen (Urbana and Chicago, 1996), 64; Lawrence Stone, 'Interpersonal violence in English society, 1300-1980', *Past and Present* no. 101 (1983), 22-33.
61 *Penrose, Account,* 12.
62 Andrea McKenzie, 'God's Tribunal: Guilt, Innocence, and Execution in England, 1675-1775', *Cultural and Social History,* 3 (2006), 121-144. Foote, *Memoirs of Sir John Dineley Goodere,* 47; *All Alive and Merry,* 22 April 1741.
63 William Jackson, *New and Complete Newgate Calendar,* 6 vols. (London, 1795); 3:40.
64 *Unparallel'd Cruelty: or, The Tryal of Captain Jeane of Bristol* (London, 1726), 19.
65 R.W. Malcolmson, 'Infanticide in the Eighteenth Century', in J. S. Cockburn ed. *Crime in England 1550-1800* (London, 1977), 197; TNA, SP 35/55 f.42, 14 February 1741.
66 *Gloucester Journal,* 18 March 1723, 24 September 1734, 20 April 1736.
67 Penrose, *Account,* 10; *London Evening Post,* 23-25 April 1741; *Daily Gazetteer,* 24 April 1741; *All Alive and Merry,* 27 April 1741.
68 Penrose, *Account,* 10.
69 *Weekly Miscellany,* 28 March 1741; *London Evening Post,* 4-7 April 1741.
70 Andrea McKenzie, *Tyburn's Martyrs: Executions in England, 1675-1775* (London, 2007), 3-4; *Daily Gazeteer,* 11 March 1741.
71 For other applications, see TNA, SP 36/53 f. 78, 18 October 1740; SP 36/58/1, f.66, 29 March 1742; SP 36/59/1, f. 110, 16 September 1742.
72 *All Alive and Merry,* 22 April 1741.
73 [Richard Smith], *The Fratricide or the Murderer's Gibbet* (Bristol 1839), 22.
74 On the popularity of broadsheets at executions, see V.A.C. Gatrell, *The Hanging Tree. Execution and the English People, 1770-1868* (Oxford, 1994), 171-3.
75 Penrose, *Account,* 9.
76 *London Daily Post and General Advertiser,* 20 April 1741.
77 *Bristol Mirror,* 1 January 1842; *London Evening Post,* 18-21 April, 1741; *Daily Gazetteer,* 20, 21, April 1741.

Chapter Five: The Gibbet
1 BA 35893/36/t; *London Evening Post,* 21 April 1741. For Smith's identification of White's burial place see *Bristol Mirror,* 26 February 1842.
2 Notes and Queries, 27 September 1856, 250.
3 For contests over the bodies of condemned felons in London see Peter Linebaugh, 'The Tyburn Riot Against the Surgeons' in D. Hay, P. Linebaugh, J. Rule, E.P. Thompson and C. Winslow (eds.), *Albion's Fatal Tree: Crime and Society in Eighteenth Century England* (London, 1975), 65-119.
4 *London Evening Post,* 22 April 1738; *London Gazette,* 18 April 1738.
5 There were 24 executions ordered by the Bristol courts between 1741 and 1785. See BA, 15267, *List of Persons Executed in Bristol Since the Year 1741* (Bristol, 1821).
6 *Grub Street Journal,* 3 October 1734.
7 *Public Advertiser,* 14 September 1736.
8 *Daily Gazetteer,* 14 September 1736.
9 Elizabeth T. Hurren, *Dissecting the Criminal Corpse: Staging Post-Execution Punishment in Early Modern England* (London, 2016), 39-40, in which several cases from the 1740s are recorded. Popular antipathy to the surgeons was based partly on the part they played in the execution (not just *post*-execution) process.

According to Hurren, 'Detailed dissection cases recorded at Surgeons' Hall reveal that a considerable number of those who were executed died in the dissection venue, not on the gallows', 60.
10 *Fog's Weekly Journal,* 11 September 1736.
11 *Country Journal,* 3 May 1739.
12 TNA, SP 36/46, David Reid to the Duke of Montague, 20 September 1738.
13 Poole and Rogers, *Bristol From Below,* 57-8; *London Evening Post,* 21 April 1741.
14 George Munro Smith, *A History of the Bristol Royal Infirmary* (Bristol, 1917), 268.
15 Stone, *Uncertain Union & Broken Lives,* 377-8; Kelly, *Mr Foote's Other Leg,* 81.
16 BA, 35893/36/t; Foote, *Memoirs of Sir John Dineley Goodere,* 48; Latimer, *Annals,* 2:232; Kelly, *Mr Footes' Other Leg,* 80-81.
17 Nikita Marryat, 'People, Patients and Preparations: Post-Mortem Journeys and the Status of Human Remains in the Medical Museum of Richard Smith Junior (1772-1843) at the Bristol Infirmary', M.Phil., University of Bristol, 2019, 89-93.
18 *Tyburn Chronicle,* 3: 146. For later examples see James Caulfield, *Portraits, Memoirs and Characters of Remarkable Persons from the Revolution in 1688 to the End of the Reign of George II,* 3 (London, 1820), 258; Henry Wilson, *Wonderful Characters,* 3 (London, 1822), 259; *The Black Register or Revelations of Crime: a Series of Authentic and Remarkable Narratives Selected from the Criminal Records of All Nations* (London, 1852), 173; Mitford, *Recollections of a Literary Life,* 2:100.
19 *Country Journal,* 12 March 1737.
20 The standard modern text on the gibbet is Sarah Tarlow, *The Golden and Ghoulish Age of the Gibbet in Britain* (London, 2017), but see also Albert Hartshorne, *Hanging in Chains* (London, 1891).
21 *London Evening Post,* 26 August 1749; *Reading Mercury,* 7 April 1783; *Gloucester Journal,* 1 May 1744; *Bristol Mercury,* 21 October 1843; BA, 35893/36/t.
22 Tarlow, *Age of the Gibbet,* 117.
23 *Bristol Times and Mirror,* 25 January 1862.
24 For example, a coastal trader was wrecked on the Swash in 1808, *Bristol Mirror,* 20 February 1808; and a boat packed with 20 passengers ran aground on it in the dark in 1814, almost pitching all of them into the water, *Bristol Times* 18 August 1814; Two men were killed there in 1825, and another in 1842, *Bath Chronicle,* 10 November 1825, *Bristol Mirror,* 5 November 1842; and two steamers collided on it in 1846, *Exeter and Plymouth Gazette,* 3 October 1846.
25 BA, Chamberlain's Accounts F/AC/Box/73/12 (1761). For the order for Mahony's gibbet see Treasurer's Account 11373/2 (1741); *Bath Chronicle,* 30 July 1761; TNA, T90/153 (1761); Tarlow, *Age of the Gibbet.*
26 Figures extrapolated from Tarlow, *Age of the Gibbet.*
27 *Scots Magazine,* 6 April 1739.
28 *Stamford Mercury,* 9 April 1741.
29 *The Lives and Trials of Cornelius York, George Masters and John Millard for Diverse Robberies and Unheard of Cruelties* (London, 1740); *Derby Mercury,* 28 August 1740; *Daily Post,* 24 September 1740.
30 BL, Add. Mss. 27951, Itinerarium Bristoliense (1772). Our thanks to Madge Dresser for sharing this reference.
31 *The Stranger's Illustrated Guide to Chepstow and its Neighbourhood* (London 1843), 3.
32 *Western Daily Press,* 2 January 1905.
33 *Western Daily Press,* 26 June 1922.
34 Ann McTaggart, *Memoirs of a Gentlewoman of the Old School,* 2 vols. (London 1830), 2: 175-7.
35 For local opposition to Prothero's gibbeting see TNA E389/247/185; *Bristol Times and Mirror,* 6 February 1905; *Western Daily Press,* 29 October 1934.
36 *Fraser's Magazine for Town and Country,* 55 (April, 1857), 450. A brief outline of the case was added in a footnote, in case readers failed to understand the reference.
37 *Bristol Mirror,* 1 January 1842.
38 Bristol Library, Fratricide cuttings book B20593. Four more relics, all attached to presentation cards and endorsed with Smith's signature are at Bristol Library SR90, Supplement to the Fratricide; and BA 13847/3, 35893/36-t and 9733/3.
39 BA 35893/36/t.
40 *Bristol Times and Mirror,* 13 July 1850, 29 September 1906.
41 Marryat, 'People, Patients and Preparations', 84; Peter King, *Punishing the Criminal Corpse, 1700-1840: Aggravated Forms of the Death Penalty in England* (London, 2017).
42 D. Halliwell, *An Unjust Hanging: The True Story of John Horwood* (Cirencester, 2012).
43 *Western Daily Press,* 12 June 1886.
44 *Bristol Times and Mirror,* 6 February 1905.
45 *Bristol Mirror,* 26 February 1842.
46 *Gloucester Journal,* 10 Feb 1741; Wilkinson, *Foote,* 1:315.
47 *London Chronicle,* 4 April 1761; *Whitehall Evening Post,* 14 November 1761; Stone, *Uncertain Unions & Broken Lives,* 113.

Chapter Six: The Dineley Murder as Parricide

1 George Lillo, *The London Merchant, or, the history of George Barnwell* (London, 7th ed. 1740), 48, end of act 3.
2 Garthine Walker interprets parricide in its denotative sense, as the killing of a father or mother, to whom a child owes allegiance. See Garthine Walker, 'Imagining the Unimaginable: Parricide in Early Modern England and Wales, *c*.1600-*c*.1760', *Journal of Family History, 41/3* (July 2016), 1-23.
3 Ephraim Chambers, *Cyclopaedia*, 2 vols. (London, 4th ed. 1741), 2nd vol. under 'parricide'; Samuel Johnson, *Dictionary of the English Language*, 2 vols. (London, 1755), 2nd vol. under 'parricide'. In *Macbeth* parricide is associated with Duncan's death by 'bloody cousins'. William Shakespeare, *Macbeth,* Act 3 Scene 1, lines 43-45. For references in 1775, see *The Crisis,* no. 22, 17 June 1775 and no. 26, 15 July 1775.
4 *Trials,* 52.
5 For Tom Billings' confession see TNA, SP 35/61, f. 147; *A Narrative of the Barbarous and Unheard Murder of Mr John Hayes* (London, 2nd ed. 1726), 11-14; *Select trials at the Sessions-House in the Old Bailey,* 4 vols. (London 1742) 3:6-11.
6 *Narrative of the Murder of John Hayes,* 7-10.
7 Ibid, 18, 20.
8 Matthew Lockwood, 'From Treason to Homicide: Changing Conceptions of the Law of Petty Treason in Early Modern England', *Journal of Legal History,* 34/1 (2013), 31-49.
9 *The Last Speech Confession and Dying Words of Mrs Catherine Hayes* (Dublin, 1726); John Guthrie, *Ordinary's Account, 9 May 1726;* Old Bailey online, OA17260509.
10 Garthine Walker, *Crime, Gender and Social Order in Early Modern England* (Cambridge 2003), ch. 4. On wifely duties as a preamble to the Hayes case, see *Narrative of the Murder of John Hayes,* 6-7.
11 *The Life and Character of Catherine Hayes* (London, 1726)*,* 22-23; *The Life, Trial and Execution of Catherine Hayes, who was burnt for Petty Treason* (London, 1810), 405-7; *Select Trials at the Sessions House in the Old Bailey, 1720-1742* 4 vols. (London, 1742), 3:21; Eugene Aram, *Criminal Recorder,* 1 (1810), 442-44.
12 *Life, Trial and Execution of Catherine Hayes,* 416; *Daily Post,* 10 May 1726; *Evening Post,* 7-10 May 1726; *British Journal,* 14 May 1726.
13 *Mist's Weekly Journal,* 21 May 1726. Billings claimed the three agreed to do away with Hayes three weeks before the event, not six, and only when Hayes proposed the wine wager did they consolidate their plan. See TNA, SP 35/61, f. 147.
14 *Daily Post,* 10 May 1726; *Evening Post,* 7-10 May 1726.
15 *Daily Post,* 5 May 1726.
16 *The Life, Behaviour, Last Dying Words and Confession of Charles Drew Esquire* (1740); *An Authentic Account of the Life of Mr Charles Drew* (London, 1740).
17 *The Suffolk Parricide* (London, 1740), 5-6.
18 *General Evening Post,* 29 March-1 April 1740; *London and Country Journal,* 1 April 1740; *Suffolk Parricide,* 8.
19 *Memoirs of the life and times of Sir Thomas Deveil* (London, 1748), 96-8; *Suffolk Parricide,* 12-22.
20 *Suffolk Parricide,* 7-8.
21 *London and Country Journal,* 8 April 1740; *The Unnatural Son: Being the Whole Tryal and Condemnation of Charles Drew of Long Melford in Suffolk, Esq.* (1740). The gibbetting is anticipated in *General Evening Post,* 29 March-1 April 1740.
22 *Daily Gazetteer,* 17 Feb 1744. For Lord Hervey's intervention, *General Evening Post,* 5-8 April 1740.
23 *London Daily Post,* 7 April 1740; *The Unnatural Son.*
24 *London Daily Post,* 11 April 1740; *London Evening Post,* 10-12 April 1740; *Suffolk Parricide,* 44.
25 On this theme, see Nicholas Rogers, *Mayhem. Postwar crime and violence in Britain, 1748-53* (New Haven, 2012).
26 *The genuine trial of John Swan and Elizabeth Jeffryes* (Dublin, 1752), 4.
27 On the Marriage Act, see Eve Tavor Bannet, 'The Marriage Act of 1753: "A Most Cruel Law for the Fair Sex"' *Eighteenth-Century Studies,* 30 (1997), 233-54; Rebecca Probert, 'The Impact of the Marriage Act of 1753: Was it really "A most Cruel Law for the Fair Sex?"', *Eighteenth-Century Studies,* 38/2 (2005), 247-62; Jona Schellekens, 'Courtship, the Clandestine Marriage Act, and Illegitimate Fertility in England', *Journal of Interdisciplinary History,* 25 (1995), 433-44.
28 *London Morning Penny Post,* 11-13, 16-18 September 1751; *Derby Mercury,* 16-23 April 1751.
29 *Captain Cranstoun's account of the poisoning of the late Mr Francis Blandy* (London, 1753), 16-17.
30 TB Howell, *Complete Collection of State Trials,* 21 vols. (1816), 18:1120-23.
31 *Derby Mercury,* 5-11 July 1751.
32 *The Bloody Register. A select and judicious collection of the most remarkable trials for murder,* 4 vols. (London, 1764), 4:38-51.
33 *Miss Mary Blandy's Own Account of the Affair between Her and Mr Cranstoun* (London, 1752).
34 *The Connoisseur,* 20 February 1755.
35 *Miss Blandy's Own Account*. See also Alexander Welsh, *Strong Representations: Narrative and Circumstantial*

Evidence in England (Baltimore, 1992); Susan S. Heinzelman, *Riding the Black Ram: Law, Literature and Gender* (Stanford, 2010); Clare Brant, *Eighteenth-Century Letters and British Culture* (London, 2006), ch. 3.
36 Printed in the *London Daily Advertiser,* 6 March 1752; the letter is foregrounded in Brant, *Eighteenth-Century Letters*, 142-7.
37 See John Brewer, *A Sentimental Murder. Love and Madness in the Eighteenth Century* (New York, 2005).
38 *Covent Garden Journal,* 10 March 1752.
39 *The whole trial of John Swan and Elizabeth Jeffries* (London, 1752, 2nd ed.), 18. Just 11 lines were devoted to the incest, without recriminating Joseph Jefferies.
40 *General Advertiser,* 13 March 1752. See also King, *Punishing the Criminal Corpse,* 55.
41 ST 6:797, 800.
42 Walker, 'Imagining the Unimaginable', 1.
43 See Billings' confession, TNA, SP 35/61, f. 147.
44 *Suffolk Parricide,* 4. Drew's 'Education was in no ways adapted to the Estate he might reasonably expect on the Death of his Father.'
45 *The Genuine Lives of Capt. Cranstoun and Miss Mary Blandy* (London, 1753), 3.
46 TNA, SP 54/41, ff. 135, 137-8, 146, 172.
47 Summer Strevens, The *First Forensic Hanging: The Toxic Truth that killed Mary Blandy* (Barnsley, 2018), appendix, derived from Horace Bleackley, *Some Distinguished Victims of the Scaffold* (London 1905), 35-8.
48 *The Rambler,* 17 August 1751. See also *Genuine Letters that pass'd between Miss Blandy and Miss Jeffries before and after conviction* (London, 1752), 31, where a fictive Jeffries hopes her guilt 'may be a warning to Parents and Guardians how they principle those under their care, lest like my Uncle they reap the fruit of their own wickedness.'
49 John Campbell, *A companion for the unmarried ladies* (London, 1752), 56-7.
50 Ibid, 57-8.
51 John Locke, *Two Treatises of Government* (London, 4th ed. 1713), 106, section 97; Ephraim Chambers, *Cyclopaedia,* vol. 2 under 'primogeniture'.
52 Stone, *Uncertain Unions & Broken Lives,* 381.
53 HL Stephen, *State Trials, Political and Social,* 2 vols. (London, 1899), 2:231-304.
54 See Martin J. Wiener, *Men of Blood: Violence, Manliness, and Criminal Justice in Victorian England* (New York, 2004).

Chapter Seven: Fictions and Fratricides

1 See especially the account of Jack the Ripper in Judy Walkowitz, *City of Dreadful Delight. Narratives of Sexual Danger in late-Victorian London* (Chicago, 1992).
2 www.OldBaileyonline. Between 1680-1740 there were 16,972 thefts, 1308 violent thefts and 1126 homicides. Of 700 selected homicides in that period, 8.6% were family related. Of these 60, only four [6.7%] were fratricides.
3 Family related homicides today account for 17.5% of the total. They are especially prevalent when the victims are women. Almost half of adult female victims [46%] were killed in a domestic homicide. See 'Homicide in England and Wales: year ending March 2020' in www.ons.gov.uk, figure 6.
4 OldBaileyonline, t17190903-33 [Mary Tame]; t16880711-9 [Charles Constantine].
5 OldBaileyonline, t17040426-40 [William Naylor]; t17080414-18 [David Bayley].
6 *London Evening Post,* 24-27 August 1765.
7 TNA, SP 54/24, ff. 279-81, 24 Sept. 1765; Martin Baggoley, 'Incest, Murder and Flight; The Eastmiln Tragedy', *Crime Magazine,* 12 Feb. 2015.
8 *Daily Gazetteer,* 18 May 1741.
9 Hal Gladfelder, *Criminality and Narrative in Eighteenth-Century England* (Baltimore and London, 2001), 5-11.
10 *Daily Gazetteer,* 11 May 1741; *The True Effigies of Samuel Goodere, Matthew Mahony & Charles White* (1741).
11 On this development see Kesselring, *Making Murder Public,* ch. 5.
12 *London Evening Post,* 20-22 January 1741.
13 *London Evening Post,* 24-27 January 1741. The letter was dated 20 January 1741.
14 *London Evening Post,* 24-27 January 1741; *Daily Gazetteer,* 26 January 1741; *Daily Post,* 27 January 1741; *London and Country Journal,* 27 January 1741; *Gloucester Journal,* 27 January 1741; *Derby Mercury,* 5 February 1741; *Ipswich Journal,* 31 January 1741; *Leeds Mercury,* 3 February 1741; *Newcastle Courant,* 7 February 1741.
15 *Boston Evening Post,* 4 May 1741.
16 *London and Country Journal,* 29 January 1741; *Gloucester Journal,* 27 January 1741. See also the *Gentleman's Magazine,* 11 (Jan 1741), 50.
17 *Common Sense,* 7 February 1741; *London and Country Journal,* 10 February 1741; *Leeds Mercury,* 3 February 1741; *Kentish Weekly Post,* 4 February. 1741.

NOTES

18 *Bristol Fratricide*, 6.
19 *Bristol Fratricide* 9-10; see also *Gloucester Journal*, 27 January 1741 and *Remarkable Trials*, 1:58-60.
20 *Bristol Fratricide*, 22-3.
21 *Bristol Fratricide*, 30.
22 *Bristol Fratricide*, 28.
23 *Daily Gazetteer*, 13 February 1741. 'The Whole being a faithful account of this Tragical Affair.'
24 *Boston Weekly News Letter,* 14 May 1741. According to Karen Halttunen, the first trial report ever published in pamphlet form in America was one of those on the Goodere case, *Some Account of the Trial of Samuel Goodere Esq.* (Boston, 1741); 'Intimacy on Trial' in Richard Wightman Fox and T.J. Jackson Lears (eds.), *The Power of Culture: Critical Essays in American History* (Chicago, 1993), 78. On the development of news networks around the Atlantic, see Ian K. Steele, *The English Atlantic: an exploration of communication and community* (New York, 1986).
25 *London Magazine,* 9 (May 1741), 183-192. There is also *A Narrative of the Murder of Sir John Dineley Goodere Bt,* printed for J. Hart at the price of 6d, that was advertised in the *Gentleman's Magazine,* 11 (February 1741), 112. No copy of this pamphlet seems to have survived, although it is likely a retitled *Bristol Fratricide*.
26 Judith Flanders, *The Invention of Murder* (London, 2011). The quote is from 'Blood' *Punch,* (Jan-June 1842), 190.
27 Krista Kesselring, *Making Murder Public,* offers a useful contextual frame for this notion.
28 Martin J. Weiner, 'Convicted Murders and the Victorian Press: Condemnation vs. Sympathy', *Crimes and Misdemeanours: Deviance and the Law in Historical Perspective,* 1 (2007), 110-25; Beattie, *Crime and the Courts,* 433. At the Surrey assizes, 1660-1800, 23.4% of all sentenced to death for murder were pardoned. This was a lower rate of pardon for every offence save those under the Black Act of 1726.
29 *London and Country Journal,* 16 April 1741.
30 *The Authentick Tryal of Samuel Goodere, Esquire,* p.8 also misdated the day of the abduction, which was 18 January not the 26th.
31 Ian Kelly, *Mr Foote's Other Leg,* 59.
32 *Gloucester Journal,* 10 February 1741.
33 Percy Fitzgerald, *Samuel Foote. A Biography* (London, 1910), 17-18; Simon Trefman, *Sam Foote, Comedian, 1720-1777* (New York,1971), 7.
34 *Daily Journal,* 7 August 1735; *London Evening Post,* 16-18 June 1737; Kelly, *Mr Foote's Other Leg,* 33.
35 Trefman, *Sam Foote,* 10, described it as a 'good estate' but it was really quite modest.
36 Kelly, *Mr Foote's Other Leg,* 34. Kelly assumes that Foote was in prison when the March 1741 trials were held. This was not the case.
37 Smith, *Fratricide,* 18.
38 Samuel Foote, *The Genuine Trial of Samuel Goodere, Esquire* (London, 1741)*,* title page.
39 BA, AC/JS/50/51.
40 There is a lot of confusion about Foote's contributions to his uncle's trial. ECCO claims Foote was responsible for the *Genuine and Authentick History*, which seems very unlikely given the bias of the account. Ian Kelly notes two, *The Genuine Trial* and *The Genuine Memoirs of Sir John Dineley Goodere.* See *Mr Foote's Other Leg,* 73-74. In ECCO there are two Worcester editions of the latter with a slightly modified title, both of which dispense with the dedication to the Bristol mayor, Henry Combe.
41 *Genuine Trial*, 17.
42 Kelly, *Mr Foote's Other Leg,* 76.
43 *Genuine Trial*, 20-1.
44 *Genuine Trial*, 24.
45 *Genuine Trial*, 24.
46 Kelly, *Mr Foote's Other Leg,*74; *Some account of the trial of Samuel Goodere, Esquire* (Boston, 1741); *The Authentic Tryall of Samuel Goodere, Esquire* (London: E. Hill, Fleet St, 1741).
47 Foote, *Memoirs of Sir John Dineley Goodere*, 10; Lincoln B. Faller, *Turned to Account. The forms and functions of criminal biography in late seventeenth and early-eighteenth century England* (Cambridge, 1987), ch. 3.
48 Foote, *Memoirs of Sir John Dineley,* 14.
49 Foote, *Memoirs,* 36; Penrose simply states that Captain Goodere was brought to a 'true repentance.' Penrose*, Account,* 8.
50 Foote, *Memoirs,* 6.
51 Mary's infidelities compromised sympathy for her in the eighteenth century. It is not until the nineteenth century that men were criticized for beating wives notwithstanding their sexual peccadilloes. See Weiner, *Men of Blood*.
52 In a later account Sir John Dineley is whitewashed. *Formidable Trials* (1765), 1:66-7, simply refered to his 'domestic jars' and elected to 'pass over in Silence what was illaudable in his Character.'
53 Samuel Foote, *Genuine Memoirs,* dedication.
54 Penrose, *Account,* pp. 6-8. On the obligations and expectations of the prison curate in London Newgate, known conventionally as the Ordinary, see Andrea McKenzie, *Tyburn's Martyrs. Executions*

in England 1675-1775 (London and New York, 2007), ch. 5.
55 *Genuine Relation of the Tryal* (Bristol and London, 1741); *Tryals*, 3-8. A copy of the first has not been found, although advertised in the *London and Country Journal*, 16 April 1741.
56 *Newcastle Courant*, 8-15 January 1743. On Vernon's Caribbean failures, see Nicholas Rogers, *Blood Waters. War, Disease and Race in the 18th century British Caribbean* (Woodbridge, 2021), ch. 2.
57 *Genuine and Authentick History*, 17; John Charnock, *Biographia navalis*, 4:245-6n. Charnock also believed Sir Edward's favouritism towards Samuel fuelled John Dineley's anger. Percy Fitzgerald seems to attribute *A Genuine and Authentick History* to Samuel Foote, but this seems unlikely given the drift of the argument in Foote's other productions. See Fitzgerald, *Foote*, 27.
58 In fact, Sir John Dineley beat off the challenge from the landlord of the sponging house where Lady Mary resided, on the grounds that she was not entitled to be there. See Isaac Espinasse, *A digest of the law of actions and trials at nisi prius*. (Dublin, 1794), p. 123.
59 *Remarkable Trials*, 1: 67; *The malefactor's register, or the Newgate and Tyburn Calendar* (London, 1779), 3: 37.
60 Faller claims, on the basis of Foote's *Memoirs of Sir John Dineley Goodere,* that the convention argument about sin and the escalating effects of delinquency held. But as we have argued, Foote was hardly impartial in narrating this familial murder, and was atypical. See Faller, *Turned to Account*, pp. 62-4.
61 Foote, *Genuine Memoirs*, 9, 14; see also a later version attributed to Samuel Foote. [Samuel Foote], *Memoirs of the life of Sir John Dineley Goodere, Bart* (Worcester, 1762?), 9-10.
62 *The Annals of Europe for the year 1741* (London, 1743), 330.
63 William Jackson, *The New and Complete Newgate Calendar,* (London, 1795), 3:40.
64 George Borrow, *Celebrated Trials and Remarkable Cases of Criminal Jurisprudence*, 6 vols. (London, 1825) 4:321-3.
65 *The Fratricide, or, The Murderer's Gibbet* (Bristol, 1839), 16, also noted as a written remark in annotated version of the poem in Bristol Reference Library.
66 *The Tyburn Chronicle* (London, 1768), 3:146; *Malefactors Register*, 3:40; *The Old Bailey Chronicle* (London, 1788), 361; Jackson, *New and Complete Newgate Calendar,*3:40; Eugene Aram, *Criminal Recorder,* 1 (1804), 363; Borrow, *Celebrated Trials*, 4:321-3.
67 Leslie Stephen, 'State Trials' in *Hours in a Library* (London, 1874-79), 3:332.
68 Samuel Seyer, *Memoirs*, 2:583. On haunted Burghope, see www.herefordshire.org, accessed 5 Jan 2021.
69 0.73% were aged 80 and above in Bristol and Barton Regis. See *House of Commons Papers*, vol 15 (1822), 119; *Abstract of Answers and Returns, Population of Great Britain, Enumeration Abstract, (1821)*.
70 Seyer, *Memoirs*, 2:583. For biographical details on Samuel Seyer, see the obituary in the *Gentleman's Magazine*, 101 (1831), 471-2.
71 Richard Smith, *The Fratricide*, 9, 11; 'My Rosinante, capering off the road,/Has trotted me into an Episode.' The description of the poem as a 'rigmarole' is to be found in Smith's introductory remarks to the editor of the *Bristol Mirror*. The poem originally appeared in the *Bristol Mirror*, 7, 14, 21 September 1839.
72 John Conybeare, *A defence of revealed religion* (London: 3rd edition, 1733) See also 'Prophecies and Miracles sufficient Proofs of a Divine Commission', in *Sermons*, 2 vols. (London, 1757), 1:269-307; Sir Henry T. De La Beche, *Report on the State of Bristol and other Large Towns* (London, 1845), 1-25; Peter Malpass, *The Making of Victorian Bristol* (Woodbridge, 2019), 35-40; Smith, *Fratricide*, 5.
73 That predicament had not changed in Smith's time. See John Habakkuk, *Marriage, Debt and the Estates System: English Landownership 1650-1950* (Oxford, 1994).
74 The Cropthorne registers reveal that the first-born son of Edward and Eleanor Goodere died in childbirth, and the second Edward, born May 1682, died in a duel in Ireland in 1708, aged 20. See Wilkinson, *Foote,* 1: 66.
75 Smith, *Fratricide*, 7, 16, 21.
76 *Bristol Mercury*, 21 February 1821; *Trewman's Exeter Flying Post*, 19 April 1821; *Yorkshire Gazette*, 30 June 1821.
77 On dying game, see Andrea McKenzie, 'Martyrs in Low Life? Dying "Game" in Augustan England', *Journal of British Studies*, 42/2 (2003), 167-205.
78 As he did with at least one of two women hanged for infanticide in 1802. See W.H. Harsant, 'Medical Bristol in the Eighteenth Century', *Bristol Medico-Chururigical Journal,* (Dec 1899) 300-1.
79 Smith, *Fratricide*, 30.
80 Bernard Mandeville, *An Enquiry into the Causes of the Frequent Executions at Tyburn* (London, 1725); Henry Fielding, *An Enquiry into the Causes of the late Increase of Robbers* (London, 1751).
81 TNA, HO 52/33, f.270, Copy of the evidence respecting the conduct of the hangman at the execution of Charles Bartlett at Gloucester, information of William Bears and others, May 1837.
82 Poole and Rogers, *Bristol from Below,* 35; Ruth Richardson, *Death, Dissection and the Destitute* (Chicago: 2nd ed., 2001).
83 Harsant, 'Medical Bristol', 309-10.
84 Smith, *Fratricide,* 31-3. See also Stone, *Uncertain Union & Broken Lives,* 377-8, who endorses the story.

85 Dyke's 'Jack White's Gibbet' first appeared in A. Whitelaw ed., *The Republic of Letters: A Selection in Poetry and Prose from the Works of the Most Eminent Writers,* vol 4 (Glasgow 1833). For the debunking see Douglas Macmillan, *Jack White's Gibbet: The Fictions and the Facts* (London, 1922).
86 Richard Smith lived on College Green or just a little way up Park Street.
87 Smith, *Fratricide,* 14.
88 John Wesley thought Bristol's Newgate worse than London's: 'so great was the filth, the stench, the misery, and wickedness, which shocked all who had a spark of humanity left.' John Wesley, *Journal,* ed. Elizabeth Joy (Oxford, 1987), 149-50.
89 Smith, *Fratricide,* 7-8; Latimer, Annals of Bristol, 2:362-3; *Public Advertiser,* 6 Oct. 1764.
90 Smith, *Fratricide,* 20, 22. On the new mode of imprisonment, Michael Ignatieff, *A Just Measure of Pain; The Penitentiary in the Industrial Revolution, 1750-1850* (London and New York, 1978); Michel Foucault, *Discipline and Punish. The Birth of the Prison,* trans. Alan Sheridan (New York, 1979). Some Canadian penitentiaries were more attentive to the wishes of ratepayers and did allow public visiting. See Janet Miron, *Prisons, asylums and the public. Institutional visiting in the nineteenth century* (Toronto, 2011).
91 Smith, *Fratricide,* 18, 21, 28-9.
92 Poole and Rogers, *Bristol from Below,* 350-1.
93 *Trewman's Exeter Flying Post,* 19 April 1821.
94 Smith, *Fratricide,* 8-9; James Thistlethwaite, *The Consultation* (Bristol, 1774), principally a satire on the 1774 Bristol election. Quote taken from a written remark prefacing the British Library copy.
95 Smith, *Fratricide,* 6, 27.
96 Shane McCorrestine, *William Corder and the Red Barn Murder. Journals of the Criminal Body* (London, 2014).
97 *Curiosities of Bristol and its Neighbourhood* 5 (January 1854) and 6 (February 1854); *Bristol Times,* 25 January, 1862.
98 *Belgravia* (January 1870), 365-9. A number of provincial papers also ran Thornbury's story, eg. *Newcastle Chronicle,* 26 November, 1870.
99 *Alden's Oxford Monthly Illustrated Journal,* 14, 2 (April 1871), 32.
100 *English Illustrated Magazine,* 20 (October 1898 – March 1899), 499-502.
101 Mary Russell Mitford, *Recollections of a Literary Life and Selections from my Favourite Poets and Prose Writers* (London, 1883), 323-335.
102 *Gloucestershire Echo,* 8 May 1933; *Western Daily Press,* 11, 13, 25 September 1934; *BBC Year-Book, 1934* (London, 1934), 112, 132, 137.
103 Henry B. Irving, 'The Fall of the House of Goodere', *Occasional Papers Dramatic and Historical* (Boston, 1907), 163-183.
104 The latest rendition is Netflix's *Bridgerton* (2021), attracting 63 million viewers.
105 'A Question of Guilt'. Mary Blandy (1980), six episode TV series, directed by Brian Farnham; Joan Morgan, *The Hanging Wood. Being the story of Mary Blandy of Henley-on-Thames* (London, 1950); Joan Morgan, *A Question of Guilt. Mary Blandy* (London, 1979); see also Summer Strevens, *First Forensic Hanging.*
106 Thomas De Quincey, 'On Murder considered as one of the Fine Arts', *Blackwood's Magazine,* 21 (1828), 208, 212.
107 Ikey Solomans, Esquire, Jnr., [WM Thackeray] *Catherine, A Story,* serialised in *Frasers Magazine* (Feb 1830) et seq.
108 Henry Mayhew, *London Labour and the London Poor,* 4 vols. (London 1861-2; Dover reprint, New York 1968), 1:15; Rosalind Crone, *Violent Victorians. Popular entertainment in nineteenth-century London* (Manchester, 2012),133.
109 Anon, *The Bloody Innkeeper, or Sad and Barbarous News from Gloucester-shire* (London, 1675); *The Bloody Palatine's Garland, being a true Discovery of the Barbarous and Bloody Murder on Sarah Walker* (Newcastle, 1740); Crone, *Violent Victorians,* 173-4.
110 See Daniel Stashower, *The Beautiful Cigar Girl* (London, 2006); Amy Gilman Srebnick, *The Mysterious Death of Mary Rogers: Sex and Culture in Nineteenth-Century New York* (New York, 1995); Edgar Allen Poe reworked the story as 'The Mystery of Marie Rogêt'; see also 'The Case of Mary C. Rogers' *New-Yorker,* 14 August 1841; 'The Mary Rogers Mystery Explained' *New York Daily Tribune,* 18 November 1842.
111 John Galt, *The Lives of the Players,* 2 vols. (London 1831), 1:294-5. See also Nash, *Collections for the History of Worcestershire,* 2:784, where an anecdote places Foote in temporary possession of Charlton long after the murder, living it up with servants and a coach and six, and happily selling off the family plate.
112 Mitford, *Recollections of a Literary Life,* 2:87; Leslie Stephen, *Hours in a Library,* 3 vols. (London, 1892) 3:334.

Acknowledgements

This book came about because a number of our shared interests in Georgian Bristol's dark underbelly began to coalesce around the Dineley-Goodere fratricide. It's a story that touches on so much: from familial property squabbles amongst the elite, to issues of civic governance, mental health, criminal jurisprudence and post-execution punishment. The circumstances of the Dineley-Goodere murder had never been fully explored, nor its lasting legacy critically examined.

Steve gave a paper on 'Mahony's Gibbet' at the UWE/M Shed Regional History Centre seminar in May 2017, and within a few years we agreed to flesh out the story of the Dineley murder as a microhistory. Our efforts were greatly aided by the discovery of a five-volumed typescript of the troubles of the Dineley-Goodere family in the Huntington Library, San Marino, California. This meticulously researched project, carried out by John Wells Wilkinson in 1936, in what was clearly the beginnings of a biography of the celebrated comedian and playwright Samuel Foote, nephew to murderer and victim in this story, enabled us to delve deeply into the family conflicts that sparked this fratricide. From there it was relatively plain sailing, once we had tracked down the many versions of the trial of Samuel Goodere and their circulation, and explored the afterlife of this fraught, premeditated murder, which attracted the attention of Victorian as well as Georgian collectors and writers and was even dramatised on BBC radio in the 1930s.

Nick presented a talk on the family quarrel and trial to the Osgoode Society Legal History seminar in Toronto in mid-October 2020. He thanks the audience for their comments, particularly Philip Girard.

As always, we are indebted to the archives and libraries whose collections and expert staff have helped us bring this project to press. These include The National Archives at Kew, the Huntington Library in California, Lambeth Palace Library, the British Library, the Worcester Archives, the team at Bristol Reference Library's excellent local studies service (especially Dawn Dyer), the Bristol Museum and Art Gallery, whose collections of historic watercolours, maps and drawings of the old city are peerless, and the Bristol Archives, whose extensive collection of manuscripts in the Jarrit Smith papers are an invaluable source for anyone studying this landmark trial.

Finally, we'd like to thank Clara Hudson at Redcliffe Press for enthusiastically bringing the book into print, and especially to the company's late founder, John Sansom. John organised the literary lunch at River Station in 2012 that set the ball rolling for a collaborative series of Studies in Regional History of which this is the fifth volume. John was an irrepressible friend to independent regional publishing; we miss him hugely and dedicate this volume to his memory.

Steve Poole and Nicholas Rogers, May 2022

Index   Illustrations in **bold**

Abseny, Joseph, gibbeted 92-3
Acton, John 17
Admiralty 29, 36-7, 39 64-5, 72-3, 80-1, 122
Aland, John Fortescue, judge 38
Anatomy Act of 1832, 141
Atkins, Elizabeth 16
Authentick Tryal of Samuel Goodere Esq, 124, **126,** 131
Barclay, privateer 37
Barrett, William 31
Beard, Mary 51
Bell Inn, Marsh Street 65
Berrow, William 37
Billings, Thomas 105-6
Blackstone, William, jurist 82
Blandy, Francis, attorney 104, 108, 110
Blandy, Mary 108-16, **112**, 147
Bobbett, Charlotte 90, 98
Bombay [Mumbai] 8
Boon, Thomas 87
Borrow, George, writer 135
Boyer, Elizabeth 106-7
Braikenridge, George Weare, antiquarian 144
Branch, Elizabeth 41
Branch, Mary 41
Brewer, John, historian 118
Brickdale, John, slave trader 37
Bridgwater 35
Bristol 29-102, 120-8, 137-46
　Brandon Hill 44, 53-4
　Bridewell 36, 42, 66, 82
　civilian-military relations 38-9
　College Green 29-30, 35, 46-51, **48**, 79, 142
　Common Council 39, 46, 85
　Exchange 34, 45-6
　Georgian precincts 35, 44-6
　Guildhall **70**,
　labour strife 41-3
　legal jurisdiction 37-9, 72-3
　Marsh Street 35, 47, 65, 84
　mercantile elite 37, 39, 44-6, 86
　murders 39-40, 143
　Newgate gaol 39-40, 43, 66, 73, 81, 88-9, 121
　newspaper press 39-41, 66-9, 100, 124, 127-8, 144
　overseas trade 30-1, 35-7, 85-6
　population 30
　press gangs 29, 35-7, 51-3
　Prince of Wales' visit 43-5
　St. Michael's Hill 35, 40, 66, 81, 86-7, 94, 135, 143
Bristol Fratricide 67-9, **68**, 122-24, 129

Bristol Royal Infirmary 85-6
Brockweir Boat 65-6, 71
Bryan, Captain Edward 40-1
Buchanan, Duncan, seaman on *Ruby,* 58-9, 64, 71, 123, 130
Burghope estate, Herefordshire, 8, **10**, 22, 23-4, 27, 49, 71, 102-3, 131, 137
Burnett, Andrew, gibbeted 92
Butterworth, Ann 41
Campbell, John, author 116
Cartagena 26
Catcott, Reverend Alexander 85-6
Chamberlayne, John, water bailiff 65
Chamberlayne, Thomas 49
Chambers, Ephraim, editor 104, 116
Charlton estate, Worcestershire 7-8, 11-12, 21, 24, 26-7, 49, 76, 80, 102, 117, 128, 131, 133
Charnock, John, naval chronicler 134
Coke, Arundel, barrister 108
Cole, Elisha, seamen on *Ruby* 58
College Green 29-30, 46-51
Colman, George, playwright
Combe, Henry, mayor in 1740/1, 37-8, 45-6, 67
Connell, Bryan 95-6
Conybeare, Reverend John 138
Court, Theodore, master of the *Ruby* 73
Cowper, William, 1st Earl 10, 15
Cranstoun, Lt William Henry 108-113, 115
Crime literature 41, 66-8, 84, 90, 95-6, 115, 120-37
Cross, John, slave trader 37
Cruel Mistress, The 41
Daniel, Thomas, alderman
Darby, Mrs. Elizabeth 53
Dagge, Abel, keeper of Bristol Newgate 73, 80, 129, 143
Davis, Maria 90, 98
Day, Nathaniel, mayor in 1737/8, 36, 38
Defoe, Daniel, journalist, writer
De La Beche, Sir Henry T., social reformer 138
De Quincy, Thomas, writer 147-8
De Veil, Thomas, Bow Street magistrate 20
Dineley, Sir Edward 10-11
Dineley, Eleanor 12
Dineley [Dinely] Sir John **6**, 7-8, 23, 27, 102
Dineley-Goodere, Edward 15-16, 24-6, 102
Dineley-Goodere, Sir John 7-10, 12-30, 35, 46-66, 91, 102, 104, 113, 117, 120-24, 130-2, 137-8, 140, 145, 147

abduction 35, 47-56, **50**, **52**, **55**, 79, 121, 145;
brutality to wife, 16-19;
debts 21-2, 26, 50, 54
dismissal from bench, 15
'madness' 75-7
marital legal battles, 18-22, 24-8, 134;
murder, 59-62, **60**, **61**, **137**
prosecuting counsel for his murder 71-5, 114
uncouth habits, 14-15, 20
Dineley-Goodere, Mary, née Lawford, 15-21, 23-24, 26-28, 69, 117, 123, 133-4, 137
Gloucester estate, 15, 26-8
infidelities, 17-21, 69, 117, 123
marital legal battles, 18-22, 24-8
Drew, Charles John, attorney 104, 107
Drew, Charles, junior 106-08, 115
Dudgeon, James, surgeon's mate 58-9, 62, 64-5, 71
Duncox, Ann, maid 19
Dupree, William, soldier 53
Durdham Down 39-40, 92-4, 96-7
Eagle, privateer 37
East India Company 8, 10
Evans, John, chronicler 144
Evesham election, 1734, 23
Executions, public 69-70, 81-4, 85-102
anatomisation 90, 98
dissection 86-90, 140-2
gallows rescues 79, 86-7
gibbeting 91-102, 136, 140
memorabilia 98-102
touching the corpse 140
Faller, Lincoln, literary historian 135
Farr, Richard, merchant 37
Ferrers, Laurence Shirley, 4th Earl 76
Fielding, Henry, magistrate and writer 140
Fielding, 'Beau' Robert, 22
Flanders, Judith, historian 124, 126
Foote, Eleanor, née Goodere 12-13, 27-8
Foote, John, later Foote-Dineley, 13, 25-7
Foote, Samuel, comedian 13, 25, 59, 128-33, 135
at Oxford University 25, 128
in debt 27, 128-9
trial pamphlets 59, 128-33
Foote, Samuel, Mayor of Truro, 12-13, 28
Foster, Sir Michael, Recorder 46, 70-1, 83, 104, 111
Fratricide or the Murderer's Gibbet 85, 138-144, **139**
Fytche, Captain Robert 29, 36, 64
Galvani, Luigi, scientist 144
Genuine and Authentick History of the Life and Character of Samuel Goodere Esq 127, 134
Genuine Memoirs of the Life of Sir John Dinly Goodere **132**, 133, 135

Genuine Trial of Samuel Goodere Esq 59, 124, **125**, 129
Gloucester assizes 43
Goodere, John, East India merchant, 8
Goodere, Edward, 1st baronet, 10-13, 22-4
Goodere, Edward, son of Samuel, 23, 26
Goodere, Elizabeth 10
Goodere, George 12
Goodere, Pennington 10
Goodere, Samuel 7, **22**-6, 28-30, 35, 40, 43, 46-90, 93, 95-7, 102, 104-5, 108, 114, 117, 120-24, 129-34, 138, 140, **141**, 142
court martial 23,
defence counsel 70-2, 74-5
murder 40, 47-66;
publicity of murder 67-70, 118-35
Gordon, William 37
Goreham, Henry, printer 129
Grove, Esther 19
Grove, Henry 19-20
Hallam, Robert 77, 79
Hanley Castle 12, 27
Hanover, privateer 37
Harding, Mary 83
Harding, Joshua, half-hanged malefactor 87
Hardwicke, Philip Yorke, 1st Earl, 21, 108
Harley, Robert, MP 12
Harris, Captain Rice 40
Hayes, Catherine 105-6, 115
Hayes, John 105-6, 114
Haythorne, John, alderman
Hobbs, Morris, publican 47-9
Hobhouse, Isaac, slave trader 37
Homicides 39-41, 118-120
fratricides 119-20
'rapier crime' 118-9
Horwood, John 98, 140, 143
Hotwells 47, 51, 53, 90, 96, 135
Hume, Major Martin A. S., historian 145
Humphries, Edward 107
Hurren, Elizabeth, historian 86-7
Infanticide 82-4
Inhumanity and Barbarity not to be Equal'd 41
Irving, Henry Brodribb, actor and writer 147
Isham, Sir Edmund, admiralty advocate 72
Jack White's Gibbett 142
James II, King of England 11
Jason, Anne 19
Jason, Sir Robert 16-21, 69, 123
Jeane, Captain John 40, 81
Jefferies, Elizabeth 108, 110-11, 113, 116
Jefferies, Joseph, butcher 104, 110, 113, 116

INDEX

Johnson, Samuel, writer 104, 116
Jones, Edward, cooper 57-8, 64, 71, 123, 130
Jones, Margaret, wife of Edward 62, 71
Kelly, Ian, literary historian 89, 128, 130-1
Ker, Lord Mark 108
Kimmerly, John 88
King, Nicholas, coroner 69
King, Peter, historian 100
Kingroad, estuary of Avon 29, 35-6, 51, 55-6, 73, 138
Kingswood colliers 41-3, 79
King's Bench prison 20, 24, 28
Kings Head, Hotwells 53
Kitchingham, Thomas 87
Knight, Charles 7
Lamb Inn, Lawford's Gate 42, 44
Laroche, James, alderman and slave trader 37
Latimer, John, chronicler 89
Lawford, Elizabeth, 15
Lawford estates, Gloucestershire 15, 26-7
Leech, Joseph, editor 93, 144-5
Lillo, George, playwright 104
Linebaugh, Peter, historian 86
Lively, HMS 35-6
Lloyd, William, Reverend 15
Locke, John, philosopher 116-7
Lowe, Godfrey, surgeon 89
Mace, William, 'Captain Rat' 106
MacGuiness, William, gunner 58-9
Mahony, Matthew 34, 46-9, 53, 56-66, 69, 71, **78**, 79, 82-5, 88, 90-1, 93-102, 120-2, 129-31, 135, 140
Mandeville, Bernard, satirist 140
Marryat, Nikita, historian 100
Matthews, Thomas 110-11
Mayhew, Henry, journalist 147
Mervin, Captain James 47, 65
Millard, John, gibbeted 96
Mitford, Mary, author 145-6, 148
Monro, Dr. John, Bedlam asylum 77
Munro Smith, George, historian 89
Murder Act of 1752, 100
Murray, Anne, wife of Cranstoun 109
Mutiny at sea 40-1, 95
Nash, Thomas 77, 79
Naval recruitment in Bristol 29-30, 35-7, 51-3
Newcastle, Thomas Pelham-Holles, 1st Duke 42, 115
Newth, Captain James 40
Noakes, Peter 77, 79
Ogle, Sir Chaloner 25
Oxenden, John 8
Oxenden, Sir George, MP 80
Pakington, Sir John, MP 11

Parricide 104-17
Payne, Henry, gibbeted 92
Penrose, Reverend John 57, 80-1, 134
Perry, Stephen, anchor smith 53
Perry, William, 2nd lieutenant, *Ruby* 64-5, 122-3
Pill, village of pilots 29, 36, 99
Poe, Edgar Allan, writer 146-8
Pope, Alexander, author 30
Porteous, Captain John 43
Porter, Roy, historian 76
Privateers, 37, 48-9, 51-3, 79, 81
Prise, Thomas, MP 8
Prothero, Jenkin, malefactor & ghost 92, 97-8
Ray, Martha, mistress of 4th Earl of Sandwich 118
Rayner, William, printer, 27
Red Barn murder 144
Reid, David 38, 88
Richardson, Samuel, novelist 112
Rochester, John Wilmot, 2nd Earl of, poet & libertine 119
Rockingham, Lewis Watson, 1st Earl, 7
Rocque, John, surveyor, map-maker 31, **32-3**, 44-46
Rogers, Mary 148
Rowland, Richard 98-100
Ruby, HMS 29, 30, 35, 47, 51, 56-65, 71-2, 75, 77, 79, 81, 128, 130, 142
Ruscombe, Mrs. Frances, murder victim 143, 147
Ryder, Sir Dudley, Attorney General 73
Sacheverell, Henry, firebrand preacher 11
Seyer, Reverend Samuel, antiquarian 85, 89, 96, 136-7, 144
Scotch Arms, Marsh Street 47
Scrope, Sir John, recorder 87
Shakespeare, William 147
Shelley, Mary, author 144
Shirehampton 94
Society of Merchant Venturers, Bristol 29, 37, 45
Sodomy 38, 88
Smith, Jarrit, attorney 26, 29-30, 47, 49-50, 53, 71, 74, 79-80, 117, 121, 133, 143
Smith, Richard, surgeon & curator 85, 89-90, 96, 98-102, 138-44
Somerset assizes 96
Spy, HMS 36
Stapleton 15-16, 27-8, 129, 133
Stephen, Henry Lushington, lawyer 117
Stephen, Leslie, author 135, 148
Stone, Lawrence, historian 89, 103
Strange, Sir John, Solicitor General 73
Surat 8

Swan, John 110-11
Swash or Swatch 93-4, **94**, 96-7, 101-2, 146
Tarlow, Sarah, historian 93
Tewksbury 40-1, 95
Thackeray, William Makepeace, novelist 147
The Fratricide 85, 89-90, 98-9, 138-44
Thistlethwaite, James, satirist 143
Thornbury, Walter, writer 145
Tockington 15, 26, 56, 129
Todd, Sweeny, demon barber 147
Trials of Samuel Goodere Esq 127
Trivett, Samuel, carpenter 53
Unparallel'd Cruelty 40
Vernham, John, half-hanged malefactor 87, 93
Vernon, Admiral Edward 67, 134
Vernon, privateer 47, 57, 69
Wager, Admiral Sir Charles 80
Walpole, Sir Robert, MP 80
War of Jenkins' Ear 25, 35-7, 51, 134
War of Spanish Succession 22-3, 134
Ward, Patrick, gibbeted 84-5
Watkins, Reverend William, vicar of Cropthorne 76
Watts, Elizabeth, 2nd wife of Samuel Goodere, 23, 80-1
Weller, Daniel, shipwright 56
Wenham, Jane, reputed witch 14
Westmoreland, privateer 37
White, Charles, 46, 58-63, 65-6, 69, 71, **78**, 79, 82-4, 86, 95, 120-1, 129-31, 135
White, William, attorney, 25
White Hart Inn 46-8, 142
Williams, Jane 82-4
Williams, Thomas, midshipman 51
Wilson, William 14
Windsor 7, 103
Witchcraft 14-15
Wood, Cyril, radio producer 146
Wood, John, architect
Wood, Thomas 105-6
York, Cornelius, gibbeted 96